The Fur Trader

The Fur Trader

EINAR ODD MORTENSEN SR.
with *Gerd Kjustad Mortensen*

From Oslo to
Oxford House

Edited by
Ingrid Urberg and Daniel Sims

UNIVERSITY *of* ALBERTA PRESS

Published by

University of Alberta Press
1–16 Rutherford Library South
11204 89 Avenue NW
Edmonton, Alberta, Canada T6G 2J4
amiskwacîwâskahikan | Treaty 6 |
Métis Territory
uap.ualberta.ca | uapress@ualberta.ca

Copyright © 2022 University of Alberta Press

LIBRARY AND ARCHIVES CANADA
CATALOGUING IN PUBLICATION

Title: The fur trader : from Oslo to Oxford House
 / Einar Odd Mortensen Sr. with Gerd
 Kjustad Mortensen ; edited and with an
 introduction by Ingrid Urberg and Daniel
 Sims.
Other titles: Pelshandleren. English
Names: Mortensen, Einar Odd, 1902–1968,
 author. | Mortensen, Gerd Kjustad,
 author. | Urberg, Ingrid, editor, writer of
 introduction. | Sims, Daniel, editor, writer of
 introduction.
Description: Translation of: Pelshandleren : mitt
 liv blant indianere i Nord-Canada 1925–28. |
 Includes bibliographical references.
Identifiers: Canadiana (print) 20220219524 |
 Canadiana (ebook) 20220219664 |
 ISBN 9781772125986 (softcover) |
 ISBN 9781772126143 (EPUB) |
 ISBN 9781772126150 (PDF)
Subjects: LCSH: Mortensen, Einar Odd,
 1902-1968. | LCSH: Fur trade—Manitoba—
 History—20th century. | LCSH: Fur
 traders—Manitoba—History—20th century.
 | LCSH: Fur traders—Norway—History—20th
 century. | LCSH: Indigenous peoples—
 Manitoba—History—20th century. | CSH:
 Manitoba—History—1918–1945.
Classification: LCC FC3375.9.F8 M6713 2022 |
 DDC 381/.4397097127—dc23

First edition, first printing, 2022.
First printed and bound in Canada by Houghton
Boston Printers, Saskatoon, Saskatchewan.
Copyediting by Kirsten Craven.
Proofreading by Kay Rollans.
Map by Eric Leinberger.

All rights reserved. No part of this publication
may be reproduced, stored in a retrieval
system, or transmitted in any form or by any
means (electronic, mechanical, photocopying,
recording, or otherwise) without prior written
consent. Contact University of Alberta Press for
further details.

University of Alberta Press supports copyright.
Copyright fuels creativity, encourages diverse
voices, promotes free speech, and creates
a vibrant culture. Thank you for buying
an authorized edition of this book and for
complying with the copyright laws by not
reproducing, scanning, or distributing any part
of it in any form without permission. You are
supporting writers and allowing University of
Alberta Press to continue to publish books for
every reader.

This work is published with the assistance of the
Western Canadiana Publications Endowment.

This translation has been published with the
financial support of NORLA.

University of Alberta Press gratefully
acknowledges the support received for its
publishing program from the Government of
Canada, the Canada Council for the Arts, and
the Government of Alberta through the Alberta
Media Fund.

In memory of
Einar Odd Mortensen Sr.
Einar Odd Mortensen Jr.

To
Karoline and Andrea
Ellie, Magnus, and Hedda

Contents

Acknowledgements IX

Introduction XI
INGRID URBERG & DANIEL SIMS

Map XLI

1 | North of the 53rd Parallel 1
2 | Alone at the Trading Post 17
3 | From Camp to Church 27
4 | From Greenhorn to Old-Timer 47
5 | Sons of the Wilderness 57
6 | Hudson's Bay versus Free Trader 89
7 | Towards New Hunting Grounds 97
8 | Days at Oxford Lake 113

Epilogue 127
A Personal Perspective on the Author and the Book
GERD KJUSTAD MORTENSEN

Reading Guide and Discussion Questions 137
Notes 141
Bibliography 167

Illustration by Birger Cranner. Used with permission from Birger Cranner's estate.

Acknowledgements

THIS WORK IS A COLLABORATIVE VENTURE, and the editors and co-author would like to thank all of the individuals and groups of people, named and unnamed, who have made this publication possible.

We would like to extend a special thanks to the late Dr. Rosalyn Ing, an Elder of the Opaskwayak Cree Nation, who provided valuable advice in the early stages of the project. We would also like to express our gratitude to the peer reviewers who provided us with constructive insights and suggestions during the revision process.

Einar Odd Mortensen Sr.'s account was originally written and published in Norwegian, and the version of the text found here is the result of numerous phases of translation and editing. Amesto Translations, Ahti Tolvanen, Marja-Liisa Tolvanen, and Gerd Kjustad Mortensen all contributed to the translation of the text that was eventually refined and edited by Ingrid Urberg.

We would also like to acknowledge and thank Dr. Arok Wolvengrey, Elder Ken Paupanekis, First Nations University of Canada, Dennis McLeod, and wintranslation for the help they provided us with the Swampy Cree sections in this book.

In addition, we are grateful for the financial support we have received for this project from the Augustana Faculty Dean's Initiatives Fund.

Finally, we would like to thank the estate of Birger Cranner (1902–1945) for kindly granting us permission to use two of his illustrations in this English edition of *The Fur Trader*. Birger Cranner originally gifted these illustrations to Einar Odd Mortensen Sr., and this is the first time they have been published.

Einar Odd Mortensen in northern Manitoba.

Introduction

INGRID URBERG & DANIEL SIMS

IN 1925, twenty-three-year-old Norwegian Einar Odd Mortensen left his job as a farmhand near Oslo to pursue work and seek adventure in the fur trading business in Manitoba. Though we do not know how long he intended to stay, or whether he was considering making this move a permanent one, we do know that he moved back home in 1928. A few years later, he married the girlfriend he had left behind and spent the rest of his life working in the family's furniture store in Oslo—an urban existence far removed from his three-year stint in what he called the Canadian wilderness at trading posts in Pine Bluff[1] and Oxford House. Though he wrote a draft manuscript describing his Canadian experiences shortly after he returned to Norway, he never completed it. Eventually, his incomplete work was pieced together and edited by his daughter-in-law and son, Gerd Kjustad Mortensen and Einar Odd Mortensen Jr. It was first published in Norwegian as *Pelshandleren: Mitt liv blant indianere i Nord-Canada 1925–28* (The fur trader: My life among Indians in northern Canada, 1925–28) in 2007,[2] nearly forty years after Mortensen's death in 1969. With this English translation, Mortensen's story is now available to a much broader audience.

Mortensen's manuscript received a fair bit of attention when it was published by Norway's largest publishing house, Gyldendal, due both to the way in which the author's family had compiled it from notes discovered after his death, and to the book's setting and northern Canadian content. This geographical region has long fascinated many Norwegians, particularly since the publication in 1931 of the account of another Norwegian temporary migrant, Helge Ingstad, who spent four years between 1926 and 1930 hunting and trapping in the Great Slave Lake region of the Northwest Territories. This book, *Pelsjegerliv blandt Nord-Kanadas indianere* (Life as a trapper among the Indians of northern Canada), also published by Gyldendal in 1931, was one of the bestselling Norwegian books of the twentieth century, and its English translation, *The Land of Feast and Famine*, first appeared in 1933.[3] Gerd Kjustad Mortensen believes her father-in-law may have abandoned his literary project due to the success of Ingstad's publication, but personal or professional obligations may also have prevented him from finding time to complete the manuscript. It is even possible that Mortensen was inspired to write down his account after reading *Pelsjegerliv*. Finally, Mortensen may never have intended to publish a manuscript, and may have written down his experiences for only himself and/or his family.

Canadians will likely be more familiar with Helge Ingstad's connection to the UNESCO World Heritage Site L'Anse aux Meadows than with his years around Great Slave Lake. In the 1960s, Ingstad and archaeologist Anne Stine Ingstad, his spouse, uncovered this Viking Age site on the northernmost tip of Newfoundland. Norwegians, on the other hand, are equally aware of Ingstad's years as a trapper in northern Canada, and Ingstad's account has had a profound impact on the Norwegian popular imagination. *Pelsjegerliv* has significantly shaped the picture of the Canadian North held by many Norwegians over nearly the past century, and it has inspired others to embark on their own adventures in remote regions of Canada. The Norwegian journalist and adventurer Lars Monsen (born 1963), for example,[4] obtained celebrity status after the 2005 NRK (Norwegian Public Broadcasting Company) television broadcast of *Canada på tvers* (Across Canada). This documentary series chronicles Monsen's 947-day solo journey from northeastern Alaska to the coast of Labrador during which he retraces some of Ingstad's footsteps.[5] The success of this television series is evidence that keen interest in the Canadian "wilderness" continues to this day, and may have contributed to Gyldendal's willingness to publish Mortensen's manuscript. Although there are some similarities between Mortensen's and Ingstad's accounts, Mortensen's experiences as a fur trader rather than trapper provide a snapshot of another aspect of the fur industry in a different geographical area. As a result, *The Fur Trader* both supplements and complements Ingstad's better-known narrative.[6]

Mortensen's text has much to offer contemporary readers. Fur trading enthusiasts and historians will appreciate the availability of another primary account of the waning days of the fur trade in northwestern Canada, one which provides a newcomer's personal perspectives of Indigenous Peoples and fur trader–Indigenous relations. He discusses issues ranging from trading post conditions and fur industry politics—including the rivalry between the Hudson's Bay Company and free traders—to travel by dogsled and canoe, northern hospitality, and Indigenous customs. Descriptions of interactions of non-Indigenous visitors, settlers, government officials, and clergy with members of the Indigenous community in northern Manitoba also receive attention and can be used by contemporary readers to discuss issues of race, gender, and class.

As historian Michael Payne points out in "Fur Trade Historiography," "fur trade posts are among the best documented communities in Canada between the mid-seventeenth and late nineteenth centuries."[7] For this reason fur trade records have often formed the basis of Canadian history during this time period, especially in the west. Despite the vast number of records that we do have, particularly from the Hudson's Bay Company, it is important to remember they provide an incomplete picture of the fur trade.. For example, though Revillon Frères was a major rival of the Hudson's Bay Company, the only full-scale extant journal we have from one of this French company's fur traders is *Northern Traders: The Last Days of the Fur Trade* by H.S.M. Kemp.[8]

Paradoxically, the journals of free fur traders are both more common when it comes to the raw number, and yet much rarer on a per capita basis than journals we have from those working for major fur trading companies. That is to say that while there are more journals, published and unpublished, by free traders than Revillon Frères traders, Kemp's single journal represents a large percentage of Revillon Frères traders as a whole.[9] Part of the difficulty in categorizing fur trader accounts is that to a certain extent free traders had always existed alongside the major trading companies, increasing in number whenever changes in the industry led to a surplus in labour.[10] Indeed, anyone with access to the necessary capital and/or credit to outfit themselves could get involved in the fur trade, especially after the Hudson's Bay Company's trade monopoly died in the wake of the Sayer Trial[11] and Confederation.[12] It helped that after 1818 annuities came to be considered the norm in Upper Canada when it came to treaty compensation, which meant that theoretically once treaties were signed in the Northwest Territories, treaty "Indians" had a steady supply of cash.[13] As Arthur Ray notes, free traders in the northwest responded by not only moving into the area, but they also began to sell substandard "treaty" or "fancy" goods that were marketed to those receiving annuities.[14] We will never know how many free traders there were, and even larger concerns, like that of H.C. Hyer,[15] are primarily known through the works of others, most notably the Hudson's Bay Company.[16]

This provenance should come as no surprise. Most fur trader accounts are from the Hudson's Bay Company (HBC) and, because of this simple fact, it is easy to treat the "Company" as being synonymous with the fur trade in Canada.[17] Logistically, this situation makes sense. As a large company that has remained in operation to this day, the HBC was able to maintain these records in ways private individuals with their finite lifespan simply were not able to. Indeed, it is often through the HBC that we have records from other fur trade companies, like the North West Company and Revillon Frères, which they absorbed.[18]

As a source of information, HBC records are problematic when it comes to the representations of free traders. While some were employed by the HBC as what one might call independent contractors, many were considered highly suspect by the HBC.[19] As former HBC clerk Martin Hunter states, "The building of the Canadian Pacific transcontinental road brought in its trail a class of very undesirable men. All rules have exceptions, I must therefore be just and not condemn all, but the majority of them were toughs and whisky peddlers."[20]

The lack of evidence from a free trader perspective has resulted in a whole host of mischaracterizations, which continue to the present.[21] Confusion arises when individuals, like historian Carolyn Podruchny, document how voyageurs used free trading, or the threat of it, as a negotiation tactic to achieve better working conditions.[22] Although her work is insightful, using the term *free traders* to refer to employees of the Hudson's Bay Company renders it somewhat difficult to distinguish them from actual free traders with no connection to the company at all.

Mortensen's memoirs provide an alternative perspective of not only the free traders but also the HBC itself. Perhaps because he did not finish the manuscript, he does not record the name of the company or companies that he worked for, but Mortensen does state that he worked for Ben Dembinsky, whom he describes as a "German Jew."[23] According to the Manitoba Historical Society, Isaac Benjamin "Ben" Dembinsky was born in Ontario in 1885, and in 1914 he moved to The Pas where he established the Western Trading Company. He opened at least five stores in Manitoba, and eventually two of these stores—those at The Pas and Flin Flon—were run as Ben Dembinsky Limited.[24] Gerd Kjustad Mortensen was able to contact Dembinsky's brother in Los Angeles, as well as Dembinsky's descendants in Flin Flon, Manitoba, to confirm that he had been active in the fur trade business in northern Manitoba in competition with the Hudson's Bay Company, Revillon Frères, and H.C. Hyers.

The promise of a job with Hyers is one of the reasons why Mortensen came to this part of the world, but as he notes in the first chapter it fell through. Having secured employment with Dembinsky in The Pas, Mortensen relocated to Pine Bluff and then Oxford House. According to his family, he was employed by H.C. Hyers while working in the Oxford House area, and photographic evidence seems to support this. It is at these two locations that most of the journal is set, and Mortensen goes into detail discussing some of the socio-cultural aspects of the fur trade, including fur trade protocols.[25] Aside from these details, we know little about how successful Mortensen was as a fur trader, though his employer, Ben Dembinsky, was fairly critical of the quality of the hides he brought back to The Pas after his first season. Mortensen does not provide us with statistics, but this lack of focus on the numbers of the fur trade is not unique. The journals of Alexander Mackenzie, some of the most famous fur trade journals, are more about exploration than the budgetary concerns of a trade expedition.[26]

Beyond this positionality, though, Mortensen's sixth chapter gives a brief history of the HBC and free traders, and he is quite critical of how the former treated the Indigenous Peoples it depended on. His assessment, however, is somewhat simplistic and at times quite racist. For example, not only does he use racist terms like *redskin*, but he clearly associates specific ethnicities with different work roles and stages of development. At times this simplification is obvious. For example, Indigenous Peoples are categorically described as uncivilized and living in an uncivilized world. At other times, however, it is less apparent, generally when it could be viewed as benign and/or engaging with a positive stereotype. For example, Mortensen feels the need to comment on how one of his Icelandic companions is a fisher, like most Icelanders are. While true in the sense that the fishing industry in Iceland is a significant part of the Icelandic economy, it is nonetheless not relevant to the text and reduces—either intentionally or unintentionally—his companion to just another Icelander. The fact that this individual is unnamed does not help.

In a similar vein, his inclusion of Swampy Cree words and phrases, while positive in the sense that he is including the language, are problematic when it comes to spelling and translation.[27] For example, his translation of *kitchi oogemoo* as "the great white man" and *oogemoo* as "master" raises questions about his conscious or unconscious perception of perceived racial hierarchy in northern Manitoba, while his exchange in Swampy Cree with one of his female customers is risqué to say the least. Rather than try to downplay these passages by inserting politically correct language, we have kept them in the original text. To paraphrase Oliver Cromwell, we want to see Mortensen, "warts and all." To avoid belabouring the point, however, we have generally only provided explanatory notes the first time these instances occur in the text.

Moving away from linguistics, Mortensen the historian is equally unreliable. For example, he ignores—either intentionally or unintentionally—the initial rivalry with the Compagnie du Nord, as well as the battles during the Nine Years' War that saw the French capture many of the HBC forts on the Hudson and James bays in his history of the HBC. Similarly, he does not mention the New North West (XY) Company and seems to downplay the actual armed conflicts that preceded the forced union of the North West Company and HBC in 1821.

In other words, like all narrators of personal accounts, Mortensen is, in some instances, unreliable. As Leonard Bell famously stated, "Observational neutrality is a fiction. Perception is never unmediated or value-free."[28] Mortensen's perceptions are clearly shaped by the time period and larger culture in which he found himself. Part of this world view was an unquestioned racism that existed that saw Indigenous Peoples as the child-like savage other, either noble or ignoble.[29] Guiding this way of framing one's experiences was the belief that Indigenous Peoples in North America had by this point in time been defeated and were now either tragic heroes or no longer truly Indigenous, disappearing in the face of civilization either literally or through assimilation.[30] If anything remained of their former glory, it could be found in the Wild West shows, other public events, literature, or film.[31] As Daniel Francis argues, all four were seen as preserving what was about to be lost.[32] Many scholars note these views often persist into the present day, especially when they helped form world views, disciplines, and discourses.[33] According to Frank Goodyear, "The popular image of the Indian fluctuates to meet the needs of the dominant culture and to justify its treatment of the native."[34] And as Theodore Jojola concludes, "Unless direct roles in the image industry are sought by native people, the process of stereotyping by outsiders will continue."[35]

It is also important to mention that while at times Mortensen's racism is subtle and arguably grounded in his myopic representation of other cultures and the culture shock he experienced, at other times it results in unintentionally ludicrous assertions. An example of the former is Mortensen's claim that Indigenous men are lazy when not hunting or freighting, which could be interpreted as a statement about relaxation after a hard day's work. An example of the latter is the veracity of his claim that Indigenous women let their underwear rot off their body. This claim is seemingly unfounded given his supposed adherence to the unwritten "hands-off" policy, although as mentioned his conversation with at least one Indigenous woman was by his own account risqué.

There are also areas in which it is hard to make a determination of Mortensen's attitudes given the way in which this narrative was compiled. For example, Mortensen left behind a collection of photographs that contain a number of Indigenous individuals. While the names of a few of the men are noted on the backs of the photos, Mortensen did not record the names of the majority of men or any of the women or children featured in the pictures. Not recording the names of Indigenous individuals in photos and first-hand accounts was a common occurrence until the late twentieth century. This practice stemmed from the viewing of Indigenous Peoples as the other, and it is the subject of a recent and robust body of scholarship examining "the unnamed Indian." However, it is unclear if Mortensen would have included names on more of these images if he had published the book during his lifetime.[36] Relevant to this discussion is the fact that the photo captions in the published Norwegian version from 2007 do not include the names of the few Indigenous individuals recorded by Mortensen. It is also important to note that in his draft manuscript Mortensen only names a couple of the Indigenous individuals he describes. This practice points towards Mortensen's othering of the Indigenous People he encountered. However, as with many things in the text, it is hard to tell what was intentional and what was a product of the original manuscript being left incomplete.

Similarly, with regard to the Indigenous Peoples included in this book, it is ultimately unclear whether they were First Nations or Métis. First and foremost, it would be a mistake to assume that the usage of the nouns "Indian" and "half-breed" in the English translation equate to First Nations and Métis. True, in the original Norwegian manuscript and his notes, Mortensen used the terms *indianere* and *halvblodsindianere*. However, neither term captures the nuances that the supposed English synonyms of First Nations and Métis have in Canada that allow for both to be Indigenous Peoples, at times with similar if not the same ancestry, while still being distinct. It is a mistake to consider any First Nations individual with European ancestry, or any European individual with Indigenous ancestry to be Métis. This axiom remains true even if that European ancestor comes from France. The Métis are those with an unbroken ancestral connection to the historic Métis homeland—the prairies and parkland of what became western Canada and parts of the United States. Admittedly, this homeland overlaps with the territory of numerous First Nations, which, depending on their relationship to the Métis, has led, at times, to conflict down to the present day. However, one would be hard pressed to find any homeland on this planet that is not contested in some way, shape, or form. Factor in Métis membership in *nehiyaw pwat*—the Iron Confederacy—and one is left with a nation that has complex political, social, cultural, and historical connections to the land and other nations, both human and nonhuman. Métis identity encompasses much more than simply having both Indigenous and non-Indigenous ancestors in one's family tree.

Similarly, assigning identity based on community and location is tempting but equally inappropriate. While it is easy to conclude that a community has a specific identity, and then based on this conclusion assign this identity to its residents, such logic is premised on the community in question being homogenous. Pine Bluff provides a shining example. According to the text, it is an Indian reserve inhabited by those identified as Indians and/or Cree. Yet a 1992 report on the community clearly states it is a Métis community, while also acknowledging an older unidentified community with close connections to local First Nations.[37] Seemingly contradictory, it is important to remember that just as the Métis homeland overlaps with the territory of numerous First Nations, historically the Métis—like many other groups in western Canada—lived in heterogenous communities. What may appear to be relatively homogeneous situations today are most often a result of government policy, classifications, and imagined community rather than ancestry.[38] This situation should come as no surprise to anyone familiar with the Métis. As mentioned, they are part of a multinational confederacy that also includes the Nehiyawak, Anishinaabe, and Nakoda, and it is not unusual for large Indigenous families with their origin from the west to contain both members with Indian status and members with Métis citizenship.

As a fur trader, it is also not entirely clear where all Mortensen's customers came from. While the local community would certainly be expected to dominate, there was nothing stopping people from coming from farther afield. Furthermore, expecting Mortensen to know in detail the identity of each of his customers is unfair. For this reason, we have kept terms like *Indian* and *half-breed* in the English translation and used *Indigenous Peoples* in the introduction. To do otherwise would suggest we are making a claim on identity without sufficient evidence. We would invite readers to consider this situation when reading the text and would like to suggest Chris Andersen's *Métis*,[39] Nicole St-Onge, Carolyn Podruchny, and Brenda MacDougall's *Contours of a People*,[40] and Jennifer Adese and Chris Andersen's *A People and a Nation*[41] for anyone interested in examining the complex history and identity of the Métis.

At the end of the day, this book is the memoir of an individual human being. In other words, while it is of interest to scholars in the disciplines of history, Indigenous studies, Scandinavian studies, and literature, it is about Einar Odd Mortensen Sr. and his perceptions. It should come as no surprise, therefore, that we learn the most about Mortensen's views, filtered through his temporal and cultural lenses.

Mortensen's frequent use of humour in his narrative also needs to be considered in an analysis of his attitudes towards Indigenous Peoples and other cultures in general, and it complicates a contemporary discussion of racism in the narrative. Mortensen does not hesitate to depict himself as a naive greenhorn, whom we laugh at and with while he confronts conditions vastly different from those he has experienced at home in Norway. While travelling on dogsled from The Pas, which he describes as a small settlement bordering the wilderness, to his first job at Pine Bluff, for example, he unwisely insists on using impractical Norwegian skis rather than snowshoes, to the bemusement of his Icelandic travelling companion. Mortensen's descriptions of encounters with hordes of mosquitoes, harrowing canoe rides through river rapids with Indigenous guides, and the process of learning the fur trading ropes are entertaining and, at times, self-deprecating. Mortensen employs a light-hearted tone while describing the culture shock he frequently experiences, and the colourful characters he describes—Indigenous and non-Indigenous—often have customs and standards regarding hygiene, dress, hunting, trading, rations, and the training and care of dogs that clash with his more urbane Norwegian sensibilities.

Mortensen also employs humour in the form of light-hearted satire as a means of both indirect and direct social criticism of the treatment of Indigenous Peoples by the Roman Catholic Church and the Canadian government. As an agnostic from an officially Protestant country, Mortensen rebuffs the attempts of a Catholic priest to convert him while he is at Pine Bluff. His satirical description of the relatively luxurious way in which this man—"his eminence"—travels to manipulatively preach to the Indigenous Peoples there is one example of negative social commentary. Mortensen's comments on the priest's role in collecting furs to cover school taxes are also critical.

Though Mortensen's use of humor and satire to highlight the negative impact of Europeans on Indigenous cultures may be interpreted as fairly progressive for his day, the influence of the time period and world in which he found himself is clearly seen in his depiction of Indigenous Peoples. To today's audience, Mortensen's portrayals of them sound quite racist, and like his contemporaries he makes no attempt to be politically correct. As previously mentioned, not only does he refer to Indigenous individuals as "Indians" or "half-breed Indians," but he also claims they "lack an understanding of hygiene" and repeatedly references the dirt on their faces and/or their smell. In part, these descriptions seem to be due to the expectations Mortensen seems to have had when he arrived in Canada. Like many of his contemporaries, it appears he learned about Indigenous Peoples primarily through popular media, like James Fenimore Cooper's *Last of the Mohicans*. In his fifth chapter he even compares his customers with the fictional characters found in this novel and laments how much actual Indigenous Peoples have changed from their supposed original state.[42] As he

The eyes of those who live on the reserve do not exactly radiate the bloodthirstiness of wild Indians. I have not seen any representatives of this group. These Indians actually appear to be peace-loving. There are no dried scalps hanging from their belts. In fact, their belts are barely able to hold up their ragged pants. The rest of their equipment reveals that they struggle through life in a constant battle to keep their rags together. They are not very successful, yet they putter along so peacefully. Such Indians are a dime a dozen. These first Indians I see remind me more of rag collectors in Oslo than the free sons of the Prairie I had imagined them to be. ("North of the 53rd Parallel," page 4)

In articulating these expectations, Mortensen reveals not only his own racist views but also his ignorance of the people with whom he was trading. While he never uses any official designation for them,[43] it appears he primarily served the Métis and the Opaskwayak Cree Nation at Pine Bluff and the Bunibonibee Cree Nation at their main village on the Oxford House 24 reserve.[44] A number of Mortensen's photographs were taken at God's Lake, about seventy kilometres east of Oxford House, which indicates he may have conducted business with members of the God's Lake First Nation as well. However, he does not mention this location in his manuscript or notes. Of these four groups, only the Métis could be described as "free sons of the Prairie," although rarely are they portrayed as stereotypical "Indians" in popular culture. The Bunibonibee Cree Nation, the Opaskwayak Cree Nation, and the God's Lake First Nation, on the other hand, are all subarctic Swampy Cree and therefore by definition neither eastern woodlands "Mohicans" nor even the Prairie-based Plains Cree. Expecting them to be like any of these groups would be similar to a Swampy Cree individual going to Norway and lamenting the fact that the Norwegians are not like the Dutch. Even if Mortensen's customers, acquaintances, and neighbours had been like the Mohicans and Plains Cree, it is highly unlikely they would have lived up to Mortensen's expectations, particularly when one considers that James Fenimore Cooper primarily based his Mohicans on missionary Joseph Heckewelder's less than ideal "ethnography" of the Lenape, rather than the actual Mahicans or Mohegans.[45]

Mortensen's assumptions, racism and positionality are particularly notable when one considers that he provides seemingly progressive social commentary for his time. We have already mentioned his criticism of the fur trade and his less than flattering comments regarding representatives of the Roman Catholic Church, but he is also equally critical of the residential school system and Indigenous involvement in the First World War. With regard to the last two, however, his ignorance of the situation mars otherwise admirable observations. For example, in describing residential schools, he states:

> *In Canada there are a number of Indian Boarding Schools, which some Indian children attend. These schools turn out the most unruly and dishonest types of Indians one can imagine. The most useless Indians that I dealt with had generally received their "wisdom" from these boarding schools. However, I am not of the opinion that these free sons of nature necessarily become scoundrels if they are lifted up into the enlightened state provided by book learning. ("From Camp to Church," page 34)*

These words accurately capture the fact that residential schools were really effective at producing damaged individuals with little real education. Unlike Canada's first prime minister, Mortensen does not blame the nature of the student but the system itself.[46] It is important to bear in mind, however, that he was not the first person to complain about the system, and it does not appear he was aware of the widespread abuse that took place in these schools, or the fact that they were factories of cultural genocide.[47]

Similarly, his assessment of Indigenous involvement in the First World War is equally dubious. In recounting the accounts of Indigenous veterans, he states:

> *They spoke almost half-heartedly about their experiences, and without any enthusiasm. They used simple words to describe enormous suffering. They participated as so-called volunteers, and of course they did not understand very much English. One day, a draft sergeant came up, and he was zealous to serve his country. These*

recruiters weren't particularly concerned with using scrupulous means, and in that way the Indians enlisted as volunteers.

Large groups of Indians were loaded on ships and sent over the ocean. They sat together in over-crowded quarters. Seasickness and other misery ruled over them in a brutal fashion, and they died like flies. But they died for their country. Those who survived were given the glorious task of emptying French latrines. Here they fought many a brave battle, and as thanks for their contribution they were, perhaps, given a medal of some sort. The only good thing about their trip abroad was that they had learned a little English. Some of them had learned it so well that they could swear like a white sergeant.
("From Greenhorn to Old-Timer," page 53)

Norway was neutral during the First World War. As a result, it was perhaps easier for Mortensen to critically consider the war itself. After all, he was not a veteran and his state was not directly challenged per se. It is possible that the veterans he met did have these experiences, but the question nevertheless exists of why the account is so similar to wider stereotypes of colonial soldiers during the war that originated with the French and their West African soldiers.[48] It seems to confirm Bell's assertion that European representations of Indigenous Peoples owe "more to other European representations" than any objective reality.[49] Either way, it is important to bear in mind that Mortensen's description of the Indigenous war experience does not necessarily accurately depict the larger Indigenous experience during the war and is complicated by the ambiguity of the identity of the people he is talking about. During the First World War at least 35 percent of the Indigenous male population in Canada enlisted, often due to the historic alliances and/or treaties with the Imperial Crown and/or a desire to use service to fight for equal rights.[50] These are, of course, idealist reasons and Indigenous individuals also signed up for more mundane reasons, like the opportunity to have a regular paycheque, the hope for direct material incentives for themselves and their communities, and/or due to the encouragement of others, including the promise of an adventure or because one of their friends had already done so.[51] Even when conscription was implemented in

1917, Indigenous Peoples were subsequently deemed to be exempt from mandatory service in part because of treaties.[52] Furthermore, it was not until December 1915 that their desire to fight was officially supported.[53] And, finally, since assimilation was one of the desired outcomes of the federal government, Indigenous veterans were distributed throughout units and saw action throughout the war.[54]

Mortensen's portrayal of Indigenous veterans also highlights the variety of topics covered in fur trade memoirs compared to post journals, correspondence, and account books, though many texts cannot be neatly placed within one genre. For example, although in theory post journals were simply business records, their authors sometimes treated them as personal journals, adding comments and information more relevant to their personal lives than the fur trade itself. A case in point is Sir Alexander Mackenzie's journal, which starts with "A General History of the Fur Trade." In addition to outlining his version of the history of the fur trade, Mackenzie also discusses how he got involved in the business and provides ethnographic and linguistic information on some of the First Nations he met while employed in it.[55] While it could be argued that these details represented valuable data for anyone involved in the fur trade, the same cannot be said about Mackenzie's assessment of the quality of Indigenous songs and dances found on page thirty-five of the journal proper.[56]

Fur trade memoirs are, arguably, more accessible to the general public than other fur trade journals and records, in part due to their broader intended audience and the editing they went through before publication. Despite Sir Alexander Mackenzie's claims to have published his unedited journal, one merely has to compare his journal with that of Samuel Black to see how polished the former is.[57] At a basic level, the authors of these manuscripts, colloquially known as "fair copies," intended them to be business reports that could be submitted to their superiors as proof of their deeds.[58] Beyond this rather mundane role, it also appears that some hoped that if they could get them published, they, like Mackenzie, could gain fortune and fame.[59] We will never know if Mortensen was aware of these published accounts and their authors and, if so, if he was hoping to follow in their footsteps by polishing and publishing his notes.

As a literary type, these fur trade memoirs fall into the larger genre of travel literature for the simple fact that they provided their European audience "a sense of ownership, entitlement and familiarity with respect to the distant parts of the world that were being explored, invaded, invested in, and colonized."[60] Sometimes this role was quite literal—fur trade companies and the colonial office in London used these journals to inform their ongoing activities and claim new territory. Other times, it was conceptual.[61] As the first European north of Mesoamerica to cross the continent, Mackenize's journals not only documented journeys of "discovery" to the Arctic and Pacific oceans, thereby making his audience aware of their existence, but also provided a brief history of the terrestrial fur trade in British North America.[62] As a result, his readers could now easily learn about these new parts of the British Empire and their inhabitants without ever experiencing it in person. In doing so, his descriptions laid the foundation for future knowledge of the area and its inhabitants by the British and other European powers as they engaged in resource extraction and development.[63] Indeed, it was Mackenzie's rather dramatic depiction of the Peace River Canyon that laid the foundation for the W.A.C. Bennett Dam in northern British Columbia.[64]

As a Norwegian in the early twentieth century, one might argue that it is highly unlikely that Mortensen was plotting the acquisition of Canada for the Kingdom of Norway. However, it is noteworthy that at the time Mortensen lived in Canada, Norway had not yet recognized Canada's sovereign rights in the Arctic due to the activities of Norwegian explorers such as Otto Sverdrup and Roald Amundsen. The recognition of Canada's sovereignty was not acknowledged until 1930,[65] and Indigenous perspectives were not a part of the conversation.

Furthermore, Mortensen freely admits to his own biased and limited point of view, stating:

If I am to add anything to the descriptions I provide of them [the Cree]...then it would have to be with a mixture of good and bad as I saw them through my eyes, emphasizing the peculiarities that struck me. Of course, I understand that this would be just one yardstick, and a subjective one at that. If one considers that I come from a country with municipal dental care and school breakfasts for children, among other things, then I will, naturally, only be giving a one-dimensional and biased impression, and a superficial description at that. ("Sons of the Wilderness," page 60)

However, comments such as these do not acknowledge colonization in any way, thus missing the point entirely. Mortensen was part of the economic colonial project in the Dominion of Canada that we call the fur trade. Indeed, his return to Norway only highlights the fact that the fur trade was extractive rather than settler colonialism.[66] He was following in the footsteps of numerous other fur traders who returned to Europe or eastern North America once their time was over. It does not matter if Mortensen was aware of this fact. After all, the twisted beauty of colonialism is that many people are unaware of their part in the system.[67]

Indeed, it is quite clear that Mortensen was part of the system regardless of how enlightened he might have been. For example, in highlighting how different the local Indigenous People are from him, Mortensen is not only helping define them but also himself.[68] In his repeated references to how dirty and/or smelly Indigenous People are he is contributing to the so-called soap saga—the idea that Indigenous People are filthy and therefore need to be cleansed by civilization.[69] Similarly, his account of being warned not to engage in sexual relations with Indigenous women, combined with his insistence that he did not, highlights the inherent problem sexual relations with the colonized represented to the colonial project.[70] For all that he was, it is important to bear in mind that he was a product of his time.

The narrator of *The Fur Trader* is a young man who both describes and, at times, challenges and criticizes the conditions, people and power structures he observes in northern Manitoba—including the Hudson's Bay Company, government officials, and the church. He has come from a society that is not only more homogeneous in terms of religion, cultural customs, and ethnicity than his new environment—accounting for the culture shock he experiences as he struggles to interact with people who have vastly different mindsets from his own—but one in which *Janteloven* (the law of Jante) dominates thinking. This term, coined in 1933 by the Danish-Norwegian author Aksel Sandemose, describes an unwritten expectation within the Nordic region that individuals are to place the good of society above personal ambition. This way of thinking continues to this day. Perhaps the "strange restlessness" that causes Mortensen to leave behind the monotony of everyday life is a reaction to this cultural mindset and/or societal expectations for conformity and convention. Mortensen never directly addresses his reasons for leaving Norway in his account, beginning *medias res* in The Pas in the late fall of 1925.[71] His account ends abruptly and in mid-action as well, before he answers the call of his family to return home in 1928.

Strikingly, Mortensen does not share any details of his family or life in Norway with his literary audience, and, according to his family, he did not share accounts of his stint in Canada with them upon his return.[72] Silences are a part of Mortensen's life and literary endeavours, and though he does not provide his readers with a satisfying ending to his Canadian adventure, he has recorded intriguing episodes.

A contemporary North American audience may note other gaps and silences in Mortensen's narrative. Except for a fleeting reference to reindeer husbandry, for example, he does not mention the Sámi experience—material many Indigenous studies scholars might want to see.[73] Similarly, although Indigenous Peoples do appear in the text as customers, acquaintances, and neighbours, this book is not an ethnography and primarily focuses on Mortensen's experiences.

It should be noted that while Mortensen shared next to nothing about his Canadian experiences with his children, he did discuss his life as a fur trader in Manitoba at some length with at least one acquaintance, Birger Cranner, a Norwegian artist and illustrator. Cranner (1902–1945) was born in 1902 in Kristiania, now Oslo, and he lived for some time in Vancouver, BC, where he married. After the break up of this marriage, he moved back to Oslo, and it was there he met Einar Odd Mortensen. They shared stories of their time in Canada, and Cranner was inspired to draw pictures of Mortensen's adventures in Manitoba. Mortensen employed the bartering ways he had used in Manitoba, and he gave Cranner some furniture in exchange for the illustrations.[74]

Einar Odd Mortensen's decision to spend time in the Canadian wilderness, and the effort he took to write about it for a potentially broad audience, is unsurprising given his era. Mortensen was born in 1902, only a few years before Norway became independent from Sweden in 1905. This marked the end of over five hundred years of unions with other Nordic countries, and during the late nineteenth century, a period in which Norwegians were developing their collective identity as they worked towards the dissolution of their political union with Sweden, their countryman Fridtjof Nansen undertook and wrote about expeditions in extreme conditions in Greenland and the Arctic Ocean. These journeys were scientific in nature, but adventure was another important motivating factor. The resulting narratives were best sellers, and were quickly translated into multiple other languages.[75]

Though Nansen's published accounts contained scientific information, they were written with the general public in mind. These and other polar expeditions not only resulted in an appetite for travel literature among the Norwegian public,[76] they also led to "the new Arctic ideal of manhood"—a phrase coined by Tor Bomann-Larsen.[77] Literary critic Ellen Rees points out how "when Nansen returned home to Norway, the public embraced him not just as a hero, but as the very embodiment of all that was positive about the nation; the newly emerging conception of the Norwegian nation was posited as active, healthy, and male."[78] Rees goes on to describe how Nansen's appearance, interests, and skill on skis "all expressed the new masculine ideal of the outdoorsman, who rejected the supposedly degenerative influences of modern society and sought a purer life in nature."[79] Mortensen's choice to work and seek out adventure in the northern Canadian wilderness indicates he, like many other young men of his generation, may well have been influenced by the "Nansen ideal." While texts such as Helge Ingstad's iconic memoir contain more direct reflections on the virtues of life in the wilderness, Mortensen is, at least, careful to acknowledge the unique aspects of the space in which he finds himself.

My last glimpse of civilization does not cause me to be sad or melancholy. Nothing can stop me now—the free life has taken hold of me, and I have laid hold of it...A new wilderness awaits me, with new experiences, new days, and new journeys in new surroundings. ("Towards New Hunting Grounds," page 97)

As mentioned, we have no way of knowing if Mortensen had read any North American fur trader journals before or after his stint in Canada. However, he was clearly aware of the fur trade since he had attempted to secure a job before he arrived in Canada with the aforementioned Hyer, a Norwegian fur trading company based in Norway House, Manitoba.[80] The closest equivalent to fur trade memoirs in Norway in terms of literary genre would be *fangstmannsbiografiene* (trapper/hunter biographies), considered to be a subgenre of Norwegian polar literature.[81] These accounts are from Svalbard, an Arctic archipelago located halfway between northern Norway and the North Pole, which became a part of Norway in 1925 due to the Spitsbergen (Svalbard) Treaty. Today, these islands are described in government publications and tourism marketing materials with words such as "Arctic wilderness" and "Europe's last (great) wilderness."[82]

Mortensen's use of the term *wilderness* warrants examination, given the fact that he uses *villmarka* (wilderness) in the opening paragraph of his narrative, and then returns to this word over forty times. Wilderness is, of course, a complicated cultural construct, and its myriad associations, definitions, and usages vary depending on factors such as time period, culture, and disciplinary perspective.[83] In recent years, the ways in which the notion of wilderness has been used in a variety of times and places to exclude the physical presence, history, and activities of Indigenous Peoples has received considerable attention.[84]

In his account, Mortensen equates wilderness with a lack of modern transportation infrastructure, and a place in which people rely on canoes and dogsleds rather than railways to move themselves and goods. Coming from the most populous urban area in Norway, Mortensen found himself in a very different physical context when he arrived in northern Manitoba. Mortensen describes a range of expectations and feelings while in "the wilderness," from excitement to loneliness, and as seen in the previous quotation, he equates this space with the new, the unknown, and possibility. Indeed, it appears adventure is one of the factors that motivated Mortensen to take a break from his urban, European existence.

Although Mortensen does not directly state that the individuals he describes who move to the wilderness to work, to escape various elements of modern life, and/or to seek adventure, are necessarily male, he does not make any effort to paint it as a suitable place for non-Indigenous women. While we know that settler women lived and worked in remote areas of Canada long before Mortensen's visit,[85] and that Mortensen undoubtedly interacted with both settler women and children in Norway House and elsewhere,[86] he only provides a few fleeting references to settler women in his text.

Mortensen acknowledges the wilderness he experiences was originally populated with Indigenous Peoples and continues to be so, but he also juxtaposes wilderness with civilization, seemingly subscribing to a type of primitivism that was common at the time. In the chapter "Sons of the Wilderness," he writes,

> *In the midst of culture's functionalist heaviness and a restlessness from the lack of a real life, we long for the wilderness and a free life. A free life, with natural joys and sorrows, where people are in their natural, primitive form. And in the boyish fantasy and boyish mind of an adult, the Indian has always lived his dangerous life as an incarnation of the free man. (page 58)*

When Mortensen uses "we," he appears to be referencing the white, European male gaze, and he returns to this theme of longing when he writes, "But the call of the wilderness was gradually heard by others who came, whether from the monotonous life of the farm or from the cities. And so new people arrived: adventurers, outdoors people and those in distress" (page 77). Viewing the wilderness as an anecdote for the trappings and problems of the modern, male life is something that William Cronon calls "a peculiarly bourgeois form of antimodernism."[87] As historian Liza Piper has pointed out, this form of antimodernism also helps "to reinforce inequitable social relations and further reify ideas about gender and race."[88] In the case of Indigenous Peoples, it erases their title to the land, their development of the land, and their connections to the land. In doing so, it renders them at best merely individuals living on the land and at worst no better than wild animals.[89] The truly insidious aspect of this connection, however, is that it was often not directly stated and/or masked by positive stereotypes, like the historical noble savage or its modern equivalent the ecological Indian.[90]

Manuscript History

According to his family, though Einar Odd Mortensen rarely spoke of his Canadian adventures after returning to Norway in 1928, he told his children he was working on a manuscript.[91] After his death in 1969, his daughter Elisabeth (Lise) Nordhagen took care of Mortensen's handwritten and typed notes, along with dozens of pictures. She did not do anything with these materials for many years, though she was careful to take them with her during several moves. Eventually she turned them over to her brother Einar Odd Mortensen Jr. and his wife Gerd Kjustad Mortensen so they could edit the material to make it accessible for Einar Odd Mortensen's grandchildren. The Mortensens discovered many things about Einar Odd Sr. while reading his unfinished manuscript, and they realized the materials might be of interest to a broader audience. After compiling and editing two chapters, they submitted them to Norway's largest publishing house, Gyldendal, for review. They were encouraged to continue their work with publication as their goal.[92]

The Mortensens received these materials in 2005, around the time that Mortensen Jr. was diagnosed with a serious illness, and the book was published by Gyldendal in 2007, less than two years before Mortensen Jr.'s death in January 2009. Due to her husband's failing health, Gerd Kjustad Mortensen did the bulk of the work, though she frequently consulted with her spouse. However, it is Einar Odd Mortensen Jr. that is credited with this work in the afterword of the Norwegian edition, a decision the couple made together at the time. This English version more accurately recognizes Gerd Kjustad Mortensen's central role in the editing of the original

Norwegian version. Kjustad Mortensen did not add any material to the notes, and she did her best to be faithful to her father-in-law's voice and conversational style as she polished those sections of the narrative that required substantive editing and reordering.

Though *The Fur Trader* is a collaborative personal narrative, its protagonist and author did not make this decision. Accordingly, the Norwegian editor, Gerd Kjustad Mortensen, has aimed not to insert herself into the text in an overt fashion. However, the editors and translators have put their mark on this work by the necessity of making certain stylistic, linguistic, and structural choices. Since Einar Mortensen Sr. did not see this project to its end, we will never know how he would have compiled and edited it if he had submitted it for publication in his lifetime. Would an older "narrating I"—to use the words of literary theorists Sidonie Smith and Julia Watson— have modified the portrayal of the "narrated I" found in the notes compiled by a younger Mortensen?[93] Would the text have been more guarded in tone or more contemplative or personally revealing if it had been edited by an older Mortensen? Neither the manuscript collaborators nor the readers of this edited text can answer these speculative questions, but raising them highlights the complex and myriad choices faced by the writers of personal narratives, particularly when the text is edited and published long after the events were experienced and/or recorded.

Since writers of personal narratives are relating their own experiences, they generally have a fair bit of control over which portions or slices of their life they choose to share, and their perspective on these experiences will change with time. Our constructions of ourselves and our storied experiences are generally in flux, depending on various personal, societal, and temporal circumstances. We will never know how an older Mortensen would have altered or framed the construction of the younger Mortensen we find in the unfinished manuscript. What we can say with a level of certainty is that if the manuscript had been submitted in the author's lifetime, a publishing house would have undoubtedly requested a more developed ending than we have here. However, we have no way of knowing if Mortensen would have provided more detail about his life in Norway upon his return.

Gyldendal asked Ragnar Kvam Jr. (b. 1942), a Norwegian journalist, critically acclaimed author, and adventurer, to write a brief preface to *Pelshandleren*. This was a sensible marketing choice. Kvam was, at the time, and continues to be, well known in Norway, not only for his research and books on Thor Heyerdahl[94] and Arctic and Antarctic explorers and expeditions, but also for his accounts of sailing around the world. When he was in his mid-forties, Kvam sold all of his possessions and embarked on the first stage of this trip, and this journey took him fourteen years to complete. Kvam begins his preface by focusing on the desire that many people experience to seek the unknown and leave their everyday, mundane lives behind. Of course, unlike Mortensen and Kvam, most people do not act on this impulse. After briefly outlining the narrative's main themes and pointing out the ways in which this text supplements Helge Ingstad's adventures and narrative, Kvam returns to his opening theme in the preface's closing sentences:

> *Let this work give food for thought to people of our time who desire to travel far afield. They will not find Canada like Mortensen and Ingstad found it. But they will find the inspiration which drove them, and their will to leave [the familiar behind]. The world has been explored with a fine-tooth comb, and there isn't more to discover, some people lament. That is nonsense. There will always be many things to discover for those who dare to travel. Einar Odd Mortensen's book gives me evidence of that.*[95]

Pelshandleren received widespread attention in the Norwegian press upon its release. Reviews and interviews with Einar Odd Mortensen's family appeared in at least five national daily newspapers from across the political and social spectrum: the conservative leaning, nonsocialist *Aftenposten*, the socialist *Klassekampen*, which markets itself as "*Venstresidas dagsavis*," or "the daily newspaper of the left," the tabloids *Dagbladet* and *Verdens Gang*, and *Dagens Næringsliv*, which focuses on business news. All of these newspapers but *Klassekampen* were among the six most widely circulated print and online editions at the time the reviews were published in the spring of 2007.[96] Regional and local newspapers such as

Oppland Arbeiderblad, *Hamar Arbeiderblad*, and *Stavanger Aftenblad* also published reviews. In addition, book notices appeared in several magazines, including *Snø og Ski*—for Norwegian Ski Association members—and *Vi Menn*, a magazine marketed to a male audience that focuses on documentary material, including hunting and outdoor life.[97]

A common thread linking the majority of these reviews and notices is the way in which they frame Mortensen's experiences and narrative in light of Ingstad's adventures and the literary quality of Ingstad's book. Ingstad references appear in opening paragraphs, subtitles, and in one case the review title—"Kom Ingstad i forkjøpet" (Preempted Ingstad).[98] Per Haddal, *Aftenposten*'s reviewer, notes, "Though this book doesn't reach the level of Helge Ingstad's account, it does speak to everyone who is drawn towards adventure in the wilderness." Haddal is of the opinion that the book is worth reading even though it was written almost a hundred years ago.[99] Kåre Bulie's review in *Dagbladet* highlights ways in which Mortensen's text compliments Ingstad's iconic narrative. "In many ways Mortensen's experiences cover things Ingstad hasn't written about. Therefore the book should be an obligatory supplement for those many people who have enjoyed Ingstad's book." Like Haddal and a number of other reviewers, Bulie theorizes that Mortensen did not complete his manuscript due to the success of Ingstad's book, and he notes that Gyldendal has basically given it the same subtitle as Ingstad's.[100] We can speculate that this was perhaps a marketing ploy. The local newspaper *Ringsaker Blad* also states that Mortensen's narrative can be read as "a supplement to Helge Ingstad."[101]

Novelist, journalist, and newspaper editor Jon Michelet, in a substantial, lengthy review in *Klassekampen*, differs from the other reviewers noted here in that he comments negatively on Mortensen's style. "*Pelshandleren* cannot be called a good book in the usual sense. It isn't well written. It is an amateur's rough work, [and] it ends abruptly." Michelet is, however, positive about the value of Mortensen's account in the way it describes the transformative changes people sometimes go through when they encounter the other. He points out how, as Mortensen's stereotypical and romantic ideas of

Indigenous Peoples of North America collide with a complicated reality, he grows to respect them. Though Mortensen's interaction with Indigenous Peoples are noted by all of the reviewers mentioned here, only Michelet uses the word *colonization* to describe the activities of Europeans and the HBC in North America. He points out Mortensen's attempts at social criticism, as well as the limitations of this criticism, noting that "at the same time, he [Mortensen] didn't recognize that he, himself, had taken on such a role [of a colonizer]." Michelet challenges privileged Western readers to critically think about their own attitudes when meeting "poor, oppressed and exploited" people on global travels and asks them if their views are all that different from those Mortensen held in the 1920s.[102]

Publicity surrounding *Pelshandleren* was not limited to newspapers and magazines. Mortensen's account was also the subject of a national radio program on NRK in which journalist Torstein Paulsen interviewed the Mortensens, the book editors. This program was first broadcast in April 2007 and has been rebroadcast several times.[103] The book was soon translated into Finnish by Marja-Liisa Tolvanen, and it was published by Minerva in 2009 as *Turkiskauppiaana intiaanireservaatissa* (A fur trader on an Indian reservation).[104]

Language Usage

Norwegians speak a wide variety of local and regional dialects, and when they write they can choose from two official written norms of Norwegian—*bokmål* (book language) and *nynorsk* (new Norwegian). People generally choose the norm that most closely resembles their spoken dialect, and *bokmål* is the dominant written norm in most parts of Norway, except in the western part of the country. *Pelshandleren* is written in *bokmål*, which is to be expected given its author's Oslo roots.

It is perhaps not surprising either that Mortensen uses some English terms in his work, at times when there is no comparable Norwegian term—for example "Indian agent" and the phrase "the bush takes him"—and at other times to show he has a working knowledge of English and is able to trade in this language. These English words generally appear in quotation marks in the original Norwegian text.

Mortensen's use of English–Norwegian hybrids, arguably a type of code switching, is also noteworthy, and we can place this usage in a broader context. Linguist Einar Haugen's extensive research of Norwegian language among migrants to the United States revealed that Norwegian immigrants frequently used English words while speaking and writing Norwegian in their new context, and these words were assigned a masculine (*en*), feminine (*ei*), or neuter (*et*) designation. Mortensen follows this practice when he writes "en teepee" (a teepee), "en greenhorn" (a greenhorn), "harnessen" (the harness), and "cashet" (the cache—note the misspelling of *cache*). Einar Odd Mortensen only spent three years in Canada, and the fact that he placed some of his English–Norwegian hybrid constructions in quotation marks shows that he was aware of what he was doing. He had clearly not fully assimilated this English vocabulary into his Norwegian speech, unlike many other Norwegian immigrants to North America.[105]

English Edition

In 2011, Ingrid Urberg met Gerd Kjustad Mortensen at the Congress of the Social Sciences and Humanities in Fredericton, New Brunswick, where Kjustad Mortensen presented a paper entitled "Einar Odd Mortensen: A Fur Trader and Adventurer in Manitoba, 1925–1928." Urberg expressed interest in using a possible English translation of the work in her course, "Personal Narratives of the North," which she teaches on the Augustana Campus of the University of Alberta. They kept in touch over the following years as they explored collaborating on the project, and Kjustad Mortensen had Ahti Tolvanen and Marja-Liisa Tolvanen, Finnish Canadian acquaintances, and Amesto Translations, a professional translation company, translate *The Fur Trader* into English.

In conjunction with her trip to New Brunswick, Kjustad Mortensen travelled to The Pas in Manitoba with Ahti Tolvanen to visit the area where her father-in-law had lived and worked. In addition to gleaning information about the location of Pine Bluff, she consulted with descendants of the people with whom Einar Odd Mortensen had interacted. During her week-long stay, Kjustad Mortensen visited the Sam Waller Museum, which focuses on the history of northern Manitoba. Museum Director Sharain Jones invited local historians to share their knowledge of the history of the fur trade in the area in a round-table setting with their Nordic visitors. It was here that Kjustad Mortensen received confirmation that there had been a Pine Bluff trading post in Manitoba.[106]

During their stay in The Pas, Kjustad Mortensen and Tolvanen became aware of and were invited to a Cree adoption ceremony held by members of the Opaskwayak Cree Nation nearby. While sharing a meal of bannock and whitefish, Kjustad Mortensen learned about the area and its people, and in turn she shared her father-in-law's story. She also met Dr. Rosalyn Ing, an Opaskwayak Elder known for her work in the areas of social justice, health care, and education.[107] Ing had travelled from Vancouver, BC, to attend the ceremony. Ing and Kjustad Mortensen exchanged contact information, and the following summer Kjustad Mortensen hosted Ing and her husband George while they were visiting Norway. Ing read the English translation of *The Fur Trader*, and she advised Kjustad Mortensen that it was critical for her to collaborate with academics that could provide a historical and cultural context for contemporary readers before publishing the work in North America.

Taking Rosalyn Ing's advice, Gerd Kjustad Mortensen asked Ingrid Urberg to review the English translation of *The Fur Trader*, and Urberg was of the opinion that the translation needed to be revisited if it were to be published in English. Urberg indicated she would be willing to both edit the translation and work on an introduction for a North American audience, and that it would be prudent to replace the original preface written by Norwegian journalist and author Ragnar Kvam Jr. with one written for a broader audience. Urberg also acknowledged the need to include annotations to provide historical and cultural context for a contemporary audience as suggested by Ing. In 2017, Ingrid Urberg approached Daniel Sims, then a colleague in history and Indigenous studies on the Augustana Campus of the University of Alberta, to ask if he would be willing to provide annotations for the narrative and co-author a scholarly introduction. He expressed interest, and they started to work together. Though Rosalyn Ing passed away in July of 2020 before this edited English edition of *The Fur Trader* was completed, her advice to Kjustad Mortensen in its early stages was intrinsic to its completion.

Norwegian Experiences in Canada

Norwegian immigration to North America has been widely studied, though much more work has been done on Norwegian immigration history and literature in the United States than in Canada.[108] This attention is not surprising, given the fact that Ireland was the only European country to send a greater percentage of its population to North America than Norway during the period of mass migration in the nineteenth and early twentieth century. As Janice Dickin points out in her introduction to a memoir by another Norwegian immigrant to Canada, Ellenor Ranghild Merriken, this movement of people resulted in Norway being "in this indirect way a colonial force."[109] It was not until 1900 that Norwegian emigrants to North America began to settle in substantial numbers in Canada, and in the 1920s, the decade in which Mortensen spent three years in Manitoba, Canada received 24 percent of these migrants.[110] While there is disagreement among scholars as to how many immigrants ended up returning to Norway after 1880, there is widespread agreement that a significant number of those who migrated to the United States and Canada returned.[111] Einar Odd Mortensen fits into this group.

    Einar Odd Mortensen's story is part of the multicultural fabric of Canada, and we have outlined how his descriptions of the Indigenous and non-Indigenous peoples with whom he interacts are of value as we confront difficult truths and realities about the past and the present. Mortensen, as we have discussed, did not settle permanently in Canada, but was like many others a temporary migrant. While identifying and analyzing the broad strokes and patterns of migration is intrinsic to migration studies, it is equally important to look at individual stories of migrants—which are frequently compelling and reveal the richly diverse and complicated human experiences behind these patterns and statistics. Some of these accounts are published during the lifetime of the author, while others, such as *The Fur Trader*, are uncovered or rediscovered by family members or historians after "the protagonist" has died. Most voices will, of course, never be heard. Einar Odd Mortensen was just one of tens of thousands Norwegians[112] who found themselves in Canada in the sixty years before and after the turn of the twentieth century, and his story—like all others—is unique and valuable.

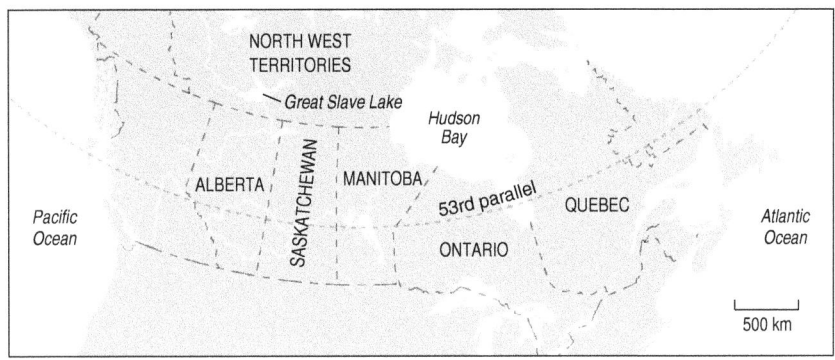

Maps of Canada and northern Manitoba as during Mortensen's time in the area, 1925–1928.

Ready for departure. Mortensen travelled by dogsled from The Pas to his first trading post at Pine Bluff, the first of many journeys by dogsled. This photo was taken at Norway House during Mortensen's second winter with his own dog team. Mortensen wrote, "This is probably the strongest dog team in Manitoba."

1 | *North of the 53rd Parallel*

EVERYTHING IS STILL UNCLEAR TO ME. All I know is that I am heading for a trading post in the Canadian wilderness. There I am going to buy pelts[1] from the Indians[2] and do some trapping myself. I will also act as general manager of the trading post.

I am here in a place called The Pas,[3] a border town on the edge of the wilderness. Or to be more precise, it is *the town* in the wilderness. I am waiting for a certain Icelander who is travelling north with a dog team. I hope to be able to accompany him to the trading post, which is located approximately two hundred miles[4] from here. The trip will take five or six days by dogsled. He should have been here several days ago, so I am starting to feel both impatient and tense. I am longing for the wilderness and the life there. What will the experience bring? How will a greenhorn[5] like me manage out there? The die has been cast and the unknown is calling to me. It is time to get started. If only that Icelander would get here soon.

There is not much to do in this border town, and it doesn't take me long to explore The Pas. There is a main street, which is about 150 metres long. Otherwise, the city consists of scattered buildings and random streets that run this way and that. All of the town's ten to twelve shops are located on the main street. They have a beautiful facade, but behind the frontage they almost look like barracks. This is how they try to make an impression here "north of fifty-three." North of fifty-three degrees is not just a geographical expression in this neck of the woods. It also signifies that we are completely outside of civilization. Here, there are a couple of grocery stores that sell all kinds of products, as well as a pharmacy, the Hudson's Bay Company[6] building, and the old French furrier Revillon Frères Trading Company.[7]

The town also has its own metal inspector. The words "Dr Smith Assayer. Same day testing of gold, silver and copper samples" are painted in crooked handwritten letters on its window. But there is no lineup in front of this shop. Nothing like the Klondike[8] is going on in the area at this time.

The town also has an inn. It contains a barbershop, a billiard table, and a beer parlour. The local white people gather in the beer parlour for a game of pool or cards, or to engage in small talk. Here you may be served illegal Canadian caviar for free. It is made from the roe of protected sturgeon.[9] The roe is harvested in Canadian rivers like the Nelson River and the Hayes River. Since this is illegal, the host keeps the caviar under the counter, and he uses it to make his customers thirsty.

There is not much traffic in The Pas, but you can see some Indian women walking around. They are wrapped in black cashmere shawls, and cross their arms to hold the shawls in place. They have come to shop. Some of them carry the family's baby on their back. The baby lies in a kind of backpack, which the women carry with a head strap. An occasional lumberjack saunters around in his Mackinaw coat, a colourful, red-chequered jacket. There is not much life in the town, and children are rarely seen.

The first thing I noticed when I got off the train in The Pas was a dog team waiting for a trapper. I haven't seen any other vehicles in this place. While sitting here and waiting in the inn, I can, from time to time, hear dog team mushers shout commands as they head out of town with their fully loaded toboggans. These sleds are about two metres long and curved up at the front. I also hear the shrill cries of some half-breed Indians[10] as they arrive in The Pas with their empty sleds. They are here to pick up loads to take to the nearest trading post. One free trader, an independent merchant, is also loading his goods in order to set out to the winter trapping grounds. At any given time, there are only a few hundred white people who live here. Their number fluctuates depending on whether the sawmill down by the river is operating or not. The sawmill and the fur traders sustain life in The Pas.

I live in a boarding house managed by an old veteran of Canada's frontier days. He is called Peg Leg because he limps around on a wooden leg. He is seventy years old now and still lives in the glory of his past. He has taken part in most of the gold discoveries in the area, and he keeps photos of claims he has bought, kept, or sold. He has hoped and gambled on trying to make his fortune in this way, living the feverish life of a gold digger. For many years he has been waiting to hit the gold jackpot. He shares these hopes with other fortune hunters. Unfortunately, such hopes rarely materialize. Now all Peg Leg is left with is this inn. He has settled down here with his colourful wife, who also can trace her family back to the frontier days.

It is easy to overlook Peg Leg's behaviour when he cheats a greenhorn for a few dollars. He does so in all friendliness and with open delight. His cheating bears no ill intent. He is merely reliving how he acted when he found himself in tough spots in the old gold strike days. Besides, his wife softens the edge of this modest cheating with exceptionally well-prepared food. This makes it easy for people to forgive her husband.

I have played a few small-stakes games with my host in the evening. We both know that he is able to deal the cards exactly as he wants. I sit and watch while he deals. He is a true master at this. He just smiles at me as if to say, "You will never understand my tricks." It is certainly not easy, for he is an old and experienced gambler. He is unbelievably dexterous, and the cards fly like a twister through his lightning-fast fingers. The deception takes place so quickly that I can neither see nor describe what he is doing. I only know that he is cheating.

The wilderness stretches out from The Pas in all directions. The railway provides a link between this place and civilization to the south. It appears as if the tracks just disappear into the swampland. The railway north towards Hudson Bay has not been completed yet. Standing here at the end of the main street next to two angry Indian dog teams tied to a tin shack, I can see the Promised Land. I am heading northwest to the place that will be my first station among fur trappers.

The Saskatchewan River flows peacefully past The Pas, and on the other side lies the first Indian reserve.[11] The reserves are the sanctuaries of the original owners of the land.[12] When you cross over the bridge you will see a sign that informs strangers about proper conduct on the reserve. There is, for example, a warning that it is strictly forbidden to sell hard liquor to the Indians. There is a serious punishment for anyone caught breaking this law. A trapper[13] would, in any case, have to pack up his traps and other belongings if the watchful eye of the land, the Royal Canadian Mounted Police, caught him offending in this way. Other than that, the sign covers how one can interact with the Indians, and specifically what one cannot do to their women.[14]

The eyes of those who live on the reserve do not exactly radiate the bloodthirstiness of wild Indians. I have not seen any representatives of this group. These Indians actually appear to be peace-loving. There are no dried scalps hanging from their belts. In fact, their belts are barely able to hold up their ragged pants. The rest of their equipment reveals that they struggle through life in a constant battle to keep their rags together. They are not very successful, yet they putter along so peacefully. Such Indians are a dime a dozen. These first Indians I see remind me more of rag collectors in Oslo than the free sons of the Prairie I had imagined them to be.[15]

The Icelander I had been waiting for arrived at daybreak today. His dog team — six large, magnificent dogs — is tied to a storage shack up the street. Peg Leg has exchanged some words with the Icelander on my behalf and arranged for me to travel with him. He will set out some time today. In the meantime, I walk shivering up and down this street. It is early in November, and it is minus ten degrees Celsius, with a biting, cold, northeast wind.

I am impatient. When a person has several years of life in the wilderness ahead of himself, he should, perhaps, not be in such a rush to leave. But for me this is a departure from everything old and familiar, a departure into the new and unknown. The hours drag on and impatience burns in my veins like a smouldering unrest. Let's go, let's go!

The Icelander loads up 300–400 pounds of flour, sugar, and various other groceries on the sled. In addition, there is a two- to three-day supply of fish for the dogs, and my seaman's bag. But this man is not in a rush, not at all. He keeps delaying his departure. Every now and then he disappears to quench his thirst. At one o'clock he finally brings out his last precious cargo, a keg of liquor.

Mortensen's dog team on the move.

The tarp is wrapped around the toboggan and tied down. It is important to both secure the load and to distribute its weight evenly so the toboggan can move flexibly over the bumps.

Now the dogs become impatient too. The lead dog takes a small leap forward now and then, and the bell on its harness shakes, producing a shrill ring. The animal looks back in an inquisitive way. The other dogs howl and howl. At times the howling morphs into a curious yawning tone. The dogs are eager to hit the trail. They live to pull. As they wait in their harnesses, they seem to have forgotten about their previous toils and struggles pulling heavy loads on rough trails. They have forgotten about the bad weather and blinding blizzards, which can cut right through them. They have forgotten about the cold. Nights so cold that the thermometer may register forty to fifty degrees below zero. Cold so extreme, their paws sometimes crack open when they step on the ground in the morning. They have also forgotten about their empty growling stomachs when there is a shortage of fish. Their only desire now is to be on the trail, and they are just waiting for the Icelander's signal. But the sled is frozen to the ground, and they must wait for his shout: "*Allez!*"[16] They are patient in the midst of their impatience.

At last the Icelander is ready. He turns the sled so that the wide runner loosens and he shouts, "*Allez!*" The dogs strike out with a joyful lunge. The journey has begun. I am on skis and the Icelander lets me take the lead. In retrospect, I realize his bushy beard may well have concealed a smile as I picked up my pace to take the lead in front of the dog team. I am only a greenhorn, blissfully unaware of the fact that when the dogs have a forerunner, they will follow right on his heels. They will stay there as long as their strength permits. The faster I ski, the faster the dogs run behind me. In good trail conditions, one might just as well try to ski away from one's own shadow as from a rested and fresh dog team.

The Icelander jogs behind the sled now and then, but for the better part of the day he sits and rides. He is equipped with extra provisions, a bottle of rum, and already after a quarter of an hour's drive he has made a marked dent in the bottle's contents. He is a strong, ash blonde man. Like many other Icelanders, he has spent time as a fisherman. Now he takes care of deliveries for the fur companies with his dog team. He delivers food and supplies to the trading posts and brings back pelts. On this trip he is travelling to Rat Portage. The river has recently frozen over and this is his first sled trip of the winter. I can't get many words out of him.[17] He looks at me with the same mistrust that is shown to every greenhorn; something we have to accept before we have walked in moccasins in the wilderness.

We follow the river upstream. The rivers are important highways in the wilderness. In the summer people travel on them by canoe, in winter by dog team. Every now and then we meet Indians on their way south with empty sleds. They step out of the tracks for us because we have a load. The river winds along, curving slightly as we navigate wide, agreeable bends. We don't notice any change in elevation. We are in typical lowlands, which are broken up by small hills here and there. The landscape is open and visibility is good.

The large marshes are covered by snow, but withered and tattered reeds and tufts of grass stick up through them. On the shores of the river there are groups of white and balsam poplars, and willows[18] grow in almost impenetrable thickets on the steep banks. Now and then a familiar white birch stands out among the other deciduous trees. Farther off on the marshes and low hills I can see some pine trees scattered about. My overall impression is one of flat marshes and forest. We follow the main riverbed of the Saskatchewan River for a couple of hours at a steady and exhausting pace. Then we turn northeast to follow a smaller tributary.

I had thought we would stop to rest sometime during the day, but the Icelander sits firmly on the sled and manages just fine without a break. It is twenty to thirty miles to the log cabin,[19] where he usually stays overnight. Although we had a late start, he plans to arrive at the cabin by evening to avoid sleeping outdoors. Late in the afternoon I have had enough of leading on skis, and I relinquish this position to the lead dog. This slows the pace somewhat.

As darkness falls, I begin to long for a rest. However, the dog team keeps going, and I hear the crisp ringing of bells on this my first night in a new world. The sound comes from far and near, depending on whether I fall a bit behind or stay close to the sled. The snow is wet, and I am unable to make my skis glide properly. The Icelander doesn't seem to care how fast or slow I am moving, but at last he takes pity on me. He even offers me some of his rum, which is by now almost gone, something which certainly makes him more generous. I decline his first offer, but when he offers it to me a second time, I accept.

A biting wind blows across the river channel, the snow is blowing, and I am so sweaty from skiing that the cold passes right through my clothing. I am really tired. First I take a swig, then he takes one, then it is my turn, then his, and then the bottle is empty. I fall asleep on the sled with a ski on either side, and the Icelander probably doesn't think it is a good idea to throw me off. I only wake up when one of my skis gets caught on a shrub beside the sled. The dogs make an extra effort as they notice something is impeding our progress. My hands grab the sled to avoid being thrown off. A moment later, I am actually pleased to hear a satisfying cracking sound from one of the skis. I have to unfasten my skis and tie them to the sled.

After this, the Icelander becomes even friendlier. The greenhorn has had his first little lesson about the wilderness. He resisted this land's travel gear of choice, snowshoes. Now I have seen the result.

This was my first time on skis in Canada. Time will also reveal that it was the last time during my three to four years in the Canadian wilderness.[20]

I have no idea how much time we have spent driving this evening since I have fallen asleep on top of our load. I don't wake up until the toboggan suddenly stops and I roll off. We have come to a halt outside an Indian cabin. Nobody comes out to greet us. The Indians hereabouts do not want to appear to be curious, even though they are as inquisitive as weasels. Finally, the Icelander succeeds in calling one Indian boy out of the house. He brings us an armload of frozen fish. This is only to be expected when a dog team arrives to stay the night.

The Icelander takes the dogs out of their harnesses and ties each of them to a separate tree, cuts the fish into big pieces and gives each dog one of them. Then it is our turn to hit the sack. The cabin has one overheated room where I am eventually able to count six people: men, women, and a couple of youths. I am not able to count the smaller ones in the dim light, but I think I see a toddler crawling across the floor.

After sitting up for a while, I gradually find it possible to breathe in the cabin's nauseating stench. The cracks in the walls aren't big enough to provide sufficient fresh air. Even if one of the walls were torn down, the smell would still have remained. We stuff some food into ourselves. This is my first night in an Indian cabin and I crawl into my sleeping bag as soon as I have removed my coat and boots, placing them under my head. For some inexplicable reason, there seems to be room for me on the floor as well.

First thing next morning it is necessary to make some adjustments to my equipment. I buy a pair of snowshoes and leave the skis there. What hurts most is leaving behind my sturdy Norwegian ski boots, which were made for me with great care and at great expense. I buy myself a pair of moccasins. At last I begin to feel a little more at home in this setting.

However, I have some problems when I start to walk on my snowshoes. I am not able to keep my legs sufficiently far apart since my hips lack flexibility. I am not able to master the slightly bent knees and springy walking style that one needs to avoid stumbling while on snowshoes. I don't learn how to use them on my first attempt. After an hour's march, I take them off and run in my moccasins for the sake of variety.

The snow is fairly firm. Several dog teams have recently passed this way so the track has been firmly packed by sled runners and snowshoes. The dogs pull vigorously. The Icelander shouts commands to his team. If he shouts "gee," the dogs turn right; if he calls "ha," they turn left.

It is important to make sure that all the dogs pull evenly and that none of them cheat. The bells are an alert system. If one of the dogs slacks off, the sound of the bells signals the offence to the driver. The cheater receives a warning shout. If this fails, the driver must walk alongside the dog and, at times, remind it of its duties with a lash of the whip.

The offender's bad conscience seems to reside in its tail. The dog tucks it shamefully between its legs, howls, and lunges ahead. Those dogs with a good conscience, particularly the older, more stable dogs who never forget their responsibilities, often turn their heads in the event of such a punishment, show their teeth and growl, as if to say, "Stay away. We know our duties and we tend to them."

The dogs run with little trouble on flat ground and over marshes and waterways. We jog behind and make sure the dogs pull evenly. While travelling over bumpy terrain, through forests and down the banks of winding rivers, we grab the rope tied to the front of the sled. This helps us steer the sled so it doesn't run into tree trunks or other obstacles.

Now and then, we jump on the sled to take a break and have a cigarette. At noon we stop to warm up and make some tea. The dogs can rest but are not fed. They have to run all day on the half fish they got this morning.

In the evening, we stop again at an Indian cabin. Another fur trader is also staying here overnight. I try to get some good advice and gather as much information as possible about everything related to trapping. I receive just the sort of information a horse trader can expect to get when he tries to pump another horse trader for information at a horse market.

The Indians in this region mainly make their living as freight carriers for the Hudson's Bay Company. In the winter they travel by dog teams, and in the summer they use canoes to visit the farthest outposts in the wilderness. In addition, they do some hunting and supplement their income by providing lodging for visitors. We give them a little bacon, flour, and other small articles. We never pay in cash. None of these Indians have any use for that.

This is the last Indian cabin where we spend a night. After this we must camp under the open sky. Tents are not used by anyone in these parts. Only missionaries and other greenhorns lug such items along with them. There is a plentiful supply of firewood so no one need suffer.

When we stop for the night, we divide up the chores. We chop wood and prepare a camp. We find a few dry pine trees and pile them up so we have enough firewood. But the very first thing we do is to tie up the dogs, each to its own tree. We cannot tie them together in the same spot because during the night they would chew off each other's ears, tails, and possibly other body parts. If we didn't tie them up, our own food would also quickly disappear. The dogs get a few spruce branches to lie on and a single fish. This is how we look after them for the night.

Then we prepare places for ourselves. We shovel away the snow to make a square of an appropriate size, trample on the bottom until it is hard, and cover it well with spruce branches. We gather a few shrubs and set these up as a two-foot barrier on three sides of the square. On the fourth side we make a fire. If there is a strong wind, we raise a slanted wall against the wind using the tarp that covers the load on the toboggan. Then it is time to melt ice and snow, make tea, fry some pork, and gulp down a simple but most welcome meal. Finally, we crawl into our sleeping bags.

Lying like this, halfway down in my sleeping bag and experiencing the warmth from the fire, I sense something new and special. I am well fed and satisfied, and feel the heat from the metre-high fire, which burns for many hours. This keeps the cold at bay.

Despite all this, as I sit by the fire in the quiet of the night, my thoughts begin to wander here and there, from the past to the future, and doubts begin to enter my mind. I am going to a trading post to be a fur buyer, initially only for this winter. However, the truth is that before leaving home a short while back, I had hardly ever held any kind of fur in my hands, with the exception of my mother's boa. And it was, I believe, made from feathers! My qualifications to be a fur buyer are somewhat questionable.

By the way, why am I really here? Well, I don't know if I can explain that properly. A month ago I was still going to work every day back home in Norway. I was doing fine and did not think about Indians or the fur trade. But people are strange creatures. We can become possessed with a strange restlessness. This restlessness can grow and grow until at last it becomes a storm. Inside of ourselves we hear a call of far-away places. Away! Away! To the South Seas? To the Arctic Ocean? To the tropics? To Canada? It doesn't matter which one you choose, it is just necessary to get away at any cost. Leave behind the days and weeks that flow by like a grey stream. Shouldn't our days offer more to us than this? My restlessness became a fever and I thought: Jump into it! Throw yourself into new experiences. Break with the old. Start swimming.

How did I come to this place? I had been promised a job in the large Norwegian fur trading company H.C. Hyer's Heirs,[21] which has its headquarters in Norway House. The company has a number of trading posts in northwestern Manitoba and all the way up to Hudson Bay.

Once I arrived in Winnipeg, I stayed there a few days to wait for a response to a telegram I had sent to the Company. Since I didn't hear anything from them, I decided to set out without waiting any longer. When I arrived in The Pas, the telegram I had been expecting finally caught up with me. It was short and to the point: "Not wanted here." Well, at least the message was clear.

After sulking for a while, I went to the office of the Western Groceries.[22] This company supplies most of the provision shipments to the trading posts. I asked if they might have some work for me. "No, nothing right now," was the reply. One of the office ladies must have felt sorry for me. She told me her father ran a pool hall in town. He had many connections and it was possible he might be able to find something suitable for me.

Her father was a Swede named Westman. He had previously worked as a lumberjack and trapper. Now he ran this gambling establishment and was a respected resident of The Pas. He knew everyone, and everyone knew him. People open up about everything and everyone over a glass of beer.

It became clear that I had several options. I was offered a job as a handyman at a hotel, but neither the job nor the hotelkeeper's daughter appealed to me. I could also have worked as a shop clerk, but I wanted a more exciting life for myself. Finally, the poolroom manager heard somewhere that Ben Dembinsky might need a man who knew a lot about furs. Perhaps this was a good fit for me? Yes, that sounded good. I tracked down this German Jew. We conversed in German, but he did not know German grammar or syntax any better than me. With broken German, I was able to make him understand that I was also fluent in many other world languages. He concluded that I, from a linguistic point of view, was exceptionally qualified to trade furs with the Indians.

Do I know anything about furs? I looked at the man and repeated that I was from Norway. I must have said it with such conviction that no further discussion of this issue was necessary. Ben was given the clear impression that, in a country like Norway, the boys become skilled with furs around the time they learn to speak.

I could start work immediately, if I wanted. Ben had a Frenchman working at the Pine Bluff trading post.[23] The man had given his notice as of Christmas, but he was not opposed to being relieved earlier. My wages would be seventy-five dollars a month for the first three months and one hundred dollars thereafter. In addition, I would receive a commission, based on total sales. This is why I am now on my way north.

We have fallen two days behind schedule so far. The fish supply for the dogs is running low. Last evening they received only half their ration. Bad weather has arrived. The going is tough, and the dogs trudge along in the heavy snow. The temperature has risen, which causes snow to accumulate on their paws. Every now and then the dogs have to chew the snow off of their paws. The wide runners of the toboggan get stuck and stop sliding, reducing our speed considerably.

In addition, the terrain is starting to get a bit uneven. This also reduces our speed. Every once in a while, we are forced to get off the river. We go ashore to avoid and move around rapids, something that is called *portaging*. In the summer, the cargo must be carried overland at these places. There is still open running water in these rapids during the winter. The Icelander goes ahead to find a way through the thick bush. He hasn't kept proper track of how far we have come due to the poor visibility. However, the Icelander is relatively unconcerned about this. For now the way is clear. We need only follow the river.

We had expected to arrive this evening, but the Icelander does not really know if this will happen. It is getting quite dark already, and we must look for a campsite. The dogs are tired of the sledding. Cheerful shouts don't necessarily have the desired effect any longer. Sometimes the dogs need a flick of the whip. However, the harness bells suddenly come to life. The dogs' tails stand erect, and they make an extra effort in their harnesses. Though they are exhausted, they disappear in an instant. They have caught the scent of smoke, and smoke means a camp or dwelling, and that—in turn—means fish and rest.

We soon catch up to the dog team. The dogs have come to a halt before the first Indian cabin on the reserve. The dogs always stop when they come to a cabin. By using the whip a bit more, we are able to make them return reluctantly to the ice. We have another kilometre to go before we are at our destination. But it isn't too long before we trot around the bend to the trading post. We have arrived. I lend a hand by unharnessing the dogs and tying them up. By now I have learned that the first task at day's end is tending to the dogs. Then we carry our load into a shed to prevent loose dogs from the reserve disturbing it during the night.

The Frenchman who has been tending the trading post is very happy to be relieved of his duties.

The next morning, the Icelander continues on his way. He will return later by the same route and take the Frenchman along for the ride south.

During the days that follow, the Frenchman must feel like I am trying to exhaust him with questions. However, I need to get as much advice from him as possible before I have to manage on my own. I must, at any rate, acquire an understanding of some main rules and the basic ABCs for this life.

The issue of the furs weighs particularly heavy on my mind. In The Pas I was informed of the prices paid for furs this season. But it is up to me to evaluate the furs and place them in the appropriate price category. I had hoped there would be a good sampling of pelts at the post so I could have developed some kind of operational standard to refer to later. However, it is far too early in the hunting season. The entire inventory at the post consists of a few weasel furs. Things do not look too good, but I comfort myself with the thought that it will be some time before the furs begin to arrive in significant numbers. In addition, there are some half-breed Indians here who also work for the company, and I expect to receive good advice from them.

We go through the accounting books and the customers, and I am able to acquaint myself a bit with business procedures. All Indians must be given cash advances. This practice is generally acceptable as long as it is recorded in the books. There is no such thing as a debt-free Indian hereabouts. However, the practice of giving cash advances is somewhat problematic. On one hand, Indians should have just enough to live on, but if the amount is too small they may sell their furs to other trading posts. If the advance is too large, they may also turn to other trading posts until all their credit expires there too.[24] Then it may become necessary to erase some of the old debts to retain the customer.

The customers are, when it comes right down to it, screened in the books. If there is a small cross by a name, it means that the person is a poor trapper and unreliable with his payments. Two crosses and the words "absolute scoundrel" appear next to other names. Fortunately, a few clients arrive while I am going over the lists so I can practice. The first is a small, dark, Indian boy. He stands silently and pulls a little bundle from his pocket—an ermine skin.[25] "Candysack," he says. Treats. That is what boys expect to get in return for an ermine or skunk they have caught in their traps. Such furs are the usual catch of women. A true Indian does not set his traps for such animals.

A few married Indian women also come into the trading post. They want flour and silk thread. The latter is an important article around here. They also have two or three ermine skins and are marked as credit worthy in the books. The Frenchman helps me serve the customers. He also writes down for me what the various skins and types of merchandise are in the Cree language.[26]

Once the women have left the store, the Frenchman tells me something in confidence. He nods towards the women and says emphatically that no white man should sleep with Indian women. I smile condescendingly and state that the women I have seen so far have not been particularly attractive, so there is no danger they will allure me.

Everybody says that when they arrive, he replies. But when white men have lived out here for some years and have not seen any white women, many start to think that even the ugliest Indian woman is attractive. Nor should I stay too long or too often on the reserve. I might visit there now and then when the men are at home, speak to the clients, trade a little, and help the sick. But more extensive involvement is not good. The white man must be a white man. He must view the Indian at arm's length to maintain his dignity.

Potential customers. Mortensen describes various types of interactions with trading post customers. At times, they came to the store, but he also visited many people in their cabins and homes. This photo was taken at God's Lake, east of Norway House. Please see the discussion of "the unnamed Indian" in the Introduction.

2 | *Alone at the Trading Post*

THE ICELANDER'S DOG TEAM HAS RETURNED, and the following morning the Frenchman is ready to join it on its journey south. I stand outside the cabin and watch as the team disappears down the river. There are a few snowflakes in the air. Strong wind gusts quickly cover the team's tracks. It feels like the last ties to my past have been erased. I am alone at the trading post.

It is as if something has been cut in two. I stand, in a sense, on a new and unknown road, and I wonder how things will turn out. I stand outdoors for a long time after the dog team vanishes from view. I totally forget where I am until I realize that I am standing outside, freezing.

I step inside the cabin. After I stoke up the stove, I eat my first meal alone. An uneasy feeling of loneliness comes over me, a kind of restlessness, which makes it hard to sit still. As a result, I start to tidy up, cut firewood, and carry it inside. I feed the dogs and make the day pass somehow, but my thoughts wander in many directions. Have *you* ever experienced a bottomless feeling of loneliness? A feeling the wilderness can sometimes leave you with?

This glorious place I have been assigned to manage is situated on a river island that is half a kilometre long. A thin spruce forest creeps over a low bluff. The name Pine Bluff likely originates from the fact that no pine trees grow here.

My log cabin is four by five metres. The furnishings are quite plain. I have a table and two chairs made of boxes, and a bunk bed. A few kitchen utensils, a sleeping bag, and a woolen blanket complete the inventory list. On the outside, the cabin is insulated with a protective coat of clay. The clay mixture is made in the fall as soon as the frost arrives, and it is spread into all the cracks, where it freezes into this protective coating.

In addition to the cabin, the buildings on the island include the much larger trading post itself. It is located about ten metres from my cabin. A counter runs across the length of the store. A makeshift display case, which was originally covered by glass, stands on part of the counter. Boxes of lard and sacks of flour and sugar are piled against the walls. The store's salt was purchased at fifteen cents a kilo and is sold for three dollars since there are, of course, shipping costs to be considered. Knit sweaters, pails, fancy-coloured pearls, and a large quantity of steel traps hang from the ceiling. This is a general overview of the store.

A poster with the words "Don't spit on the floor"[1] hangs over the counter. One of my predecessors has apparently tried to improve the standards of the place. The poster hangs there, even though most Indians are unable to read English. If they had been able to read the poster, they still wouldn't have bothered to follow the request.

A fish shed and a storage shed are also located on the trading post site. The food for the dogs, the fur stock, and most of the merchandise inventory are kept there. The dog team is tied up outside the storage shed. These five Indian dogs do not look at me with friendly eyes. The lead dog, a black female, stares and growls at me as she lies there. The first time I approach her, in a cordial manner I might say, she snaps at my hand. As I turn my back to the dog, I instinctively take a big leap. Something just tells me to do so. As a result, the dog is only able to snap at the back of my pants without damaging my nobler body parts.

The dogs raised and cared for by white men are altogether different from Indian dogs.[2] White men's dogs have a different temperament and they obey voice commands. They rarely need to be whipped. In this part of Canada, it is necessary for every white man to learn to be a good dog breeder and team driver. It becomes just too tiring to drive a team of five or six Indian dogs over time. It takes more out of the driver than the dogs.

The Indian reserve[3] is on the river's west shore. From my cabin, I can see most of the Indian cabins through a thin forest. The reserve has a total of forty to fifty cabins and teepees, all clustered in small groups along the edge of a ridge.

Customers begin to arrive. On my second day alone, I escort two Indian women into the store. They have brought a pair of moccasins, and want tea and lard in exchange. In addition, they must surely be both curious about and eager to meet the new Mister *Gooshoo* or Mister Stupid.[4]

The moccasins reveal that the women are trying to take advantage of my ignorance in trading affairs. However, I have been advised as to what moccasins should look like. These prove to be made from patched and holey leather. "No good," I say. So they leave and return later with another pair in better condition. I must have given them a good price for these. The next day, numerous moccasin sellers visit me, but I have been advised to only purchase a limited quantity of this footgear. In no case should I waste good merchandise on moccasin trading.

The Frenchman has marked a number of goods as unsalable, and I can exchange these for moccasins or furs of lesser value. But it is not always that simple. Although I am able to count to ten in the Cree language, it is quite simply beyond me to negotiate prices in that language. I am not familiar with the local manners or customs either. One day, two women, who bring nothing but moccasins, come into the store. I find some underpants in one container and show these to them. The underpants have been labelled as outdated merchandise, and I think they could be a suitable trade for the moccasins that they take out of their shawls. But they just laugh and giggle at my offer. I take their giggling to be a sign of shyness. Since there is no changing room in my store, I discreetly turn my back to them and rearrange the shelves a little. When I turn around again a bit later, the moccasins, the underpants, and the Indian women are gone. I had no way of knowing that it is not a custom in this part of the world to wear underpants.[5]

Fortunately, there are no more customers that day. The loss in revenue from these women's visit is limited to half a dollar. I will not be able to identify these two dirty women from among the others who visit my store. After all, I only caught a quick glance of them in the dark trading room.

Cabin maintenance.

The first Indian man who comes to my store does not have anything of value to offer either. He pulls an ermine pelt from his pocket. I try to appraise it the way only a greenhorn can. I estimate it to be of average quality, and he is given suitable merchandise. His facial expression does not reveal anything. I could just as well have studied a stone as his facial expression. Well, these are not momentous events, but this is how my life begins as a trader out here in the wilderness.

One day, I pay my first visit to the Indian reserve. I have learned to use the snowshoes well enough now so that I can go out in public without feeling totally out of place. Although I have been advised not to linger on the reserve for too long at any one time, I have to take a good look around there. I need to show myself to my customers and become more familiar with my surroundings.

Most of the cabins are empty and locked. This means that the door is tied shut with a leather strap. The men are out trapping, at least most of them. Often the entire family goes along. There are mostly women on the reserve from fall until Christmas. A few old Indian men who are no longer capable of trapping also remain in the camp. A trapper becomes old somewhere between the ages of forty and fifty. Chasing prey is an exhausting job.

The cabins are very similar. They are built of logs and have clay spattered on the exterior. Each cabin has only one room in which one, two, or three families live. The amount of wealth and number of family members determine how many families live in each one.

These cabins are always overcrowded. One seldom sees an Indian cabin with a reasonable number of people living in it. Though it does not take more than a few days' work to build such a cabin, they are still always too crowded. I believe their way of thinking is that if there is room for twelve people in the cabin, why have fewer people there? I also believe that they enjoy living in close quarters.[6] It is easier to foster a sense of solidarity when everyone is gathered in the same place. Once a cabin has been built, it does not appear as if anyone thinks of adding on a room later.

There are some differences between the cabins. Wealthy Indians, those who are skilled trappers, have installed stoves or cheap ovens in their dwellings, items purchased during years when furs were plentiful. In general, the cabins contain a lot of spit and a lot of rust. I think it is better to spit at the oven than on the floor, at least from a hygienic perspective. So this habit may not be so bad after all.

The poorest people have clay fireplaces that function well in the winter. However, when rain pours down the chimney in the spring, summer, and fall, these fireplaces are not very effective.

The floors of some cabins are made of raw timber, but most have dirt floors. Some cabins also have a window, but these are usually stuffed with old rags. There are no furnishings except the oven. You will not find benches, shelves, or a bed. People sleep on top of furs placed on the floor. During the day, the furs are thrown against the walls. Cooking pots and other utensils are stored on the floor.

One cabin stands out from all of the other Indian dwellings. It belongs to MacEever, who is listed in the ledger as a good trapper and a reliable payer of his debts. He has a small organ in his cabin.

A missionary or a clever salesman likely palmed it off on him. The family is extremely proud of it, and every now and then the organ is even played a bit.

Every cabin has an outside structure for food storage that we Norwegians might call a *stabbur*.[7] In these parts it is called a cache.[8] The cache stands on four pillars with a platform on top. The poles are about three to four metres in height. Food is placed on the platform for safekeeping. The poles protect the food from wolverines, foxes, and other four-legged food thieves. The tarp or spruce branches on top of the goods keep ravens and other winged freeloaders away.

Pieces of moss suspended on strings hang outside some of the cabins. These are used as diapers for the smallest children.

While the men are out hunting, the women of the reserve must try to keep themselves and their children alive as best they can. They rarely get anything from the store on credit. An Indian man will not accept his wife's credit. Some men do have an agreement with the trading post that their wives can spend a dollar or two on goods every week. This provides them with a little flour and tea.

The people survive mainly on fish from the river. The women fish with nets a little downriver from the trading post. This work can be quite demanding, but the women are used to it. The women set their nets under the ice. This is something they have supposedly learned from the Icelanders.[9] First they chop holes in the ice, two to three metres apart, based on the length of the net. Using a pole, the women run a rope from hole to hole under the ice. Then they tie the other end of the rope to the net and use it to extend the net. They chop the holes in the ice during the fall before the ice gets too thick. After this, they only keep the first and last holes open, and over the winter big piles of chopped ice build up around these net holes. The fishing net can be used all winter long.

When they come in the morning to check their nets, the women tie one end of a rope to the net and the other end to a stick on the ice. When they pull up the net, the rope remains under the ice. They immediately set out the dry nets they have brought along.

It is extremely hard work to handle wet nets in the bitter cold. The water freezes quickly between one's fingers. Many have suffered frostbite doing this work. It is not uncommon to see Indian women whose fingers have been injured from working daily with nets. I later observe that some of them have to keep their hands together while eating. Their fingers are no longer of any use.

Women also go trapping for grouse and rabbits. Rabbits are especially desirable because of their fur. The women dry the skins, twist them together, and make rugs and bedcovers out of them. In addition, they make moccasins and mittens. They are also skilled embroiderers. They create patterns and use both silk thread and pearls in their embroidery.

The women pass their days doing handcrafts and domestic chores and gathering firewood. They seem to find it difficult to gather wood for several days at a time. I have never seen an Indian man gathering wood for the family. Gathering wood and fishing are considered women's work.

It is relatively quiet on the reserve now. Occasionally, some of the Indian dogs visit me. They like to come by when I am stooped down in the bushes. They prefer to come from behind and growl and show their teeth to each other. They start fighting over the fruits of my labour even before they appear. This is very strange and foreign to me, but it is something I get used to little by little. Indian dogs mainly eat what humans have already eaten. They are the tireless cleaners of the camps.

My own dogs stand impatiently in their chains. It seems like high time to go for a drive. We have now become somewhat better acquainted with each other. I have fed them fish twice a day, and as a result I'm not afraid they will ambush me. I should really try to go for a run with them. Their harnesses hang ready on the wall of the shed. I take them out and position them on the ground in front of the sled. One by one, I harness the dogs. Finally, it is the lead dog's turn.

"*Allez!*" I shout cheerfully to them. I should have given the command more calmly. The dogs charge ahead at a furious pace and I am barely able to jump aboard for the ride. However, I am not able to get a grip of the guide rope. We jump over a little snowdrift. After that, I am no longer riding on the sled. The dogs vanish behind the trees without me. After running some distance, the dogs stop because the sled gets stuck in some trees. As soon as the lead dog stops and no one is guiding them, the entire team is in chaos. The traces get tangled and the dogs end up in a glorious dogfight. That is always a good way for the dogs to pass time. I have to take out my whip to get the dogs under control in order to untangle the harness. Then I take a firm hold on the guide rope, settle into the sled, and we drive onto the river ice. We move at a furious pace since the dogs have been inactive for so long. In the end, everything goes well and the dogs are able to run off their excess energy. They actually obey my verbal commands too. When I want to stop, I just jump off and pull the guide rope tightly. Then I let out a calm "whooooaaa."

Whenever I go out with the dogs for a breath of fresh air after this, I always place some heavy boxes in the back of the sled. It is simply foolish to go out for a drive with a rested dog team and an empty sled.

One day, when I set out for a run with the team, I take along some traps from the store. It might be time to test my trapping skills. If the Indian women, and even the small boys, constantly catch things in their traps, I should probably be able to get something too. First, I follow the river for some distance upstream, looking for any kind of animal tracks. I eventually find a small point that is nearly free of snow. There, under an old tree root, I locate a hollow with three entrances. Then I place a pile of fish for bait under the root and set a trap at each entrance.

I return after three days. It seems I have caught something in my first three traps. Yes, there truly are animals in all three traps. These turn out to be a skunk, a squirrel, and a jay. One can get fifty cents for a skunk.

The skunk is still alive and I can hear it growling. Since a barking dog does not bite, I am bold enough to bend down towards it and give it a hard blow on the neck. It dies from the blow. However, I didn't know that a skunk growls with its behind. The growl turns into a whistling sound, a sound that I realize originates from the fine spray the animal directs at me. For the first time I realize the skunk has a bladder in his behind that it uses to protect itself. This is something I have never forgotten. This defence mechanism is unique. The smell is beyond words. One has to experience it. The smell clings to my clothes and there is no way to get rid of it. I wash my clothes several times and hang them outdoors for an entire month. One day, the wind has blown away one of the garments, but the smell remains. I end up having to discard my clothes.

Even if the skunk had been dead, I wouldn't have avoided being sprayed by it. I would doubtlessly have skinned it the usual way. Only later do I learn that a skunk must be skinned under water.[10]

A dog-racing event at Cross Lake, sixty miles north of Norway House, March 6, 1926. This is the only one of Mortensen's images that contains all three of the following: a specific place, date, and event. However, he does not mention Cross Lake or the dog race in his text.

3 | *From Camp to Church*

MOST INDIANS TRAVEL A COUPLE OF DAYS BY SLED from the reserve to their hunting grounds and return home when their food and other supplies run out.[1] However, there are also a number of trappers who travel farther away, a distance of three or four days from Pine Bluff. Representatives of the Hudson's Bay Company, as well as free traders, come to visit them in these camps. It is also part of my job to visit these trappers a couple of times during the winter. I didn't have time to make these trips before Christmas, but some days into January I am ready to do so. It has likely been a while since other traders have visited them.

One day I prepare my sled, loading it up with various provisions, including salt, some clothing, ammunition, tobacco, candy, and a small selection of other useful items. Fish for the dogs completes the load.

The half-breed Indian who accompanies me knows the location of the trappers' camps. It feels somewhat festive to lock the door behind me, hitch the dogs to the sled, and set out. This is the coldest time of the year. The thermometer registers thirty to forty degrees below, so this is not a mere pleasure ride. It is necessary to tie a scarf over my face and breathe through it to spare my lungs. Every time the scarf freezes, I turn it over. The hood of my parka—a roomy outercoat—is lined with fox fur, and it provides remarkably good protection in the biting wind.

The snow has been hard packed by the wind, and there are some snowdrifts as well. We keep to the west side of the rivers and lakes because the snow is deeper on the other side. The wind has mainly been blowing from the north and the east. The Indian runs in front of the dogs. He runs in his moccasins, only putting on snowshoes when we are in the forest or other places where the snow is deep.

We rest a couple of times during the day, and build a roaring fire in the evening. The tree trunks, two to three metres in length, will burn until morning. When it is very cold, the Indian gets up in the middle of the night and sits by the fire to keep warm. He is not dressed warmly and only has a woolen blanket for the night. I can't understand why the Indians don't freeze to death given their scanty clothing.

At first, I keep the food in a box that I share with the Indian. It is very well stocked by Norwegian standards, but I soon discover that the man cannot be allowed to freely eat whatever he wants. If so, the box would be empty in no time. From now on he will be given his portion and nothing more. I have similar experiences later on as well. If an Indian is given his entire weekly ration of tea, sugar, and jam all at once, staple items as common as goat cheese on bread at home,[2] then everything is gone in two days. Indians make their tea as black as gunpowder and as sweet as syrup, as long as they have these supplies. After that they have to manage as best they can. It is of no use to feel sorry for them.[3]

The first couple of days we cover fifty kilometres, and on the second evening we arrive at a trappers' camp. I take the cargo into the cabin and stack it in one corner before we settle in. It is taken for granted that we will spend the night there. We do not even ask about that.

I make some dough for bannock, the fur traders' bread out here. I spread the dough in a frying pan and tilt it on the fireplace so it will bake thoroughly. The man in the cabin stands near the fireplace. He coughs and spits in his hand, and then holds out his hand to examine its contents. No, there is no blood. Tuberculosis is what these people fear the most.[4] It follows them like a threatening nightmare and when they cough they can never be certain what it might imply. This time the inspection reveals nothing, and the man throws the contents towards the fireplace behind him with satisfaction. This lands on my bannock. His wife quickly comes to the rescue and smears the substance all over my bread. Of course, the wife is only trying to wipe it off and her words are very well intentioned: "Mister Gooshoo's poor bannock," she says. They are pleasantly surprised when I give them the entire bannock, while I begin to prepare a new one. By the way, I am not able to swallow any of that one either.

Afterwards I offer the Indian a cigar and transport him to the state of euphoria that comes from possessing and smoking tobacco. At this stage, I view the cigars as promotional items, but later I learn that such gifting is only an unnecessary sales expense. After giving him the cigar, I unpack the merchandise.

Someone throws me the fur of a red fox. It is a down payment on debts. At first an Indian will hold back, smug and self-satisfied, if his trapping has been good. If it has not been good, there will likely be lots of head shaking and talk of Wittigo—the Indians' devil—who for some reason has been after him.[5]

Here it is the young boys who trade first. Then the man signals to his wife. She goes out and returns with something in her handkerchief, which she hands to her husband. He takes it and with a feigned air of indifference, tosses it to me. The family follows the scene with excitement.

It is a silver fox, a quarter silver and of the type that is all the rage these days. It is a beautiful fur and is difficult for me to evaluate. I tactically choose to appraise it high, and then raise the prices of the goods I sell to him to make up for it. I can enter the sums in the account books later. In this manner, the Indian appears to receive much more for his fur than what we get for it later in Winnipeg.

We sit and trade all evening. I let a watch worth one dollar go for ten, referring to the good relationship between us. I charge only twenty-five dollars for the bison hat that I bought in The Pas for six dollars. The price of a rifle easily increases by 600 to 700 percent. But it was worse in the days when the Indian had to pay for a rifle with a stack of beaver pelts—that was the currency—and the stack had to be as high as the length of the rifle.[6] And the rifles were quite long back in those days.

In this way we roam from camp to camp. I need to use a pocket mirror the whole time to keep an eye on my appearance. This is not really for the sake of vanity, but rather to guard against the cold. Although I have an Indian with me, he politely leaves it up to me to discover the effects of frost. One morning, as I am sitting and talking with him, I get the feeling that everything is not as it should be. And sure enough, my nose and the skin around it are as white as snow. This is what frostbite looks like.

On the fourth night I sleep outdoors. My intention had been to sleep in my new host's canvas tent, but there is also a sick girl lying inside. Her breathing is laboured, her chest quickly rises and falls, and her eyes have a feverish shine. She coughs up phlegm the whole time and spits into a tin cup. Soon, tuberculosis will take her life. The others think it strange that I don't want to eat anything, but I am not able to swallow a bite in these surroundings. I also offend the family when I prepare a place to sleep outside the teepee.

The next morning, I wake up to a long, drawn-out cry: "uhuu-uhuu." The girl has died during the night and the women sit in the teepee, pulling their hair in front of their faces and mourning with a monotonous song of sorrow. "Uhuu-huu, uhuu-huu."

We continue to wander from one campground to another. Some of the trappers live in cabins, others in teepees.[7] These are the Indian tents with a smoke hole at the top. Earlier teepees were usually covered with animal hides, but these days they are made of canvas. Only the top part is made of leather, preferably from moose or caribou. That is less flammable than canvas.

The teepees are smoky and crowded, but in the cold weather it can be good to sleep shoulder to shoulder. Besides, they have the same conveniences as the cabins. The Indian cabins here in this remote place are even more primitive than those on the reserve—small and draughty.

The better off an Indian is, the farther away from the reserve he traps. The same rule prevails here as elsewhere: it is expensive to be poor. These things are mercilessly connected. If a man is a poor hunter, he acquires few furs. If he has few furs, he receives little credit, only scant supplies, and few traps. The traps are expensive out here. However, they are not among the items that have increased most in price. This is because the Hudson's Bay Company has always had the principle that goods directly needed for hunting should not be too expensive.

With scant supplies and few traps, one cannot travel very far, and the closer to the reserve one hunts, the less game is to be had. This chain of events leads to an inevitable fate. This simple law of economics has a firm hold around the necks of these sons of the wilderness.

The white hunters out here have, to some extent, been able to avoid this situation. They move farther south in the spring to directly sell their catch, and they drive their own supplies up north. They also have a greater number of traps than the Indians. Indians usually work with 60–120 traps, while the white trappers have 250–350.

The white folks usually lay out their traplines in a set direction, for example south or west or some other point of the compass. This makes it easy to maintain the traps, and they are able to look after many of them. The Indians set their traps based more on topography and their knowledge of various animals. In most traps, including fox traps, they mainly use bait, and this bait is usually fish. A beaver's genitals are worth their weight in gold as bait.

There are great differences among the Indian trappers. Some know the lifestyles and habits of animals through and through and set their traps just where they need to be. This knowledge, coupled with the greater diligence that some have, results in greater trapping yields. As a result, some Indians are able to provide comfortably for their daily needs. They own more than one set of clothing or more than one shawl, and they are also debt free.

One week follows another. My life alternates between trips to the camps and the more quiet life at the trading post. I have set out my own trapline, but my catch does not nearly meet my expectations. It has become clear to me that out here you cannot just reap where you have not sown.

There is a church service today. Yes, Pine Bluff has its own church—or at least something that they call a church. It is a room that is only used on special occasions. Here there is a stove and some roughly hewn benches, running across the room. In one of the corners some beams have been assembled to make a platform. Even out here in the wilderness, the priest can stand above his fellow human beings.

The Catholic priest has arrived. He has two dog teams and two Indians with him. One sled carries food and a tent, among other things, and his eminence sits in the other. His sled has basically been converted into a bed, so he does not have to exert himself. He visits this place twice a year; partly to preach the message of Christianity, partly to collect furs for the school tax. The dog team is tough and strong, and this is how the priest has braved the cold and the loneliness of the wilderness for a few days in order to spread his dear teachings.

This journey is guaranteed to bring him lots of respect where he comes from, a place where the wilderness is always thought of as something horrible. But it is certainly not much of a hardship when one travels for a couple of winter days in this style, seated and well bundled.

The priest also comes to pay me a visit. He is a very pleasant person. We chat and he finds out that I am some sort of Protestant. Our conversation becomes rather intense since the priest clearly wants me to covert. As his orthodox, incredibly orthodox, way of thinking becomes apparent, I tell him that I am not only a Protestant but pretty well an agnostic, and actually a bad one at that too. He works hard to get me to convert, but nothing comes of it. He promises to pray for me and to include me in his evening prayer.

Later in the day, the people gather in the church, and I join them there too. The congregation consists mainly of women and their offspring of various ages. The atmosphere is rather peculiar and strange, at least in my eyes. If the priest hadn't been so familiar with the order of service, he might have had difficulties gathering his thoughts. The little ones crawl freely around on the floor. Every now and then a four-year-old may want some milk, and comes over to his mother to have his thirst quenched from nature's own spring. And the four-year-old is allowed to do so. The Indian women breastfeed their children until they are five to six years old. And while the four-year-old is satisfying his needs, a one-year-old who is clinging to his mother's back begins to wail. He discovers his brother's attack on his only food source and perhaps fears that his chances of survival are threatened.

The priest can only speak English and has brought along a translator who proves to be a sly fox. The priest first preaches for twenty minutes, but the translator manages to complete the translation in five minutes. The translator also moderates the tone of the speech a bit. The priest speaks mainly about punishment, Satan, hell, and fire and brimstone. The members of the congregation sigh the whole time and their heads nod slowly. This is followed by some singing, simple and monotonous. When the priest's sermon is over, everyone kneels and I follow suit. The priest goes around handing out big cards where purgatory and the place even worse than that are graphically depicted. He also mentions he will return in the spring. The priest says it is the wish of the great Heavenly Father that he be given a generous number of pelts. The pelts are handed out generously by the Indians, particularly after a good muskrat season.[8]

After the sermon there is a wedding. From a practical standpoint, the couple is already bound together, but since the priest is here they might as well have a church wedding. The couple steps forward, embarrassed and with downcast eyes. The priest speaks. The couple remain silent, even when they are expected to respond. "Say *ehe*,"[9] says the priest. No reply. "Say *ehe*," repeats the priest. No reply. Finally, the priest says "*ehe*" on their behalf and the ceremony is over.

The congregation appears to be very moved while they are here inside the church, but the feeling does not appear to last, at least as far as I can tell. I had many opportunities to observe this later while in Canada. The people may come out from a fire and brimstone sermon that has thoroughly examined sin in all its forms. But no sooner are they out of the church than they appear to have forgotten everything. They may lie with someone else's wife just behind the church wall. I saw such things many times.

The priest continued on his journey the next day. He dropped by and praised me because he hadn't heard any stories about me. He also promised to come back in the spring to fetch the furs. This is how the Indians pay their school taxes. The priest also gets a considerable number of furs as his share.

In Canada there are a number of Indian Boarding Schools, which some Indian children attend. These schools turn out the most unruly and dishonest types of Indians one can imagine. The most useless Indians that I dealt with had generally received their "wisdom"[10] from these boarding schools. However, I am not of the opinion that these free sons of nature necessarily become scoundrels if they are lifted up into the enlightened state provided by book learning.[11]

Spring approaches. The ice turns bluer, the snow gets soft and wet, and sledding becomes laborious. When I am out with my team in the warmer weather, the sled sticks in the wet snow and the dogs pant and tire easily.

The days at the trading post become hectic. Soon the store must be closed for two or three weeks, and the Indians won't be able to reach me. Food and other supplies must be taken to those who are hunting muskrat along the rivers. Most trappers have returned to the reserve from their winter locations where hunting ebbs out around the middle of March. Soon the muskrat hunt begins. Those with a poor winter hunt count on the muskrat to bring in essential extra income.

The ice conditions on the river become increasingly difficult to manage, and at last traffic to the trading post comes to a complete stop. The half-breed Indian has left to hunt muskrat and I am now alone. I can't go anywhere until it becomes possible to travel by canoe.

One Sunday morning, after a frosty night, I take a risk and visit the reserve. I must find out how the muskrat hunt is going. I stay there for a couple of hours and when I set out on my return trip, I have to rely on my luck and a long stick. I have taken the stick along so I have something more than a straw to cling to if the ice doesn't hold, and it doesn't hold. Everything goes well for some time, but then the ice breaks. I manage to get myself back onto the surface of the ice but soon fall in again. I'm in serious trouble and I splash about in the ice-cold water. I feel how the current takes hold of my feet, causing me to lie diagonally in the water.

A few Indians stand on the shore watching my progress. It is highly likely they are concerned about what is going to happen to

The spring breakup often led to dangerous ice conditions for people and dogs alike. As Mortensen notes on this photo of women stuck on the ice with their dog team, "They cried for help, and I ran to get a rope. I also brought my camera."

me. In any case, they wave and shout, but I don't understand what they are trying to tell me. Soon they settle down.

It is my long stick that saves me. After a combination of swimming, crawling, and plunging about for an hour, I finally get to dry land. I try to force myself to rapidly march to my cabin but have lost all feeling in my legs. My entire body feels strangely awkward. Back in the cabin, I manage to drink some tea and climb under my woolen blankets. Words cannot describe what it feels like to pour burning hot tea down my throat and sense warmth flowing through my body again.

Four hours later I hear voices outside. Three Indians have come to look after me. They have come by canoe since the river suddenly opened up after I got back. The ice has broken up into smaller floes and everything is moving.

Now it is spring indeed. Spring up here in the North, with the opening of the waterways, is not the beginning of a new season but the end of winter. The departure of the ice is the event of the year, the first true day of spring. The hunting is mainly over, for better or for worse, as Wittigo wills. Now the lazy, wonderful days of summer beckon. No sub-zero temperatures, no checking of traps, and no struggling with the dogs.

For the trader, the opening of the rivers means it is time to bring the furs purchased in the winter to the auctions in the city. The anticipation starts to mount. Will prices go up or down? Will I have a profit or a loss, or will I break even?

The food inventory has decreased lately. There have been no bananas, milk, or sugar for weeks. However, the canoes will soon bring new groceries. The time of want will pass. Maybe there will be a bit of fresh fruit and other delicacies that the civilized world can offer.

Spring is also the time of the muskrat hunt. Rat hunting has its very own appeal since it doesn't involve much hard work, and springtime is an ideal time for the hunt. To sleep outdoors during these mild spring nights, and make money on top of it, that is the life. A life with many advantages and few struggles. This is why the Indians eagerly await the start of the rat hunting season. Some young men are particularly excited, because if they catch fifty to sixty animals, they will earn enough money to allow them to get married. Hides are worth a dollar each.

The muskrat also provides food. Yes, I said food. It is a delicacy, at least according to the Indians. I must admit I was taken aback when the half-breed Indian at the trading post surprised me with a rat meat dinner. "Never," I said—but I said it in Norwegian so the Indian did not understand me. Eventually, I dared to take a little bite, certainly the smallest piece of food that a skeptical diner has ever sampled. The morsel of food was, however, too small to have any taste at all. By using various gestures, such as rubbing his stomach, the Indian got me to understand that this was a kind of top Indian culinary experience. Only then did I dare take a piece that was a bit larger. I survived and the morsel stayed down too. And that is not all. It really tasted quite good. Rat meat is actually tender and tasty, similar to veal, and the rat tails are a much sought after delicacy. These are dried and smoked and then chewed. Rat meat can also be prepared in this way.

The next day I caught a fat, wet frog for the Indian, a large bullfrog specimen, and threw it in the pot. The frog would provide considerably more than a mouthful, and I served it to the Indian with great anticipation. "They eat a lot of these down south," I explained and added, "yummy." Surely he would allow himself to be convinced to try this, since I had been convinced by him. However, he pointed at me, implying I should go first. I tried to explain that in the country I came from—a land that would take countless days to reach by canoe—the custom was to wait to eat until the guest had eaten. Unfortunately, the man would not allow himself to be persuaded.

I must admit that I had an ulterior motive for serving the frog. I had encountered dried frogs and such rarities further south, and I very much wanted to witness a person eating a fresh one. Frogs are said to be a delicacy, but man is often a doubting, suspicious creature. Though I wanted to convince myself that it was a delicacy, I wanted to see someone else confirm this first. I declined to dine on the frog myself. "I'll put it aside so it has time to cool," I said. "Then it will be even better." That could well be the case.

The muskrat population varies considerably. The number of pelts we buy may fluctuate by several hundred percent from one year to the next. The muskrat has, you see, many enemies in addition to hunters. The muskrat multiplies in nature according to a fairly general and prevailing principle—the smaller the animal, the greater the number. With several litters per year and four to six little ones in every litter, the population has to amount to something. But nature often gives with one hand and takes away with the other. In Norway, we have a saying: "Nature is wisely arranged." However, I have never been able to understand how such an arrangement is particularly wise or smart.

Nature can take the life of a muskrat in many ways, particularly in the fall. For example, if a dry fall is followed by a bitterly cold period that freezes most ponds, small lakes, and shallow swampy rivers to the bottom, a rat is finished. The muskrat will have dug out small hollows where it lives, and from these there are tunnels leading to free-flowing water. If the water freezes to the bottom, the muskrat becomes trapped in its hollow and freezes to death. It is true that it has the option of digging a tunnel up to the surface. However, when it comes up, it will either be eaten by other animals that enjoy rat meat, or it will freeze to death.

Another weather-related condition that can be fateful to the muskrat is the surface flooding of lakes and rivers in autumn after they have already frozen. If this happens, water enters the tunnel and the den and the rat drowns. Though a rat is able to swim underwater, it is not able to live like that.

With this simple combination of temperature, water, and hunger, nature holds the rat population in check, and humans try to catch those animals that remain. In some years the rat litters are actually very small. The fertility rate seems to decline after severe winters, when the food supply is poor, and wild rice and swamp plants are scarce.

The muskrat is so feared at home in Norway that we have not dared to import it. The fear of this valuable furbearer is probably partly rooted in the fact that it is called a rat. It is also due to people confusing the muskrat, the true fur rat, with its South American variant. There are many areas in Norway, however, that would be ideal environments for muskrats to breed. There have, of course, been other arguments made against the muskrat. At any rate, it is North America's most valuable furbearer, and is most widely distributed in those areas of Canada and Alaska that are rich with lakes and swamps.[12]

In spring, when the muskrat's fur is at its best, one hunts it by breaking into the animals' dens. These protrude like small mounds from the marshy ground alongside rivers. Traps are set and are attached to a stick. One can also dig down to the tunnels or locate the air holes in the ice. Another method is to make air holes, chisel out a small shelf, and then set traps on the ledge. Bait is not used. One only needs to be familiar with the muskrats' habits.

A little later in the spring, muskrats can also be easily shot. One need only lie down on the riverbank and imitate the twittering of the female, even though the Hunting Act prohibits attracting them by this method. At this time of mating and life's pleasures, the male rat comes swimming by, happy and full of expectations. Its pointy nose sticks up out of the water. Its ears are closed and almost hidden inside its fur coat. Both its body and its tail are squeezed together on the sides to facilitate movement in the water. The back feet are webbed, and with them he rows quickly ahead, making a little wake on the surface of the river as he swims directly towards what it thinks is a waiting female rat. It is an easy target for a small calibre rifle. When a female calls at the right time, the male appears to throw all common sense aside.

The muskrat's lifestyle greatly resembles that of the beaver. It holds to lakeshores and riverbanks, preferring calm waters with an abundance of reeds and other marsh plants. They are very cautious and if they suspect danger, they dive with lightning speed. One can hear a little splash as its tail hits the water. The other members of the colony hear the warning and immediately vanish. The tail of a full-grown male is twenty-five to thirty centimetres long, as long as its body, so it functions as a fairly effective warning device.

It is wonderful to launch the canoe into the water and set out on the spring's first paddling trip. A short distance downriver from the trading post is another island that the half-breed Indians call the Island of the Dead. Someone probably died here in the past.

Much of the snow has blown off here, and the heather is starting to emerge. I go ashore and it is strange to feel the soft moss under my moccasins. I really want to caress it with my feet and I tread carefully on it.

A row of canoes made from birchbark lie on the south shore of the island. I tip over the closest one. The canoe is light and from underneath rises the unbearable stench of a half-decomposed Indian. The Island of the Dead is truly an island for the dead. It is an Indian burial ground. Under the inverted canoes lie deceased Indians in varying states of decay.

The Indians have a custom of laying the dead on the ground and covering them with these overturned, canoe-like, birchbark boats. A free man should not be shut inside the earth. "The white men live from food which has grown in the earth and they are buried in the earth. We Indians live on what runs on the surface of the earth, and we want to sleep our final sleep in the trees." This was how one

Indian expressed it. Some Indian tribes further to the south actually place their dead in the trees. Due to the influence of the Catholics, some Indians have started to bury their dead in the ground.[13]

April is the beginning of the spring thaw. Now, by the end of June, one can be confident that summer has truly arrived. The time to get moving approaches. The trading post will be closed and will not open again until the fall. Since the Indians have no more hides, keeping the store open would only result in increased debt. The Indians have a short memory, and they are accustomed to the fact that there is nothing to buy in summer. The summer is also a delightful, lazy time for them, when nature sets its table to a far richer degree and with more variety than during the harsh winter.

I pack the dried hides into bales, each variety separately, using the trading post's handmade press. Every 20-30 kilo bale must also be sewn into its own canvas bag. The store inventory is taken and the door is locked. There are no shutters over the windows, there is little merchandise remaining, and we are safe as far as the Indians are concerned. It may be that, in their innocent ignorance, the Indians sometimes shoplift things that are useless to them, such as a bar of soap. However, they are not up to the task of breaking in by destroying a cheap padlock. Civilization has not succeeded in getting a strong enough hold on them yet.

My dogs remain here. An Indian woman will feed them until the fall. The Indians release their own dogs to run free. The summer is a wonderful time for the Indians but a bad time for their dogs. In a manner of speaking, the dogs are let out to pasture and they must survive on their own. Since the dogs do not chew cud or live on grass, summer is, for them, a time of hunger with few good meals. Here in the north the dogs' lives vacillate between these two extreme combinations. In the winter: food and hard work, and in the summer: no food and no work.

Life in this remote place would be nearly impossible in the winter if the Indians didn't have their dogs. Actually, it would be totally impossible. Indeed, the dogs are as important for transportation for the Indians as the camel is for the Bedouin or the reindeer for the Lapp.[14] However, all that is forgotten with the transition from the sledding to the canoeing season. The Indians have no use

The lazy days of summer.

for the dogs at this time, so they must fend for themselves as best they can. The Indians no longer seem to remember the dogs' great efforts during the winter. Appreciation for their faithful sled dogs resembles the Indians' thankfulness to the white person when he extends a helping hand in difficult situations.[15]

It is clear from the dogs' appearance that summer is a lean time for them. They end up emaciated, and it appears that the only thing holding them together is their skin. However, the dogs have a remarkable ability to keep going, and they engage in a continuous struggle with their masters. They steal everything they can, although the Indians make sure there is nothing in the camp for the dogs. If they happen to creep into camp, they are greeted with catcalls, kicks, and stones, but not with food. When one dog has gotten a hold of something, whether it is edible or not, the other dogs set upon the poor wretch, demanding their share of the spoils, more annoyed than the Indians.

Dogs during their work season.

It has been said that dogs that prowl about the camp take everything that is not nailed down, and if something is nailed down, they tear it loose. What type of food do these dogs find for themselves in summer? We consider the forest to be full of wild game and other food, and this is indeed accurate, but it is not very easy for a domesticated animal to hunt. Rabbits are an exceptional source of meat, if they can get a hold of any. Mice and fish are also part of a dog's diet. During the summer and the fall, the dogs eat berries, such as lingonberries.[16] It is amusing to watch them stripping the bushes like master berry pickers. On the other hand, it is sad to watch these sled dogs chewing on berries and leaves like vegetarians. In addition, they eat, as previously mentioned, human waste of every imaginable and unimaginable sort.

When the Indians begin to gather the dogs together for the winter after a rough summer and fall, they resemble piles of bones held together by scruffy hides. At that point the Indians need to begin caring for the dogs, so they get some meat on their bones and gather strength for the approaching sledding season. When they start to pull again, the dogs have forgotten the thanklessness of their masters and burn with a desire to get back into the harness. Like the

Indians, they have a short memory, and they view the summer like the Indians view the closing of the trading post in the spring: it is meant to be.[17]

I say goodbye to my winter haunts. Pine Bluff disappears behind me. One last glimpse of the outlying cabins before the river winds around a bend, and we paddle away. I am travelling with two canoes and four Indians. Where we struggled with dogsleds in winter, we now paddle at a rapid pace on a wide, quietly flowing river. From time to time we come to a portage, where canoes and cargo must be carried over land.

I sit in the stern of the first canoe and review the events of the winter as if in a film running through my mind. I summarize all I have learned. I am no longer "Mr. *Gooshoo*," but "Mr. *Oogemoo*"—master.[18] I have learned a lot and the Indians know it. But what have I learned?

First of all, I have gotten to know the Cree Indians. Despite their expressionless faces, I know what they think when I am trading with them, and I know how to deal with them. If their faces do not reveal anything, their conduct does. The more politely they behave, the greater scoundrels they are. The fewer skins they have, the more demands they make about establishing credit.

I have also learned to drive a dog team and run behind a sled for the greater part of a day, jogging with my legs bent and wide apart. I also own several pairs of snowshoes, some large and some small, for use in a variety of conditions. When I am out on the trail, I know how to make camp and prepare a good bed for myself under the open sky, even in biting, sub-zero temperatures. Next autumn I want to purchase some good puppies and train them myself.

Am I a trapper? No, I must be honest and admit that I have not become a trapper. I don't want to reveal what I caught over the winter, but I have learned from my blunders and gained some appreciation of what trapping is all about.

I have, however, learned a great deal about pelts and how to distinguish between a good and a bad fur. I know how to appraise their thickness at the shoulders, and am able to discern which furs have good tails and long outer hairs. I am also familiar with the various qualities of marten pelts: the dark valuable ones, and the light ones. I know how to sort the rough, light fisher pelts from the less valuable ones.

In a word, when the canoe runs ashore in The Pas, I feel like an old-timer.[19] The winter has given me experience and a fine van Dyck beard, which makes me appear ten to fifteen years older than I am. An old-timer indeed, tried and true! This feeling gradually vanishes during the coming days while going through the hides with Ben Dembinsky, the German Jew on whose account I have been buying them. First of all, the pelts are of poor quality, and secondly I have paid too much for them. I certainly don't get any praise, that's for sure. I have also unknowingly bought patched hides. As far as beaver pelts go, I have failed completely by not paying attention to the most important quality: the size. Dembinsky says that the hides were either all small last winter, or the Indians have held back their best ones and sold them to others.

I am proud of some bear hides, but only for a moment. Bear hides are not on the list of furs to be purchased, and I accepted them partly for their novelty. Dembinsky appraises them at three to five dollars per hide, and I now realize I must have greatly amused the Indian who sold them to me.

Nonetheless, on these days I learn a great deal about fur. Dembinsky talks and gestures, brings out hides for the sake of comparison, and only now do I learn something about furs. It is likely that he is, in part, so eager to explain these things because he is thinking about the commission we had agreed to before I started. As he goes over our affairs, it appears to me as if it is I who owe him money.

Despite everything, the year as a whole seems to have turned out to be an average one. He wants me, at any rate, back in the autumn and generously gives me two months of vacation—without pay.

Mortensen describes trading with Indigenous women, men, and children in Pine Bluff. He labelled this photo "Two Cree girls with black cashmere shawls," though its location is unclear.

4 | *From Greenhorn to Old-Timer*

THE DAYS PASS BY AND DECEMBER HAS ARRIVED. It gets light around eight in the morning, and darkness already returns by about four in the afternoon. It is snowy, cloudy, and grey all day long. Winter is here to stay. At times the thermometer reads thirty degrees below zero. At these temperatures the cold cuts right through the log walls and clay caulking, and it is difficult to keep it warm inside. There is not the slightest chance that the lard in the store will begin to melt, no matter how much wood I burn. It can be quite uncomfortable when the cold north wind nips at your ears, but you just need to dress well for the cold and then there is nothing to worry about.[1] Nevertheless, it is still most comfortable indoors.

As a rule, I get up in the dim dawn, and while still inside my sleeping bag, I hop over to the stove to add wood to the fire. Then I jump back into bed. I lie there and watch the shadows from the flames in the oven play on the wall, and feel the warmth spread into the room.

I have no cares to speak of. When the snow blows outside and the wind whines through the chimney, I stretch out luxuriously in my sleeping bag and take it easy. When customers come to the store and I am in my cabin, they often come over here. They stop and stand in the doorway, saying nothing.

Otherwise, the days here at the trading post are filled with basic routine tasks. Outside the cabin I have firewood that an Indian has gathered for me, but I chop it myself. The dogs must be fed, and I give them fish once or twice a day. Sometimes I boil corn porridge to feed them for the sake of variety. After breakfast I open the store and warm it up. Maybe there will be a customer, maybe not. I have never been informed that the store has to be open at particular times, and if I am not here the customers can wait until I come back.

The meals I prepare for myself are fairly simple. For breakfast I have coffee, oatmeal, bannock, and fried pork. The main course at supper is pork and beans—one of the trappers' national dishes—along with small sausages or corned beef. I have brought along a couple of boxes filled with cans of each of these food items. There are a few potatoes in the basement, but they are sweet due to frost damage. I also shoot some game now and then. I trade for rabbits and shoot a few ptarmigans, which I cook. Ptarmigans are fairly easy to shoot with a small calibre rifle, since they are quite tame. An old Indian woman brings me some boiled whitefish, which is delicious.[2]

One day when I am out for a run with the dogs on a trail close to the reserve, I see an entire row of rabbits hanging three to four metres above the ground in the trees. They have been caught in traps called spring pool[3] traps. The Indians bend down a poplar tree and attach the snare line to the top. When a rabbit runs into the snare, the poplar springs up with the rabbit, and the animal remains hanging in the air. This prevents the foxes from getting a hold of them.

A week before Christmas I spot three dog teams approaching the reserve from the north. The trappers are returning home. This will mean more trading. I go through my accounts and make a list so I can easily locate information about people when they come into the store. Later that day, two more dog teams return to the reserve. The day passes, but not a single customer comes into the store. Only some young girls drop by to purchase tea, candles, and tobacco.

The next day also passes without customers. I am in the store until nearly ten o'clock in the evening before I finally leave. As soon as I have started to undress, someone knocks on my door and a swarthy Indian slips in. I give him one of the household's two box chairs to sit on while I dress. We go over to the store and sit there looking at each other. "Nice weather," I say. "Oh yes," he says. "Many furs," I say. "Oh yes," he says. But where is the load of furs I assumed he had brought? The man lights his pipe and smokes for a while. My god, this man appears to have plenty of time. Then he looks around, opens his pocket, and spits into it. I consider this to be a polite gesture, but nevertheless I put an empty tin can in front of him. He continues to spit into his pocket. Then suddenly he pulls a silver fox fur from his jacket and throws it to me. "Cash?"[4] "No cash," I reply.

The accounts show the man owes 130 dollars and I offer ninety dollars for the fox fur. Of this, forty dollars will count as payment towards his debt and he will receive merchandise worth fifty dollars. All right, the matter is settled. He gets a pair of trousers and some silk cloth for his wife. He also buys a pair of three-dollar moccasins. I had bought them a few days earlier from his neighbour's wife for one dollar. The Indians do not trade among themselves. They come to the trading post, even if the end result of this roundabout method might be considered slightly unsatisfactory.[5]

I had, as mentioned, expected this man to bring a big load of furs. However, even though planning for the future is not particularly important to these children of nature, they are always hesitant to trade their entire catch.[6] In order to soften him up a bit, I give him one of the two-cent cigars that I have reserved for customers.[7] His dirty face breaks out in a beaming smile. It is a great moment in the life of an Indian when he can hold his own cigar.

Life in the store gets busier over the following days. The room is full when there are six or seven men there at the same time. The others wait outside. I collect a portion of the debts, and the fur inventory increases. The women have been given ermine skins and they gather around me, eager to sell them.

There is also another trader around here, a half-breed Indian. He stays over on the reserve, and is an employee of the Hudson's Bay Company. His main task is to collect debts owed to the Company. At this time of the year he doesn't have much merchandise to sell and most of the customers come to me.

During this time, the Indians mainly buy clothing, such as sweaters and colourful silk fabric for their wives. When the women get a new dress, they just put it on over whatever they are wearing. Among young Indian men, blue suits are very much in demand. One day I noticed an Indian on the reserve who had just bought one of the most expensive suits. When I met him in his cabin, the man was lying on the floor in his new suit. He had not even bothered to hang up his jacket. But this is the sort of thing that makes a trader happy; after all it increases our sales.

The customers do not usually come until the afternoon or evening. They only drop by earlier in the day when they are preparing for a new trip. But even then they may linger in the store until evening.

Now and then they try to trick me. A man arrives one night with something he calls a white fox. It is sewn together from rabbit furs with the tail of a white fox attached. However, he does not succeed. When I occasionally feel like I am paying them too much, I try to make up for it later in another way. I increase the prices of the goods I sell or skimp a bit on the amount of cloth I give them. The principle is catch as catch can.[8]

Now that the Indians have returned, I spend more time on the reserve. I visit the cabins, take a seat, and say almost nothing, but I greet everyone by holding out my hand. "I have learned to say "*Minni kissi khao.*"[9] It means "nice weather." "*Ehe*"—yes, they reply. "*Misteet makeso?*"[10] Many fox furs? "*Ehe*," they reply again. This is how I go from cabin to cabin. It is part of my job, and I must, of course, keep in constant contact with those people who owe me money.

Now and then I visit a cabin when only women are present. "*Neema kaskenema monia oogemoo,*"[11] cracks one of the younger women to me. Everyone starts to giggle loudly. This is a standing joke on the reserve and it means: "I am dying to do something to the white man." "*Nina minikino wipatch nehentemon,*"[12] she continues. "Soon we will have fun together." After some time has passed, I learn to respond: "*Getch noat.*"[13] That means: "Yes, that's for sure." This causes the pleasant atmosphere to turn uncomfortable.[14]

Otherwise they sit there and remain occupied with their domestic chores. One may be skinning an ermine, another may be embroidering moccasins, and yet another may be breastfeeding a child or picking lice. There is a plentiful supply of those.

On Christmas Day, I receive a visit from a white trapper for the first time—George Dane—who arrives for his annual visit. His current camp is located four days by sled from my trading post. As his name indicates, he is a Danish Canadian and every winter he makes trapping forays into the wilderness. When he visits a trading post, he only does so to trade a few low-quality furs for essential supplies that he has run out of. He sells the rest of his furs in The Pas or other towns where he also buys food and other supplies. There is no doubt it is to his advantage to trade in this manner.

The visit of the Dane to the trading post at this time of the year is an annual spectacle.[15] Earlier in the fall he had left behind a keg of wine and a jug of rum. Like other heathens, he likes to celebrate Christmas and prefers to do so with white folks. During Christmas there should be peace in the forest. The trapper removes his traps, so even the animals are given a few days off.

George Dane makes himself at home at the trading post. This type of visit also cheers me up. At first I prepare meals for both of us, but I soon get tired of this and he has to look after himself as time goes on. I am impressed by his appetite, and I realize that much larger quantities of food can fit into a human stomach than I had ever imagined possible. At his first meal with me, he starts by eating two whitefish, each weighing one kilo, and then a half kilo of bannock bread, together with a hearty portion of peas, meat and pork. In addition, he downs a bucket of tea. This seems to satisfy him and appears to do him no harm. He belches contentedly and crawls into his sleeping bag. His little black shaggy dog, which resembles a Norwegian *buhund*,[16] climbs in after him.

I must also admit that the Dane is one of the dirtiest white men I have ever seen, and it is no small thing to make that statement. Most people would, at the bare minimum, bathe properly before Easter and Christmas. The Dane has skipped the Christmas bath, and I don't believe he is particularly concerned with cleanliness at Easter either.

I get the Dane to look over the pelts I have purchased to review my blunders. He teaches me to see the differences in quality among fox pelts. It turns out that I have paid too much for some damaged furs. When a fox sits on the ice during the winter, its hairs often freeze to the ice and come loose when the fox moves on so that only the undercoat remains. I have only checked pelts to make sure that the hair is even. Now I learn new things about the length of the pelt, its colour, and the quality of the neck fur. The Dane also grabs the tips of the tails of some of the pelts I have purchased and shows me that if a fox is not properly skinned, and part of the tail remains, this piece will rot and the tip of the tail will fall off. I have already purchased a few of these worthless pelts.

The rest of the time we talk about the fur trapper's favourite fantasy: an abundant year of trapping on Great Slave Lake, an Eldorado that haunts, entices, and captures the imagination of every fur trapper. These trappers will never become properly rich, but they all have one thing in common. They expect and believe a year of plenty will come their way. A year when everything is ideal: lots of animals, beautiful animals, and good fur prices.

There may be years when nature gives abundantly, providing animals in unimaginable numbers, seemingly with no limits. However, trappers don't long for these conditions so they can take it easy for some years. On the contrary, such conditions will provide money for more equipment, so the trappers can travel farther afield. The farther away they travel the better, because then they might find richer hunting grounds.

When the trapper sets out in the fall, he finds his trapping territory and then builds his little log cabin in the course of two or three days. Once again, he has a chance to achieve the great catch of his dreams. Maybe he can pay off all his debts, and there will be a large, large sum of cash left over.

But the days go by. A few animals end up in the traps, but far from a huge influx. The winter passes. This looks like just an average year, perhaps even a bit below average. Or it looks like it will be hard to pay off debts and purchase new equipment for next autumn. The funds may only allow for hunting in the poorer districts. But if...

The years pass in this way. The lean years consume the fat ones. There are not just seven lean and seven fat years, but many lean years and a few fat ones. But they survive the years, and they still have their hopes. And even if they have had a relatively good year and have played around in town for some time, the wilderness calls them back again. The loneliness and struggles, the blizzards and the cold, empty traps and debts to the company—nothing can hold them back. The life of the free man is still out there. The dream about

Great Slave Lake or other distant lakes is kept alive. They will just have to travel there some day.

George Dane departs a few days into the New Year. I must admit that I prefer solitude as well. George will not return before summer approaches, certainly not before the muskrat hunt is over. George and the muskrat hunt is truly a story in its own right. George was a pioneer in this area, being the first to use a dog, and his shaggy dog had quite a reputation. Some say the dog was able to smell a rat dwelling from a distance of several kilometres. Although these tales are not entirely true, the dog was indeed able to locate nearby lodges, and this gave George his own unique method of catching rats.

When George Dane departed, he left behind a large number of little travelling companions. I was so covered with fleas that I had to conduct a thorough cleansing ceremony. This created certain difficulties. I ended up stripping naked in the forest, pouring paraffin on my underwear and burning them. That is how I got rid of George Dane's pesky remnants.

Every once in a while, I also receive a visit from the two half-breed Indians who are attached to this trading post. They are out in the field trapping on the company's account, and also buy pelts from the surrounding Indian camps. I especially enjoy interacting with one of them. He speaks a bit of English, and I am able to expand my knowledge of this and that when he acts as a translator.

This man acquired his limited ability to speak English during the 1914–1918 World War. You see, many of these Indians participated in the war, and I often heard them talk about their experiences. They spoke almost half-heartedly about their experiences, and without any enthusiasm. They used simple words to describe enormous suffering. They participated as so-called volunteers and, of course, they did not understand very much English. One day a draft sergeant came up, and he was zealous to serve his country. These recruiters weren't particularly concerned with using scrupulous means, and in that way the Indians enlisted as volunteers.

Large groups of Indians were loaded on ships and sent over the ocean. They sat together in overcrowded quarters. Seasickness and other misery ruled over them in a brutal fashion, and they died like flies. But they died for their country. Those who survived were given the glorious task of emptying French latrines. Here they fought many a brave battle, and as thanks for their contribution they were, perhaps, given a medal of some sort. The only good thing about their trip abroad was that they had learned a little English. Some of them had learned it so well that they could swear like a white sergeant.[17]

Thomas Mamanewatum, an elderly acquaintance of Mortensen. Location unknown.

5 | *Sons of the Wilderness*

THE IMAGE OF REDSKINS[1] I had originally constructed turns out to be an illusion. Or perhaps it is more accurate to say that I came to the North American continent one hundred years too late if the reality of what I saw were to have matched the colourful and bloodthirsty image of the Indians that most of us have created in our minds.

In any case, Cooper's last Mohican has long since departed from these parts. Chingacoock has gone to the eternal hunting grounds, and the Deerslayer has not been seen since he waved his last goodbye from the edge of the forest.[2]

But how do we imagine them to be, these sons of the wilderness, and what do we want them to be? The answer is, of course, as we once imagined them in our boyish minds: as representatives of things unknown, of things yet to be experienced, unrestricted by ordinary, everyday life. These images match our expectations. Somewhere deep within all of us lingers the memory of our youthful dreams, though we are constricted by our prejudices, chained by our daily worries about rent and food budgets, and bound by our social ambitions. We are buried in the routines of daily life and years that fly by faster and faster as our minds settle into habits, and we are no longer able to see the world with a child's directness.

In the midst of this, our dreams of adventure and our discontent with things we haven't attained nag at us, as we long to be something we are not, to live a life we are not living. We yearn to travel—to escape from reality. In most cases, this means we think we should have accomplished more in life. These daydreams reveal our disappointment that we don't have what others have. They reveal our inability to be fulfilled by our work, and they prevent us from seeing what we have achieved. They reflect the hazy belief that with another profession, in another place, we would find fulfillment and be more successful.

Some people react to these daydreams with disappointment, and bitterly criticize what others do and say. They only see the negative things in life. In others, these daydreams lead to a different reaction. Wilderness—that is the song some of us can hear within ourselves. In the midst of culture's functionalist heaviness and a restlessness from the lack of a real life, we long for the wilderness and a free life. A free life, with natural joys and sorrows, where people are in their natural, primitive form. And in the boyish fantasy and boyish mind of an adult, the Indian has always lived his dangerous life as an incarnation of the free man.

An Indian—that is a known entity. I could ask the reader to sit down and draw a picture of an Indian. How would you draw him? You would not have to think for a long time. The Indian would stand there immediately, ready and complete. We can draw upon many models.

Indian figures from our boyhood, when we imitated them as best we could while playing in the fields and forests. We did this with a feather in our hair, a tomahawk made of wood, and, for those who were well off, leather pants with coloured fringes. This is how they appeared in the comic books about Sitting Bull[3] and the cheaper ones about Old Waverly.[4] This is how these sons of the wilderness sneak into our imaginations, and we can see them there in front of us as if they were real.

We meet him on the warpath, far away from the protective fences surrounding our apartment buildings; a really good, old-fashioned and typical Indian, one with a feather headdress hanging down his back and with dried scalps on his belt. We meet him stealing along a desolate and lonely path—but our rifle sounds first, so it is we who survive.

And the Chief sits by the campfire in council with his men. The peace pipe has been extinguished, and the tomahawk has been dug up. The scalps, hanging from their belts, grimace. The torture post has been raised and soon a captive warrior will be brought out. He is likely to be rescued at the last moment, just as the heat from the fire begins to reach him and the suspense reaches its peak. Some nearby tree trunks move, and they turn out to be enemy Indians. Suddenly, they throw away their branches and other botanical accessories. A knife quickly cuts the prisoner's rope and everyone is safe.

Yes, this is how we imagine the Indian and Indian life to be, and this is how we want to draw him. He is given a fine headdress reaching down his back, a wild look in his black eyes, and a nose that curls menacingly like the beak of a bird of prey. Shadows creep forward in the forest, someone leaps over a menacing chasm, a tomahawk whizzes through the air, accurate and fateful, and a bowie knife relieves the fallen enemy of his scalp. An "Ugh" echoes through the forest and the victor vanishes silently.

The Chief gathers his people by the campfire, and the Medicine Man predicts the future by looking at the entrails of animals and the magical flames. The Chief stands there threateningly in his deerskins and scalps while he issues his orders for the next day. He is in total control of his people, bloodthirsty in his hatred and extremely lithe. Ugh!

But he is different today, that is for sure.[5] The first Indian Chief I met was the one on the Pine Bluff reserve. Two weeks after my arrival at the trading post, he and another man pounded on my door at two in the morning. They had gotten a hold of some firewater and were quite intoxicated. On a sudden whim, they decided to come and visit me to do some trading.

"Me, John Chief, me tobacco," the Chief said and hit his chest. I was so sleepy and angered by the disturbance that I responded with some strong language, expressions that would even have impressed and drawn the envy of an old sailing ship captain. But my words had no effect on these fellows. The Chief remained calm. Finally, I had to throw both of them out. They remained in the yard, crawling around a long time in the snow before they were able to get to their feet. Then they swayed arm in arm back to the reserve. I almost regretted that I had gotten angry. I hadn't thought an Indian Chief would allow himself to be thrown out so easily, at least without returning to take my scalp or do something else to get back at me. However, I kept my hair and the good-natured Chief was all smiles the next time he came to buy flour and sugar on credit.

Of course, you can still find Indians decked out in brilliant feathers and with bloodthirsty expressions and so on. You can still encounter these types on the prairies farther south and west.[6] They make their income as tourist attractions.[7] Here we can meet the Indian heroes from our childhood. They are almost more elegant than we had imagined. The feather ornaments nearly reach to the ground. Most of them are great Chiefs, they say, and they know how to perform with the appropriate bloodthirsty gaze in their eyes when the situation or the tourists demand it.

But, otherwise, I have not discovered any similarity worth mentioning between those Indians that I have met and those that I had expected to meet. The only features I recognize from Cooper's books are the impassive faces. Rarely does an Indian's face light up with any kind of movement.

The Indians I move among are Cree Indians.[8] If I am to add anything to the descriptions I provide of them in other contexts and places in this book, then it would have to be with a mixture of good and bad as I saw them through my eyes, emphasizing the peculiarities that struck me. Of course, I understand that this would be just one yardstick, and a subjective one at that. If one considers that I come from a country with municipal dental care and school breakfasts for children,[9] among other things, then I will, naturally, only be giving a one-dimensional and biased impression, and a superficial description at that.

First, let's look at appearance. The Cree Indians are small, 150–160 centimetres tall, with dark complexions and slight builds. Their faces are usually broad. In addition, the Cree men are black-eyed and beardless. A few isolated tufts of beard are all they can manage as far as that goes.

In terms of outward appearance, they really are a disappointment at first, as their daily clothing has lost its Indian characteristics, with the exception of the moccasins. They wear all kinds of trousers and jackets, as well as overalls made from blue cloth or wind-resistant material. Women usually dress in ginghams, which sounds fancy, but this is merely the English name for dresses made from blue cloth. They use their shawls as head coverings. Men prefer black felt hats but often have to settle for a cap.

The type of shawl women value most is black cashmere, rather than colourful or speckled ones. These can be worth one hundred dollars if the husband is a good hunter and can afford it.

On special occasions—and on some not so special ones too, just as long as there is an occasion—they love to dress up. A festive atmosphere and a certain Indian style becomes evident when they put on their ornamented deerskin jackets, and their long cuffed gloves and moccasins—both richly embroidered with silk thread or beads.[10]

The typical summer garb for an Indian includes galoshes. Yes, that is right, galoshes just like the ones we use. It seemed pretty strange to me the first time I saw an Indian wearing galoshes over his moccasins, but I quickly learned to stop being surprised. Otherwise, I would have had to go about in a state of wonder the whole summer long.

I first noticed the galoshes in Pine Bluff when I went to look over the trading post's storehouse. I thought they must be hanging there due to a combination of a pretentious salesman and a foolish trader. However, it quickly became apparent that the galoshes were a very, very important ware. The thought of an Indian creeping around in the forest wearing galoshes may sound strange, but that's the way it is.

Indians have somewhat different clothing customs than we have. They never take their clothes off when they camp outdoors, and rarely remove them indoors either. When the women buy new underwear, they simply put it on over the old pair. The old ones remain there and rot, basically disappearing on their own.[11]

One can, at any rate, smell an Indian, particularly the women, even if your sense of smell is much weaker than average, and even if the Indian is some distance away. The smell can be explained by the fact that these Indians completely lack an understanding of hygiene. There are probably some exceptions, but if they wash, then it is mainly their hands and areas around their nose. In any case, I remember being quite struck by an elderly, somewhat religious Indian who accompanied me on one of my trading trips. He carried a washing basin made of tin. He made a strong impression on me, I remember, first by washing up in a little bit of water, and then afterwards by throwing the dirty water out and immediately putting flour in the basin to make bannock.

This lack of cleanliness also causes variations in the Indians' appearances. The racial characterization "redskin" does not fit, at least not for these Indians. These are brownish grey. The brown is from the sun and the grey from dirt. As a result, their colour can change depending on the amount of precipitation. Their skin is a cleaner brown colour after long periods of rain.

Lice and fleas accompany the dirt. The first of these zoological creatures have a particularly nourishing dwelling place, living in human hair in great numbers. This provides the opportunity for many intense delousing hunts.

It should be clear by now to the reader that these Indians do not seem to be particularly warlike or bloodthirsty. In fact, any potential bloodthirstiness is avoided. If we, for example, have a little boxing match just for the fun of it, and someone gets a nosebleed, they immediately give up. They do not display any fighting spirit in that sense.

Most Indians are weak when it comes to athletics and sports, and they are inferior to the white man in competitions. They do not even distinguish themselves in target shooting. But if the target is a living creature, such as a moose, then their aim is very good. Live animals are, after all, the only targets they have known. If a white man had experienced the same conditions, he would certainly be equally skilled. When the Indians see an animal, they always want to shoot it, whether they need it or not.

The Indians' concept of work differs greatly from ours. Perhaps they might be best described as people who work in fits and starts, who work intensively and give it their all for a while, and then take a complete rest. This is not altogether unknown among us either. The Indians work for the day, save little, and take every day's cares as they come. They may have a small amount of meat cached away, but apparently only because it is necessary to shoot an entire animal. Animals cannot be shot in daily meal-size portions. I have never seen an Indian store up more firewood than needed for the day. Every morning the women haul the day's firewood home. Even blizzards and drifting snow have not taught them to build wood piles by their cabin walls. Only once during these years did I see stored wood and that was at the home of Noah the one-armed.[12] He lived up north on the shores of Hudson Bay in a treeless and stormy area.

The word "work" to Indians in this area, if I understand it correctly, can best be translated as "hunting and transporting." The Indians of this area are not physically strong, but they are very tough and have great endurance when needed while hunting or canoeing. In these situations, they can be as industrious as ants while on the move all day from four or five in the morning.

During the summer portaging, it is incredible to see how much these slight men are able to carry. I particularly admire the pace at which they work. Although they have to tramp through rugged terrain and swamps, ascend steep hills, or plod over shrubby patches in the forest, they move along at a jog with incredible ease while carrying their heavy loads. I often wonder how their necks can tolerate this.

If the men are not hunting or moving freight, they are lazy.[13] Then they usually lie on the cabin floor, smoking, spitting, and talking while they let the women do the work. If the women are sitting around in the evening sewing moccasins, skinning animals, or doing other chores, the men sit there doing nothing. But this custom is not only seen among Indians.

The Cree Indians are skilled canoeists. On many occasions, I have felt shivers go up and down my spine as we paddled through foaming rapids, which boiled and pounded against our fragile canvas boats. Only a little tumble against a stone, or a bigger tilt in the powerful current, and we would be off to the afterlife.

In these situations, an Indian's brain functions with lightning speed and clarity. Instincts, both inherited and developed through experience, function at their peak when split-second reactions are required. With a slight flick of the paddle and a rapid assessment of the colour of the water and spray conditions, the canoe whirls between life and death. This most fragile vessel darts and turns amidst the churning foam and stones, and the deeper water. It is important to choose a route through the deepest and darkest water. Though much of this appears to me to be happenstance, it is evidently based on the Indian's knowledge of the river. But still...

The river's water level fluctuates and the strength and direction of the current changes as the water rises and recedes. The colder it is, the heavier the water. It isn't enough for the Indians to be familiar with the river's course and currents on one particular day. The conditions could be totally different the next time they travel through the rapids. As a result, the Indians often appraise the situation from the riverbank before embarking. Now and then a canoe gets into big trouble, but usually everything goes well.

One might think that these Indians are highly skilled in all water-related activities. This isn't the case, at least not for the Indians I have dealt with. In adventure books, the Indians are always good swimmers, both above and below the surface, diving and splashing about like fish.

But the Cree cannot swim and they appear quite clumsy in the large York boats. Even in canoes they display little prowess as seamen. But the caution they display is probably due to the fact that they cannot swim, so they do not want to take unnecessary risks. In addition, they don't mind paddling. If, however, they have to choose between a tiring portage on a river or shooting the rapids, they often take the gamble. But they shun sailing. It is only when they have a tailwind that they might raise a tarp as a sail. I have never witnessed the Cree Indians taking advantage of the wind in any other way.

Some say Indians never take risks on the rivers. But anyone who has been on a lively paddling trip, for example through the Devil's Rapids, would strongly object to this statement. Just put a white man in a canoe with a couple of Indians to ride through such rapids. I will wager a hundred to one that the white man will get shivers down his spine and continue to feel the effects of the trip in his body for the rest of the day. Until his dying day, he will not hesitate to confirm that Indians take risks. If the canoe capsizes or is cut open, however, we can no longer speak of risks. That is the end of all the helpless people in the canoe.

We always associate the idea of nature's bounty with people living in a natural state. They do not have to sow, just reap. Animals wander the forests and fish swim in the lakes. Everything is there for the taking. But it is not always a simple matter to go to the forest to get some meat, or to the lake to pick up some fish. From time to time the land shows its hard and merciless side, cruelly and with no joy. Empty traps and Wittigo's displeasure often force the Indians to live with great frugality, a condition that we would not accept.

Here is a little story to provide a glimpse of the difficult conditions experienced by the Indians, and the toughness with which they meet them. A winter encampment inhabited by about fifty Indians was hit by an illness, which resulted in hunger and despair. Finally, all of them succumbed to the illness except for one woman and her small child. The woman would not give up, so she took her child and set off towards Nipigon House.[14] She had no dogs so she had to travel on foot, pulling a small sled on which she had packed all of her possessions. The food she had brought along was soon gone, and the traps she set remained empty.

At last the woman came to a cabin where she hoped to find some food in the cache, but all she found was some fish line and a fishhook. The woman chopped a hole in the ice and tried to fish, but no fish was hungry enough to swallow an empty hook. In the end she resorted to cutting a piece of flesh from her leg. A fish took this bait and with the first fish she had both food and more bait. She kept herself and her child alive until spring came. Then she was able to reach other people.

Even in her old age the mother had the scar on her leg as a permanent reminder. However, when the child reached adulthood, he forgot the scar and its story. He was mean to his mother and she basically starved to death.

In addition to the eternal hunting grounds to which Indians wander after this life, they also have earthly hunting grounds where they make their living. Hunting is their main means of support and every family has its own "hunting ground,"[15] the boundaries determined not by written agreements or contracts but tradition. Indians do not hunt in each other's territories. That would only have led to poor yields, and there are enough areas to go around. Indians are not required to pay hunting fees. A white trapper, on the other hand, must obtain a licence and have his paperwork in order before he can hunt.

The Indians' hunting grounds are located in several areas since the animals have a variety of habits and seasons. Mink prefer to stay near rivers, as do otters and beavers. Foxes are often found around the edges of lakes. They find rotten fish washed up along bays and the mouths of rivers, and they have to be satisfied with this type of food. Animals like the lynx stay in the forest since they require thick underbrush and terrain with good cover. The marten frequents swampy terrain with large clumps of trees.[16]

Every family tries to have as many of these varied terrains as possible within its hunting grounds, and this is easily arranged given the landscape here. Hunting brings pelts, and with these families can obtain flour, sugar, clothing, tobacco, and other goods from the trading post. Hunting and fishing provide the rest of the food they need.

The Indians in this region are not farmers, although some white men from time to time try to interest them in this venture. Some years ago, a man was elected to the Canadian Parliament who had a burning desire to teach the Indians on some reserves to grow potatoes. Seed potatoes were sent up north accompanied by directions on how to grow them, along with a strong message about the many benefits that would result from their proper cultivation.

It is quite possible that a few families made an honest and sincere attempt to grow potatoes by planting them in the ground. However, the enthusiastic potato representative probably had no idea what the chances of success were for this type of crop in the remote wilderness. Furthermore, he likely knew nothing about the farming interests of the Indians. He had, at any rate, overlooked certain uses for the potato that the people out here immediately pursued.

Most of the potatoes they received were certainly used, but in a completely different way than intended. You see, some Indians on the reserves had interacted with white people while working for a logging company. There they had learned something about other uses of the potato, beyond basic farming. As a result, they purchased sugar and raisins, and in order to get a hold of some yeast they sent a canoe to a trading post twenty-five kilometres away. With these ingredients they started fermenting a batch of potatoes, and then waited patiently. As the starch turned to alcohol, the excitement rose among the shareholders of the "spud distillery."[17] One day, when their anticipation had reached a boiling point, and the moonshine bubbled with an enticing smell, they gathered round and drank all of the wonderful liquid. It was an orgy of excess on a grand scale, worthy of a group of gold miners. As the stomachs of the celebrants became bloated, their heads grew lighter. They got so drunk that people told stories about it for a long time afterwards. One of the Indian women in attendance was so moved that she began to dance naked, so the party turned into an event of exceptional abandon.

In all likelihood this agricultural reformer was either not re-elected or he voluntarily gave up his plans. In any case, no more potato shipments arrived at that Indian reserve.

There have also been attempts to introduce the Indians to fur farming. The thought was that Indians could earn a better income from this livelihood, and they could supplement it with trapping. However, this turned out to be a hopeless endeavour. As one Chief said: "We cannot even care for our dogs. How are we going to manage to raise wild animals?"

Indeed, we can say with certainty that hunting is the Indians' main livelihood. It provides them with goods for trading, and it gives them food—abundantly or scarcely according to whether Wittigo is with them or against them. The Indians are survivors, in good and bad times.

The Indians' appetite is just as great when they have food as it is small when they have nothing. Rationing is not part of these Indians' way of life. If they are given a week's supply of sugar or jam while on a trip, it is gone in a couple of days. They would rather have sweet, syrupy black tea for two days and only water for six than have regular tea for eight days.

If you take Indians along on a long trip, they will, in the beginning, complain a great deal about the food, both the quantity and the type. If they get a lot of meat, they will complain that they aren't getting any fish, and if they get fish, they complain that they aren't getting any meat. If they are served both meat and fish, they will complain that they aren't getting any flour. After listening to such things for a while, one gets used to the complaining and then the Indians stop complaining.

The Indians here like tobacco and they smoke a lot. The pipe is almost a necessity for them. Some have learned to chew tobacco and they want sweet tobacco. Alcohol is also in high demand among many of them, but the Canadian Government has done a lot to cut off access to liquor.[18] They have more or less succeeded in this, but the Indians still find opportunities to get drunk every now and then.

A Hudson's Bay Company employee told me a story, which certainly isn't very couth, but reveals the great ingenuity of the Indian in this regard. It also demonstrates that the alcohol question could perhaps be better resolved in other ways.

A couple of Indians on a reserve had gotten a hold of some whisky from a passer-by, and had become quite tipsy. They were all smiles as they staggered around the village, arm in arm, gesticulating. Two 20-year-olds thought that this looked quite tempting, so they went to the trader looking for some firewater too. The trader had no whisky to sell, but he promised to help them and made a brew from water, sugar, vinegar and a little Worcestershire sauce. The water was partly comprised of his own urine.

The boys had their drink, and later they were seen on the reserve mimicking the two other drunkards to the best of their ability, swaying about with abandon, and uttering little cries of delight. This was perhaps a somewhat exaggerated imitation of the howls of drunkards, but a good act all in all. It was a fine drink, they said.

Among the terms we normally associate in our minds with Indians is the word "Chief," and this is still in use. Every Indian reserve has its own Chief. The Canadian Government has undoubtedly found it to be tactically wise to have this arrangement: both in order to feign a certain connection to the past and to have a specific person to deal with from each reserve in the present.[19]

The Chief, who is elected by the Indians, is the reserve's spokesman when dealing with the representative of the government—the Indian agent.[20] The Chief has a large belt, provided by the government, to reflect his status, but in reality he is a person of no great importance. However, his task is to uphold order and he is accorded a certain respect. Most of the Chiefs I have met have been quite talkative individuals. They might be compared to a certain type of politician, a type not unfamiliar to people in Norway either. In addition, a Chief has two advisors, called counsellors, under him.[21]

Indians have forgotten most of their past and almost all their old customs, but some things have been retained.[22] In addition to Chiefs, Medicine Men are still found, but it seems to me that Indians would rather seek out one of us white men who live in the wilderness. We often have to assume the role of Medicine Men, even if our knowledge of medicine doesn't qualify us to do anything invasive. So while the Indians have their own Medicine Men, they prefer to go to a white Medicine Man too.

As a matter of fact, I didn't have any medicine to speak of with me during the first winter. However, I found forty-eight bottles of a medicine called Painkiller,[23] which the Frenchman had left behind in the old warehouse. The bottle appeared to contain a bit of alcohol and naphtha + aqua, items which are usually found in medicines. One day I let an Indian take a swig from a bottle. I thought he had a worrisome cough and I wanted to lend him a hand. This man was one of my best customers. I don't know if his cough was cured, but he certainly became intoxicated from the stuff.

The results? The cough spread at a terrific speed. All of a sudden the entire reserve had caught it. Before I knew it, I had given out so much Painkiller that my entire stock was basically depleted.

I don't know which ailment the medicine was intended for, but it was potent stuff and only the most serious illness could have escaped being cured by it. Personally, I was only able to manage a couple of teaspoons in a cup of tea, and even that was a really powerful dose. The Indians drank the medicine straight, which led me to think their taste buds could not be all that refined. On the other hand, they were very susceptible to the intoxication brought on by the Painkiller.

I later learned of free traders who were in the habit of selling the same Painkiller for a hefty price. Many Indians are exceptionally fond of any alcohol they can get their hands on and this was the only lawful way to serve alcohol. However, there did seem to be some exceptions. The Catholic priest who came by every spring to collect the school tax from the Indians usually brought along a barrel of wine that he donated to his taxpayers. The muskrat and weasel pelts he collected from the Indians were more a payment for the wine than for the school tax.[24] No one interfered with the dealings of this man of the cloth, so presumably the wine could be considered a medicine.

The white men seemed to take advantage of their knowledge of medicine in many ways. Joe Lees was one of those who had developed his own special medical treatment. Joe had at one time worked as a driver for a doctor. During the long drives he had acquired an extensive medical vocabulary, as well as different medicines. He gave up his employment as a driver some years ago to become a trapper and hunter. The Indians also considered him to be a kind of doctor, and he gradually learned to take advantage of this. Joe was lazy by nature and his laziness increased as his hunting dwindled and his clientele grew. Most of his clients were women.

When Joe entered a cabin he sent all bystanders outside. Then, as I was later informed, he gave his patients a somewhat intimate form of treatment. An unusually large number of women fell ill when Joe Lees arrived on a reserve. At last the men thought that this doctoring was going too far. The Indian agent, the special representative and spokesman for the government, was tipped off about this doctor's unusual treatments and set out to study the matter more closely. The police investigated the matter and it was the policeman in charge who told me this story. The upshot was that Joe Lees was sent out of the region and he had to set up his business on other hunting grounds. However, many blue-eyed children were born on the reserves where he had practised his personal brand of medicine.

I personally favoured castor oil for treating patients. It was an effective and easy-to-administer substance that didn't taste so bad either. Again and again people complained of pains in their stomachs, the result of eating to excess after a successful hunting trip. But from time to time neither Painkiller nor castor oil worked.

On the second of my trading trips this winter, I visited a camp where there was a sick Indian. He had been out on the ice to retrieve a sack of fish. While swinging the sack onto his back, he slipped and fell so awkwardly that the sack hit him and apparently dislodged one of his kidneys. A certain jiu-jitsu move can have the same result.

This injury caused internal bleeding, and when I arrived on the scene, he had been in bed for two days and there was blood in his urine. His wife sat there rocking her head, combing her lousy hair, and crying out in sorrow. My medicine box was of no help in this situation. The man was dead the next morning.

Like other children of nature, the Indians are at the mercy of the baser rather than the loftier powers. The thing these children of nature fear the most is Wittigo—which can be roughly translated as "the devil incarnate," a being which it somewhat resembles. If the hunting goes poorly, it is Wittigo's doing. If a disease is ravaging the Indians, that same character is viewed as the cause. If a rifle jams, Wittigo gets the blame. His evil spirit hangs over the people as a threatening nightmare. When a storm whips up the snow so that the driver of a team cannot even see the lead dog, it is immediately clear who is to blame. Once Wittigo is out and about playing his games, there is little the Indians can do. Wittigo is in full control. The Indians have no counterforce to pray to, to believe in, or from whom to receive consolation. They have no benevolent god or powerful All-father.[25] As a result, a distinguishing characteristic of these Indians is to meet adversity such as sickness with passivity.[26]

Some Indians rank a little higher on the religious social ladder, at least externally, and have converted to Catholicism or Methodism. There is, as a matter of fact, a bitter enmity between these two faiths, and a determined battle for souls rages between them here as elsewhere. It is, of course, not sufficient that people are saved, each by his own faith. They must be saved in a certain way following certain rituals, in other words the way I and my religious group require.

I cannot say how devoutly Christian Indians really are, but I know that they sometimes hold evening prayers at home. I have, at any rate, heard them pray and then end their prayer with a belch. After they have done this, they take no interest in Christian matters for the next twenty-four hours, so their Christianity does not go very deep. But they have learned a little from civilization.

Civilization has also brought them other good things. Many of the Indians can both read and write in the Cree language, although one would hardly expect to find paper and ink in an Indian's cabin. The written language is very simple. They do not have a letter alphabet but a syllabic alphabet. There are a total of thirty-six alphabetic characters, and the Indians are supposed to be able to learn these in a very short period of time. A Methodist missionary named James Evans "invented" the Cree alphabet about one hundred years ago.[27] The structure of the language is relatively simple, and with the thirty-six symbols they are able to communicate the essentials.

A lot of foreign words have been mixed into the Cree tongue. Goods and terms that have come into use through trading with the white man do not have Indian words. They use the English words in a slightly altered form by adding endings or by changing the pronunciation. The English word sugar becomes *sugoa*.

The Indian tongue did not originally have any swear words,[28] but it is obvious that the Indians—particularly the half-breeds—who want to swear have had a rich selection of English swear words to draw upon. Some have been very adept at learning. If one has ever driven a dog team with Indian dogs, then one understands that a longstanding deficiency in the Cree vocabulary was resolved when these words were introduced.

In their dealings with the white man, the Indians consider themselves to be the original owners of the land, and they feel that they have been defrauded by the whites. Therefore, in return, the Indians try to cheat all white people at every opportunity. They also assume that all whites are wealthy, and as a result the Indians have no qualms about taking advantage of them.

There is no advantage to being a greenhorn here, but instead one must act like an old-timer. A gullible tourist would be fleeced. The Indians who are hired to give canoe rides to tourists have, in fact, learned to strike. They flop themselves down, and blame it on an illness that can be cured with extra gifts or additional portions of food.

Thankfulness is an unknown concept when dealing with the white man. If you do a favour for an Indian, it is forgotten as soon as it is done. The white man, it seems, owes them everything. You may help them in an emergency by giving them food and clothing. You can give Indians presents and provide free medical services and so on, but as soon as you need a service in return from them, they demand the full price. This is what the trader in the North runs up against immediately. He may come with a fully loaded *toboga* to an Indian camp where there are neither furs nor food, only misery, hunger, need, and passivity. He helps them, and gives them food, traps, and ammunition. He journeys on with the message that he can come back in six weeks. Then he will be given pelts as payment. But if another trader visits the camp before he returns, you can be sure that this other trader has been given all the pelts they have.

When the Indians believe that they own the land, and that the white man owes them everything, they are forgetting that they too once took over the land without any payment. Originally, they came from the south. The large tribal wars and the wars between white people—for example, in the Quebec and Montreal regions there was constant unrest between the English and the French for years—drove a number of Indians north to the great forests where there was peace and quiet. Undoubtedly, it wasn't the strongest tribes that had to move. However, they did not take the land from anyone, since no one controlled the land when they arrived.[29]

Among themselves, the Indians are kind and helpful and take no payments from one another. Generally speaking, the Cree are mild-mannered people, and if they become angry, it passes quickly. Families do not usually have many children. Death seems to take many of the little ones. The incessant kissing of young children, regardless of how tuberculosis-ravaged the kisser is, combined with a primitive understanding of hygiene, are practices that faithfully act in death's favour. I have never seen an Indian lose his temper with a child. Perhaps a child is corrected with a couple of words, but nothing else. I have never seen an Indian strike a child. If a newborn baby is a son, great paternal pride is on display.

Perhaps I should also mention something about other moral codes among the Indians. I thought a lot about these practices before I became accustomed to them. I was often astonished, for instance, at how faithfully some Indians continued their affairs with the wives of other men. "The moccasin wire"[30] reports when a woman's legal husband is away during the hunting season, an opportune time for the other man to return home to the camp. The suitor purchases food and dress cloth for the woman, and these gifts often fill a need since the husband may not have left his family much when he embarked on his journey. The woman is also deeply grateful if she can get a little sugar and flour.

When the rightful husband returns home, rarely at an inopportune time, the other man is long gone. However, the wife makes no attempt to conceal the silk scarves or the other gifts she has received. As a rule the husband gives her a beating, but she is happy to pay in this manner. A beating is soon over, but a silk scarf will bring pleasure for a long time. I never observed any signs of jealousy in connection with this swapping custom. Of course, I have seen jealousy and ambushes and revenge in adventure fiction about Indians, but only there. It may be that the two male Indians try to avoid one another for some time after such a visit, but they don't confront each other for a more intimate showdown the way white men would have done.

Among married couples, the whole matter is not considered all that dramatic. They borrow wives from one another as we see in certain modern circles in the civilized world. If a man from another tribe visits and the husband is away, the extension of hospitality goes beyond just food and drink. I have witnessed many such peculiar encounters while staying overnight in cabins on my travels.

At one time, I had an Indian in my service whose task it was to run in front of the dog team. He was heavily into this lifestyle. When we bedded down for the night in our hosts' cabins, I always took the bed near the door, even though the winter winds would blow right through the flimsy log walls. I would place my forerunner on the other side. But often, when I woke up, this runner had disappeared across the floor to entertain the daughter of the house or the daughter-in-law.

One evening while I am lying in bed and speculating into whose bed my runner has crawled, the elderly housewife lets out a sudden, shrill scream. She lights a candle and surprises the runner in the middle of the most intimate diversions with her daughter. I become very worried, fearing that we will be thrown out of the cabin, and it is no fun to end up outside at night when it is 30–40 degrees below zero. However, my fears are unfounded. The entire household joins in a ringing, mischievous storm of laughter that rolls over the guilty parties. There are no other verbal reprimands. On the whole, such moments appear to serve as a popular form of entertainment. When the old wife's howls break the silence and intimacy, everybody is immediately aware of the situation and enjoys the amusing diversion.

Generally, the shyness of Indian women seems somewhat strange to a white man. While they are natural and uninhibited while feeding their young ones, they are equally shy about exposing their lower body parts. It is a rare sight indeed to glimpse an Indian woman's legs above her ankles.

I have been told that many a white fur trader has also participated in this sharing of other men's wives, lingering too long on the reserves and taking advantage of the women while the men are out hunting. There is always a price to pay, as the affair quickly becomes public knowledge. The Indian women don't hesitate to talk about these encounters, which provide variation to their daily routines. On the contrary, they enjoy boasting of them, even if such boasting inevitably results in a beating. However, the beating is the end of the matter between the spouses. As far as the trader involved is concerned, he erases the husband's debt, a debt which inevitability exists. It is highly likely that Indians think this is a clever way to deal with debt, since they do not appear to me to have any moral scruples on such occasions. But they have, of course, learned some business ethics, and know that it is not good business to give away something for nothing.

Many a trader has incurred considerable losses for his company with this kind of conduct. The Indian does not only erase his debt to the trader concerned, but at the same time he turns to another trader with his fur business, at least for a while. After a period of time, when the debt at the new trading post has reached an appropriate sum, the Indian may forget the incident and re-establish the relationship with the familiar trader who is closer.

These relationships have resulted over time in the introduction of French and Scottish blood into the Cree population, and into many other tribes as well. They do not shy away from mentioning such mixing of blood. It does not matter whether the kinship is through a legal marriage or an extramarital relationship. "My wife, who is John McKay's daughter," is a phrase I have heard many times during my first year. At one time John McKay was a trader here. He was a Scot who played the bagpipes to ward off his loneliness, scaring many Indians with his music. Whoever has listened to sad Scottish folk tunes played on the bagpipes will have to admit that such music, heard in the wilderness on a dark night, would scare just about anyone. But John McKay was obviously not always alone, and his leisure time occupation is proudly remembered by his descendants today.

Every year in July, the tribe gathers for a treaty or a *ting*,[31] which is probably the best way to characterize this gathering. Attending this assembly are the Indian agent, representatives from the Royal Canadian Mounted Police, and most often a doctor. There are Indians everywhere, as well as a huge number of dogs. As the dogs wander from tent to tent in their hunt for something to eat, they are driven away, kicked, or have stones thrown at them. Small children and the puppies play together and enjoy life. The entire scene is the very picture of the carefree days of summer.

The women have gathered at the tent entrances, holding upside-down tin pails between their legs. Every now and then a small snap is heard from the lid. The women comb their hair and search for lice. When a louse is found, and that seldom takes long, they immediately place it between their nail and the bottom of the pail. There is a snap and then there is one less louse in the world. The hunt extends to other areas besides the hair. The women lift up their long breasts, inspect the folds of their stomach, and search for lice in the folds. Snap, snap, snap. This summer hunt continues without interruption in front of the white man who has stopped to watch.

These are only minor, informal events at the treaty assembly. There are other matters that bring the Indians together. Here they are paid their annual bonus: the twenty dollars they receive from the government as compensation for the rights they have relinquished. This is one of the few times they have cash in their hands, but not for long. The money is soon spent. They turn to the nearest trader to buy candy, silk, and beads for sewing on moccasins, or they purchase fine clothes. There is a kind of unwritten agreement that the money from the government must be used in this way. Other necessities like clothing and food are still bought from the trader, preferably on credit.³²

Various legal and other questions are also dealt with at the treaty assembly. Paternity questions are common legal issues, but the details of the cases can be quite unusual. I can provide an example from a hearing in a paternity case, where a certain Catholic missionary was very unfortunate. The Indian agent asked the girl whom she had been involved with, or as he put it, which men she had slept with. The girl began to conscientiously rattle off a list of names, and it was evident she had a good memory that went back further than needed. At this point the missionary interrupted and explained to the girl that she only had to name those she had been with over the last ten months. A knowing smile then spread over the girl's face and she said, "Oh, you mean those I've slept with after you, eh?"

A more or usually less well-trained doctor is present at these meetings. He has an enthusiastic and dedicated clientele. Patients come to him in a steady stream with real and imaginary ailments. The doctor is also required to do a dentist's work and pull teeth, but that is clearly a procedure requiring more strength than dentistry skill. Usually both the policeman and the Indian agent must hold onto the patient while the doctor summons up his strength and pulls. The Indians' teeth seem to be permanently attached to their jaws and are not designed to be pulled out.

The modern Indians have been shaped by their own past and the white man's present. Interactions with white people have given rise to certain changes. This area was originally inhabited only by Indians. But the call of the wilderness was gradually heard by others who came, whether from the monotonous life of the farm or from the cities. And so new people arrived: adventurers, outdoors people, and those in distress. As a result, the modern mixed culture was born. It really cannot be called a culture because it has no obvious customs that connect lives in a steady, commonly experienced rhythm. It has no superstition; superstition being, of course, nothing but faith. Now there is some use of ceremonial dress, and some wearing of galoshes. A little consultation with the Medicine

Man, and a little use of castor oil. A little bit of faith in Wittigo, and a little bit of Methodist faith. A little bit of everything, but nothing in full. There are conflicts between the new and the old; a bit of red and a bit of white.[33]

Many believed that mingling with the white people would be a good thing. The white people would influence the Indians, marry them, and raise them up. For when a nonwhite person adopts a white person's culture, we always assume that he will "be lifted to a higher level." Well, be that as it may, in this case it usually went the other way. The white people sank down to the level of the Indian. Their culture was not strong enough.[34]

We can discuss whether it has benefitted the Indians to make their living by trading their hunting yields. Many may be of the opinion that they were happier when they were still living as nature's children, and got their living directly from nature without intermediaries.[35] However, such discussions lead us nowhere. No culture is ever complete and imperishable. All of mankind is an unwilling tool in its own progress, in the hands of its own inventors. We do not know where the human spirit will lead. No one can fully predict the effect of a new invention; nobody knows the impact of their own deeds. A person transforms his surroundings and his tools, without understanding the consequences.

The guides of humankind lead us forward towards a new land, but the guides themselves are blind. They lack objective yardsticks and comprehensive backgrounds. People are driven by their faith, their will, their hunches, their yearning. And they always find something. They find a small, new tool, words that can go through the air, material that can be blown up, or knowledge about the human mind. They can increase crop yields, and learn about galaxies and the composition of matter. They can master molecules and know the peculiarities of the electron. But no one knows where this will lead us.

Many say that the Indians must have been happier in times past, but do we know what happiness is? First of all, we know little about this concept. It is just a word, some letters that describe an indefinable dream, an unclear longing for something better. And even if we knew what happiness was, who has said that happiness is the goal?

Isn't happiness actually the drowsy state of the human mind? Isn't it stagnation?

This is our way of fumbling along. We believe a little, doubt a little, and seek to find a nail to anchor our faith to. Why? Because in our innermost beings we are a mixture of faith and doubt, which is a passive tool for our own spirit as it searches for new hunting grounds. We detect new horizons beyond the distant blue. We pursue a prey whose shape we see through a fog and in a dream. But we do not know which weapon we should use to capture the prey, or how far away in the future it roams.

The hunting grounds of reality are just the outward form where our inner humanness roams restlessly from camp to camp, from season to season.

This photo and the following images appear to be of Einar Odd Mortensen's neighbours and customers. Several people appear in multiple pictures. Please see the discussion of "the unnamed Indian" in the Introduction. Unless otherwise indicated, Mortensen did not specify locations for these photographs.

Mortensen captioned this photo "Two real old-timers. Elijah Hook and Thomas Mamanewatum."

Taken at God's Lake.

Local trappers and working dogs.

Daniel Muswagon.

Einar Odd Mortensen and an unidentified young woman.

Einar Odd Mortensen and a young girl.

A group of hunters and trappers.

6 | *Hudson's Bay versus Free Trader*

THERE IS A SET OF INITIALS one constantly encounters here in the North. You see them displayed in many forms and in many places: on Indians' woolen sweaters, on canoes, on buildings, on steamboat packing crates, and on train freight. The initials are H.B.C.

Some newcomers once asked an Indian what these letters meant. The answer was: "The Company." "What words do these letters stand for?" asked the strangers. The reply: "Here Before Christ."[1] Well, the Hudson's Bay Company isn't quite that old, but it has been trading with the Indians for two and a half centuries. The Indian's expression accurately captures the status of the Company in Canada and the way many Company employees view themselves.

Most people consider H.B. to be the sovereign ruler and main buyer of Canada's fur riches. We free traders view H.B. as our common enemy.[2] We wholeheartedly hate the Company, and all of us fight against it. I do so too, even though I have never had any direct dealings with the Company, and it has never done me any harm. This dislike is the heritage of every free trader. All of us who work against Hudson's Bay, or, to state it more clearly, do not trade furs for H.B., are free traders.

There were two French adventurers, Pierre Radisson and Médard Groseilliers, who backed the founding of the H.B. Company in order to get revenge. Their actions were motivated by the fact that in the 1660s they had traded with the Indians in the Hudson Bay area and had taken large quantities of furs back with them. They had, among other things, sixty thousand beaver pelts. However, a few corrupt officials in Quebec, acting in the name of the French authorities, took all the furs from the men, contending they did not have valid trading permits for this region. The officials gave them no compensation for the furs they confiscated.

In retaliation, these two French adventurers travelled to England and convinced a few Scottish noblemen to send an exploratory expedition to Hudson Bay. The year was 1669. The expedition was successful, and a shipload of furs worth two million crowns was brought back to England.

The King of England, Charles II,[3] granted "the governor and a company of merchants and adventurers trading around Hudson Bay sole rights to lands everywhere which had tributaries that drained into Hudson Bay and which were not the domain of any other Christian state."[4] This was cleverly formulated, not only because this included a territory larger than a third of Europe's landmass, but also because the granted land was Indian territory. Since the Indians could not be counted among the so-called Christian nations, the grant also included their lands.[5]

Right from the beginning, the Company assumed an arrogant and condescending attitude, which has characterized it and the conduct of its employees ever since. In the beginning, the Company's trading ground rule was that the Indians should bring their furs to them.

The Company built its outposts on the shores of Hudson Bay and this was where the Indians were to bring their catch. It was of no concern to them if the Indians had to travel a thousand kilometres or more. The H.B. man sat by the little service window of the building and paid them whatever he saw fit for their furs.

Later, the Company had to change the way it did business because its competitors were gaining control of the market by using other methods. Otherwise the Company's men would, in their conservatism, still be sitting in their buildings by their small service windows.

For the first one hundred years, H.B. completely dominated the fur trade market. The Company could charge a pile of beaver pelts as high as the length of a rifle, for the rifle. But H.B. found itself with rivals, since all rivers did not flow into Hudson Bay. The northern half of Alberta and northwestern Saskatchewan — areas that make up Canada's richest hunting grounds — contained waters that emptied out in other directions. When the English conquered

Eastern Canada, many French traders went back to their native land, and the trappers who had been in their service found themselves unemployed. These trappers started working for the Scots who organized the North West Company.

The North West Company men did not sit idly at trading posts around Hudson Bay. They moved into H.B.'s fur empire, partly on the Company's own territory, partly farther west where H.B. had no territorial rights. The new company established trading posts in these regions and did not even care if it happened to build in areas H.B. had claimed. The boundaries were, as a matter of fact, often vague and were a frequent source of contention. The headquarters of the new enterprise were located in Montreal, and a new competition for furs began.

Things became quiet at the H.B. trading posts. Understandably, the Indians did not care to travel one thousand kilometres when there were trading posts closer by and when, in addition, they were better paid for their furs at these posts. There was a noticeable decrease in the fur shipments sent by H.B. to England, and the Company had to change its way of doing business by spreading its trading posts over a wider area to keep up with the competition.

For years these two companies criticized and attacked each other. Conflicts arose over old trading grounds and new markets. They clashed over those trading posts that were located on the other company's claimed territory. The Indians were the great beneficiaries of this fighting. Fur prices were determined more sensibly, and in the end the Indians only needed to pay 10–15 beaver pelts for a rifle.

The game continued and H.B. developed a new strategy. The Company no longer bought only furs but also began to buy North West Company traders by offering them better wages. A war almost broke out between the companies, and now and then actual physical fights occurred.

In 1821, the Canadian and British government took the combatants by the scruffs of their necks and forced the two sides to merge into one company named the Hudson's Bay Company. The English still won the fight in the long run.[6] After the merger, the Company once again had a monopoly on the fur trade until new competitors appeared, and the battle for furs intensified once again.

Fifty years after the merger of the companies, H.B. was forced to sell its lands to the Canadian government.[7] However, it retained its trading rights, and that was the most important thing for them. H.B. continued to maintain control over its huge territories through its trading posts and without military support. Naturally, the fur trade was the cornerstone of all its operations.

Trade brings power, they say, and in this land the traders have raised their billowing flags as a sign of their power. The Indians have never risen up against their trading lords either.[8] H.B. was dependent on the work of the Indians, and the Company ruled over them. The Company ruled by trade, however, instead of arms. H.B. also contends that it allowed Indians to live their own lives. After all, the white people would end up influencing the lives of Indians even if they allowed them to live their own lives. This was just a natural result of trading and the new goods that accompanied it.

One must also remember that before white people started to purchase furs in the early 1600s, these pelts had no monetary value. At that time Eastern Canada was under the control of the French, and England had numerous colonies on the American[9] east coast. The western part of Canada was a no man's land. The H.B. Company currently has 150 trading posts scattered over a vast area, and the Company's employees believe they represent the real power here in the North. The Company tends to employ Scots as trading post managers in northern Canada. The Scots are hired at a relatively young age on long-term contracts. Tradition is the guiding light of these managers. They view the new free traders that violate the H.B.'s old ways of doing business with disapproval.

The Company has, without a doubt, been important for the Indians up north, but through their fur trapping, the Indians have been even more important for the Company. With increased competition, the Indians have started to get better prices for their furs, but they have also received lower quality goods as payment.

H.B. can rightfully say that they have often helped hungry Indians during poor trapping winters. Indeed, they have even saved Indians from starvation when they had stopped hunting and fishing altogether and were just waiting to die. They gave up because they believed that Wittigo was after them. However, the Company kept track of this aid. Of course, it is not a good thing to kill the goose that lays the golden eggs.[10]

While the H.B. Company has been a lasting and firm link in the trade between the Indians and the surrounding world, the free traders have been a more inconsistent intermediary. Some free traders have warred with the H.B. Company for years for a variety of reasons.

A free trader is filled with enthusiasm when he first arrives. His intention is not to remain in the wilderness but to spend a few years here, save money, and return to the civilized world with his savings to finance a new career. Some are successful in this. However, for others the adventure proves fateful—"the bush takes him." He descends to the level of the Indians and becomes a "squaw-man."[11] Perhaps he also becomes a subcontractor for the H.B. He does not work at a trading post, but receives his own small supply of merchandise to trade with the Indians during the season.

The free trader has other opponents to battle besides the H.B. He might be under the thumb of some big wholesaler in Winnipeg. God forgive him if it is a poor year for furs, as sometimes happens. In that case he has to beg the wholesaler to renew his credit, which is no fun at all. Then he is not able to specify what goods he requires for trading either. The wholesaler sends the free trader whatever he sees fit, and that is the downfall of many a free trader. It may also be that the free trader is smitten by gold fever. He becomes possessed by a rumour of a new gold find, so he closes his store and runs after an imaginary Klondike without a second thought for the Indians.

The Hudson's Bay Company pays better attention to the Indians by keeping their trading posts open year-round. The free traders, on the other hand, generally close for the summer and trade only during the season. Most free traders come here for a few years and then disappear.

A few free traders have kept their heads above water. One of them is H.C. Hyer, who was originally a Norwegian. In Norway his name was Høier, which sounds more familiar to me. Hyer started as a trapper but soon saw the opportunity for something bigger and seized it. Hyer was not driven by greed but by the game itself; the struggle with the H.B. Company. He did not give up easily and mastered the skill of living alone. He was unmarried and could not tolerate having women around. For more than sixty years he managed on his own.

Old H.C. Hyer was one of the very few who stood their ground against the powerful Company without going under. This old man of honour struggled for fifty years against H.B., and nothing succeeded in breaking him. H.B. tried to place obstacles in his way at every turn, and Hyer reciprocated. Hyer had the ability to see through his adversaries. Once H.B. sent an Indian with his furs to Hyer not only to sell the pelts, but also to trick Hyer into revealing where he planned to break his winter trails. Hyer simply grabbed the Indian, removed his clothes, and painted his whole body blue. Then he sent the painted being[12] back to his bosses with the message that he had gotten off easily. Hyer guaranteed that the next visitor sent on this errand would not receive such gentle treatment.

Many have attempted to take advantage of Mr. Hyer, and just as many have received a good licking. If someone tried to cheat him at the trading post, he would leap over the counter in one movement, and his angry stare was notorious among the Indians. As he leaned forward, almost sitting on his haunches and letting out a series of the worst Norwegian curses, his angry, dangerous eyes saw right to the bottom of the offender's soul. This was followed up with a more hands-on treatment, which was also quite persuasive.

Hyer provided strong competition for the H.B. Company, and he was well liked by the Indians. He was fair and uncomplicated, but he could not tolerate dishonesty. People took care not to irritate him unnecessarily given his strong personality. Hyer liked animals, particularly dogs. If there was deep snow that made it hard for the dogs to travel, he would often cut down a spruce tree and pull it behind him. He walked ahead of the team, breaking trail.

Hyer died when he was over eighty. His memory lived long after him.

Canoes replaced dog teams once the spring breakup had occurred. Paddling on Roenase Creek, one of the many waterways in northern Manitoba, between Island Lake and Norway House. The man in the photo is one of two Indigenous men who accompanied Mortensen on this trip.

7 | *Towards New Hunting Grounds*

IT IS VERY EARLY ON A SEPTEMBER MORNING. The nighttime darkness is slowly giving way to a new day that sprinkles its light over the sky, lakes, and forest. The cool air flows through us like a refreshing drink. We push our canoes into the water. With a few rotations of the outboard motor's flywheel, the gas evaporates in its chambers. The piston compresses and the spark plugs sparkle with their tiny flashes—puff, puff. The monotonous, pounding noise echoes with unforgiving loudness in the endless stillness of the morning. The throb of a busy, mechanical life drowns out nature's quiet pulse.

I am on my way north towards the Oxford Lake[1] winter outpost,[2] which is a twelve-day[3] canoe trip from Norway House.[4] We are three men, two redskins in addition to me. We are travelling in two canoes, pulling one of them behind us.

The buildings of Norway House disappear out of sight behind me. In front of me awaits a two-year assignment in unknown country. My contract binds me for this length of time, but my last glimpse of civilization does not cause me to be sad or melancholy. Nothing can stop me now—the free life has taken hold of me, and I have laid hold of it. I know more about it than I did last year, and my enthusiasm has not diminished because of that. A new wilderness awaits me, with new experiences, new days, and new journeys in new surroundings.

At the start of our trip we travel mile after mile on mirror-clear lakes, interrupted by wide rivers. I am pleased with our speed and the Indians are not overworked as long as we are able to use the outboard motor.[5] For the time being the trip is not at all strenuous for me. The Indians do all the paddling and carry everything when we portage. I am, by now, a bit more familiar with the Indians and know that when I am with them I have to be the *kitchi oogemoo*,[6] which means the great white man. This means I must not stoop to do too much labour since this would significantly reduce my position of authority. Other than that I have been advised to be on good terms with my travelling companions. They are both good hunters and prominent men in their own tribes.

The landscape around us is somewhat low and compressed, as if a giant hand has lain on it and pressed it flat with a few parts of the land swelling up between the fingers. As we struggle forward along the shore in our low canoe, however, the land appears more varied. Rows of pine-covered, dome-shaped hills stand out against a glowing blue sky. The familiar silhouettes of large, healthy spruce trees resemble beautiful straight pillars. When daylight strikes it, the granite bedrock adds a touch of red to the scenery. The warm sun shines strongly, clearly highlighting all the variations and details of the landscape in the clear autumn air.

Occasionally, an abandoned Indian cabin comes into view, but there are no humans to be seen. Only a few abandoned[7] Indian dogs howl on the shore and try to follow us in the hope that we might take a break and toss some food to them. But they soon give up.

On the first day the outboard motor functions faultlessly, and by evening we have travelled a distance that would have taken two days to paddle. We settle down at an old campsite, one of a number that have been created one day's journey apart along the regular transport routes to the trading posts.

I have very limited conversations with the Indians at first. I only drop monosyllabic words from time to time, partly because my limited language abilities do not allow easy and free conversation, and partly because we are still sizing each other up. The Indians do not know how much of an old-timer I am, and I do not know to what extent they view me as a greenhorn. "Good weather," I say. "Yes," they reply. "Many foxes last year?" "Yes." But I don't know if they mean "yes" or "no." "Many muskrats at Oxford Lake?" "Yes." "Many cross foxes and silver foxes?" These furs are highly valued and there are supposed to be many in these parts. Red foxes are most common in the rest of Canada. The men shrug their shoulders. I ask about the assistant manager at Oxford Lake. No—they don't know what he is like.

We get somewhat better acquainted in the evening. One of the Indians prepares our sleeping places and points out a spot intended for me. I act as if I don't understand what he wants and take the spot he has prepared for himself. He protests, but I act as if I absolutely cannot understand what he means. I know that if an Indian has prepared the campsite, I must take the sleeping place he has reserved for himself if I want to sleep somewhat comfortably.

This small maneuver concerning the sleeping arrangements works, and because of it I gain an advantage and a certain authority. I have proved myself to be an old-timer and the Indians do not attempt to fool me again. After a while the man begins to prepare a new sleeping place for himself. He cuts more spruce branches and selects a completely different spot.

The second and third day we travel through burned forests—burned, burned. Charred stumps jut up and the ground is black and lifeless. Only here and there do some green sprouts come into view, as if lost and puzzled. They stand as if helpless in this large, scorched area. The fire has raged for miles and miles, and humans were unable to stop it.

Forest fires have always been the curse of dry summers, and in earlier times people were entirely helpless against them. The fires just raged until they died down by themselves, unless rainy weather came to the rescue. Only in recent years has it been possible to intervene with the aid of airplanes and firefighters.[8] However, if one has seen these thousands of square miles of scorched forest where charred trunks stand blackened and dead, it seems impossible to imagine that the situation could be effectively controlled, even with a good air patrol system. Airplanes are stationed in Norway House, and with them it is possible to gather information about the fire, including in which direction it is moving, and to decide if anything can be done. They can, for example, determine if in some days the fire will reach a large lake where it is possible to do something. By clear-cutting wide belts over the narrow peninsulas that often connect the lakes, firefighters may be able to contain the forest fire.

These ravaging forest fires are not always caused by the careless use of fire or poorly extinguished campfires during dry summer days. Winter campfires often cause the fires. During that season, there are few who think about the danger of fire. In actuality, the fire on a thirty-degree-below night requires a lot of wood and a high flame. Then the heat sometimes works its way down through the permafrost to the moss. The fire remains there smoldering, hidden so deeply that neither snow, the cold, or the melting spring snow and rain are able to extinguish it. The fire creeps deeply into the marshy ground and barely remains alive. As the summer progresses, it is able to move its way up to the surface, and one fine day the whole landscape is ablaze.

After midday we have some problems with our motor, and while we are repairing it, one of the Indians points to a spit of land: "Bear!" Then I also catch a glimpse of the champion of the forest. His brown, furry body blends into his surroundings. It stands there without moving, peering through the trees. The Indians begin to paddle closer with careful strokes, but the bear stands his ground, squinting curiously. The Indians gesture to me to shoot—this is a great compliment—and they put me ashore a short distance below the point. The Indians themselves shoot everything that moves, whether they need the meat or not. However, they now extend this courtesy to me and allow me to take care of the job. I feel excitement in my body as I creep closer. The Indians' enthusiasm has clearly taken hold of me. I am the proud hunter about to fell his first bear, and there he stands with his side towards me looking out over the lake. I am very close and the bear has not heard me approach. I raise the rifle, take careful aim, and then—bang! The bear jumps and falls to the ground. After a couple of kicks with its paws it stops moving.

I have a bad taste in my mouth as I inspect the prey. Is this hunting? My first bear? Pride? A trophy? A chance for a photo? I am embarrassed the rest of the day and my conscience bothers me every time I think about the animal. A poor creature that watched someone pass by with curiosity and trust. Unsuspecting and gullible, it just stood and stared until a rifle was aimed at it. This is neither hunting nor excitement. The power differential is too great. I experience no feelings of pride over the fallen prey, even though it was my first bear. Nor can I justify the matter by saying that we did this out of necessity, since we don't use much of the animal. We only take enough meat to feed ourselves for a couple of days.

In the meantime, the Indians have found a campsite nearby, so we do not travel any farther but settle down for the night. The outboard motor needs proper servicing and one of the Indians has already mounted it on a stick between two trees and taken it completely apart. I hope that he is also able to reassemble it without my aid, since I do not know anything about this piece of machinery yet, even though it is very simple. But before going to work they do what every Indian does when game has been shot: they cut inch-thick, fat strips of meat from the bear. We put them on the ends of sticks and roast them on the campfire. The meat acquires a pleasant smoky flavour that has an incredible impact on our appetites. We eat as if we have not tasted meat for ages. Regardless of how much I eat—far more than I had thought possible—the Indians still eat at least twice as much.

We spend the first days of our journey travelling in a leisurely fashion on lakes and rivers with weak currents. The outboard motor works continuously and smoothly transports us from one meal stop to the next. Then the journey becomes more strenuous. We have left the flat muskeg[9] marshland, and the land begins to rise. The river becomes rocky and difficult to navigate, and our progress is often interrupted by waterfalls and rapids, both big and small. In these situations we have to go ashore to make difficult portages. It is a bit misleading to say "we." I only carry the outboard motor and my personal possessions, which, for that matter, do not weigh very much. As the others struggle with the canoes and the cargo, I pass my time by fishing or shooting something to eat for dinner. But I do have to keep an eye on my companions to some extent. When the men go ashore at a place where the water is so shallow that the canoe cannot be brought right up onto the shore, and the distance to the bank does allow them to keep their feet dry, the Indians don't hesitate to toss a bag of flour into the water to step on so they don't get wet.

These portages, paths for bypassing rapids, vary in length. On the fourth day we come to the longest one. It is three to four kilometres

Loading a York boat at Norway House.

Rough water ahead on God's River. Mortensen wrote, "The best place for fishing trout that I know of. They weighed from 2.5–10 pounds."

long, but this time we can pull the canoes and cargo on cars that are found on tracks running along the river—remnants from the past. Previously, H.B. only used large York boats[10] to transport cargo to their trading stations. In order to get these boats around rapids, they had to pull them on timber logs over land. But this portage was too long and it was too much work to pull in that way, so they built tracks on the timber logs and pulled the York boats on cars. The cars are still functional, even though the saga of the York boats has ended on these rivers.[11]

This portage, called the Height of Land, is also the highest point on our route. From now on the land descends as we travel towards the northeast in the direction of Hudson Bay. There are still many portages and a lot of hard work ahead of us. I admire the Indians' technique. It is amazing how much these small and slight men manage to carry.

First they place a long, doubled-up strap on the ground and tightly secure the load. They can carry 2–300 pounds, which is an unbelievably heavy burden for a white man. When the load is attached to the long carrying strap, the free loop is placed over the forehead and they carry the load with their foreheads. A little bit of the weight is distributed over the back, of course, but most of the weight is on the neck. This method of carrying requires a lot of practice. My attempt, at least, caused my neck muscles to become so stiff that I had to turn my whole body when I wanted to look to the side. But the Indians easily move with their 2–300-pound burdens. In addition, they do not walk but jog!

On the sixth day the Indians begin to talk about the Devil's Fall.[12] There is much debate as to whether we should run these falls by canoe or carry the cargo overland. The portage is long and steep and does not lend itself to carrying loads by foot and on the forehead. The Indians decide on the water route. I ask them how it usually goes when the falls are run. They shrug their shoulders and answer that it generally goes well. A couple of years ago a missionary and a half-breed attempted to run the falls and nothing has been heard from them since. However, that is not common.

Now we hear a distant low roar from the first part of the rapids. Gradually, the river flows faster and the roaring becomes louder until the rapids rumble like thunder. The deafening sound pounds more and more against my eardrums, which is uncomfortable. In front of us we see foam and mist rising from the riverbed. We leave one of the canoes behind on shore and we will return for it later.

One of the Indians sits in the front of the canoe and the other in the back while I am placed in the middle. Actually, I would have preferred to stay on shore with the other canoe and to have taken the portage on foot, but I was too embarrassed to suggest that. Now I have to try my luck. The Indians shout and scream continuously to one another, but I don't know why since there is no way they can hear each other. I can't understand anything either, even though I am sitting right in the middle of them. This shouting is typical of Indians when they are excited. Shouting appears to be primarily an expression of their emotional state.

The man sitting in the back of the canoe does most of the steering and selects the canoe's course. With small, lightning-quick movements he changes course a few centimetres now and then to avoid rocks and suspect spots. If the canoe were to be caught in a whirlpool or hit a rock, both we and the load would certainly be lost.

Our speed increases, pitching the canoe forward even more. I firmly grip the sides of the canoe and I have a feeling that the tip of the canoe is pointing straight down. That may be an overstatement. My senses are surely playing tricks on me. I try not to follow things too closely and, to be honest, I shut my eyes and no longer see anything since I simply have no desire to face my surroundings. Just sitting in my place as a silent spectator, not at all familiar with this travel technique, causes me to feel very uncomfortable and tense. I merely know that if something goes wrong, it will go seriously wrong. I sense every little move the Indians make, and I feel as if the canoe is alive under me.

Then, suddenly, the terrible rumbling stops. I only hear a steady rushing sound and our speed decreases. The water no longer pulls at the sides of the canoe and we glide into calmer waters. We have successfully traversed the rapids. I am filled with a sense of relief and must stay behind to rest while the other two go back up to retrieve the second canoe.

We paddle north and east at a steady pace. After ten days we take a course more directly east and leave the river we have followed till now. We carry our cargo overland through the forest in order to reach another waterway so we can follow the river to Rat Lake.[13] I try to follow our route on the map, but it isn't so easy to get oriented. The maps in this country are based, to a large extent, on the mapmaker's imagination, aided by various Indian accounts. There is often a large discrepancy between the map and the landscape.

After Rat Lake we come to a section of the route that, I gather, the Indians are not particularly fond of. It is supposed to be unusually strenuous and intimidating, but it remains unclear to me why it is considered to be so demanding. Little by little, Rat Lake narrows and marsh formations start to dominate the flat landscape. The vegetation loses colour, and everything becomes yellow and dreary. The trees are dry and thin and stand out on the dank marshland; white moss and bitter groundwater do not provide good nourishment. The river turns into a small brook that bends lazily between the marshes. Many times it stands completely still as if it does not really know whether it is a river or not.

After having paddled for some time through the marsh, we run into a partially submerged York boat that is in a state of decay. At one time it ran aground and since then it has lain abandoned in the middle of the marsh. I did not believe that the river could possibly become narrower, but it does. It meanders around more and more bends and the water takes on a pudding-like consistency. We have difficulty moving ahead in the canoes and we end up poling more than paddling. It is also difficult to make our way round the bends.

The water becomes even thicker until it is nothing but a big, dark brown, muddy porridge in which we get stuck. For a long time we attempt to struggle through the porridge, but the mud becomes so densely packed around the paddles that we are completely immobile.

It is still early in the day. The sun blazes down on us with all the strength it is able to mobilize. We have agreed to clear this muskeg portage before making camp. Therefore, there is nothing else to do but to climb out of the canoes, find firm footing in the muskeg, and pull the canoes along behind us. We fold up our pant legs as high as we can—we certainly don't want to get wet—but it doesn't really help since we end up standing in waist-deep water. It is not possible to carry anything through these marshes. One can be satisfied as long as they do not sink more than a half metre into the soft mud.

The reader should, by now, be able to imagine the scene. We are wallowing in a swamp that has been formed from rotting plants. It is neither solid nor liquid, but on the other hand it isn't bottomless either. Now and then we are unable to find anything solid to stand on, so we must lie down on our backs or stomachs to distribute our body weight more evenly so we do not completely disappear.

Above the marsh the sun blazes down from a cloudless sky, radiating intense heat. In the middle of the swamp there are three people who are trying to get through with their two heavy canoes. But this is not the full picture. Finding ourselves in this type of swamp environment, before the autumn frost has set in, we soon understand that we are not quite alone after all. Certain small winged members of the local fauna quickly discover us and faithfully follow us.

Yes indeed, mosquitoes. There is no way Norwegian readers can comprehend what that word signifies in this Canadian marsh setting. You may talk about the mosquitoes in Norway, in Røros and in Finnmark.[14] However, this is a poor basis for comparison and is basically just a joke. These winged creatures of the Canadian wilderness have an altogether different appetite and energy level. Different species of insects seem to have specialized in preying on different body parts so they can enjoy their victim as effectively as possible. The blackflies attach themselves to the lower parts, the mosquitoes gather around the upper body, and the sandflies take care of the other parts.

I can't defend maintaining my *kitchi oogemoo* status as we move through these marsh formations. As a result, all three of us struggle side by side. After many hours of wading in the mud and dragging the canoes, we reach an area where the water flows a bit more freely. Now we can move ahead, with some difficulty, by paddling. We reach open water again, though the landscape around us continues to be mainly swampy. The landscape has begun to slope slightly so the water understands when it should act like a river and when it should act like a lake.

We go ashore at the end of a point, which is to say that I disembark while the other two go back to retrieve the second canoe. Perhaps I should have accompanied them and helped them haul this one too, but for the moment I am too tired and too exhausted to do anything but rest. When the others leave, I make camp. I boil some tea, which I drink up, and fry some pork, which I eat up, while the mosquitoes continuously eat me up.

It isn't my intention to describe how these attacks against an innocent man take place. Our language does not have words to adequately convey the situation. However, I can say that I will remember this evening and night for the rest of my life. This night didn't make me crazy, but that wasn't due to a lack of effort on the part of the mosquitoes. They did their very best. I tore my mosquito net apart in the middle of that night, but I don't remember the exact words that came out of my mouth.

Since the mosquitoes have paid me so much attention through the years, I have to reciprocate by writing some pages about them. My reprisal will unfortunately be incomplete because my account cannot harm them, but still—it brings a certain satisfaction to me. And this will be the last time I talk about mosquitoes. But later on, when I write about the summer, the reader must, in order to get the full picture, constantly imagine a quiet accompaniment of mosquito music. A constant, tireless buzzing and humming sound produced by mosquitoes fanning their wings over people and animals as they go about their activities.

The mosquitoes can be heard in other ways, both directly and indirectly. They are the cause of fervent and bitter swearing around campfires when they no longer hover over a person but attack. They are heard as an extra crackling in the flames of the fire and in the matches lighting a pipe—it is the mosquito committing a kind of *hara-kiri* in the flames. A canoe is paddling over a lake. Something grey, a bit greyer than the surroundings, buzzes over the canoe the whole time. It is the mosquito stalking its prey. A greenhorn is sleeping by a campfire. Suddenly, he begins to act like a madman, and it would be inappropriate to repeat the words that flow out of his mouth. His mosquito net is torn. The wilderness is a paradise, an Eldorado for fishermen and hunters, lake after lake, river after river, forest after forest. But in the summertime many anglers have to flee. For this wilderness is often a piece of hell with throngs of devils. It is mosquito season in Canada's wilderness.

During my first night in the muskeg, I am anxious to find out if these myriads upon myriads of humming mosquitoes are all that nature has to offer of these evil spirits. Is it possible they are only providing a little introduction? I recall some numbers from a traveller who took a mosquito census in various areas.

On the first day the man kept his hand open for five seconds and 5-10 mosquitoes started to sting him. When he came to Buffalo Country, he repeated this and there were 15-25 mosquitoes in the same period of time. In Nyarling the number had increased to 20-40. At Great Slave Lake he counted 50-60. When he had come to the Barren Grounds, 100-125 angry mosquitoes landed on his hand, still within the same time frame. Counting the mosquitoes had, by now, become problematic. Even though he killed the mosquitoes by striking them against his hand, it was difficult to accurately count the small corpses when they were all piled up.

I don't carry out any such count myself, but I realize it must be pleasant to be a mosquito-eating bird in these parts. All they have to do is to fly a short distance with their beak open, and after a few flaps of their wings, mosquitoes—dinner's main course—fill the space between the tip of their beak to far down their throat.

The only animals I envy are the frogs that swim and leap around our feet in the swamps. I have never seen mosquitoes on them. Day and night the low hum of mosquitoes hangs in the air. Low hum may be a rather modest expression. When one has gone to bed, it almost sounds like a distant waterfall.

Initially, I am somewhat relieved to discover that the stingers of these mosquitoes point directly downwards and are not slanted. That means they do not carry malaria, but they still manage to plague people in a brutal fashion. Mosquitoes, sandflies, and blackflies—the words may sound innocent, but the innocence ends there. Innocent? No. That doesn't seem possible once we have given it some thought. The only innocent-sounding one would be the sandfly. That word sounds rather impersonal, but the other words: mosquito, blackfly, mosquito, blackfly? Aren't they somewhat ideal examples of the onomatopoeic concept? Don't these words completely describe the sound of these beings?

Just listen: Mosquitoes — the hum of small, white wings; mosquitoes — seemingly innocent and tiny. But a warning from this cursed pest: Be on guard. I will succeed anyway. Chase me away. Now I come back buzzing easily and frivolously, mosquito — quickly, sharply, and elegantly my stiletto will find its way to a vein. Mosquito, sting, smart.

Blackfly. We can hear right away what the word encompasses: a little devil packed full of energy, black and savage, at the ready. Blackfly, no hum, no elegance, straight at the target, and no detours.

The sandfly's name isn't personal, but its attacks are very personal indeed.

How do we deal with mosquitoes? What is helpful? How do the Indians react to them?

Recreational travellers who do not have to make the trip may, perhaps, turn around and head home. There was recently news of a rich American who was travelling in my area. He had planned to go trout fishing in some of the first-rate rivers a little to the southeast of my post. But I soon heard that his travelling party had turned around. Despite being well equipped, they were not able to keep the mosquitoes away. They had not been stung enough yet. It has been said that when someone has been stung a million times by mosquitoes, they will become immune or at least accustomed to these nuisances. But even though I am convinced I was bitten this many times, I didn't notice any increased immunity or tolerance.

We have mosquito nets, leather gloves, and, for the most part, appropriate clothing to help in the battle against the mosquito. These items are extremely uncomfortable in the summer heat, but one can, at any rate, get used to them. However, I do not become accustomed to mosquitoes.

Many insect repellants have been recommended to me and I have tested them. I am sure they have fulfilled some of the expectations of the manufacturer. He has made money from his products, but I am not aware of any satisfactory results beyond this. They may help for a few minutes, but this does not mean much when there are 1,440 minutes in a twenty-four-hour period and the mosquito season lasts more than two months.

The Indians, on the other hand, suffer less from the mosquitoes. I don't know the reason, but a possible explanation is smell. A typical characteristic of many mosquito repellants is their powerful odour, and the effectiveness of the substance seems to be in proportion to the strength of this odour. If one is aware of how strongly the Indians smell, they can easily surmise that the Indians' scent is stronger than all the other substances that humans have, using ingenuity, attempted to create.[15]

The only thing that helps in addition to mosquito nets and gloves is to sit near the smoke from the campfire. But if you do not want to suffocate, you cannot sit there too long either. One quickly discovers that a special trait of the Canadian mosquito is its almost supernatural resilience and enterprise that borders on the fantastical. Even if it is dealt a crippling blow, it will continue to crawl and drag itself to a new position where it can use its stinger to inject its distinctive poison. This substance prevents the clotting of blood, so the mosquito can quench its thirst without fibrinogen coagulating and blocking the source.

The first time I arrived at a lake where a fresh wind was blowing after having been at an extremely hot and mosquito-infested muskeg, I rejoiced. Now the wind would blow them away. But these northern mosquitoes do not allow the wind to push them around anywhere—not at all! Even the smoke-cured, strong-smelling Indians do not totally avoid being plagued by the mosquitoes. The Indians never use nets or gloves and don't worry much about mosquito bites, even if their necks swell from having been bitten so many times. They too must suffer to some degree.

This night, my first in real mosquito country, is the longest I can remember experiencing. The next morning I didn't lie half asleep, as was my custom, watching the Indians attend to the camp. As soon as dawn broke, I got up, ran to the river, and lay down in the water so that only part of my face was visible above the surface. My neck was swollen and my entire body itched and burned like fire. It was a pleasure to lie there protected from my attackers and let the water cool my stiff, burning body.

The next morning, after paddling for a couple of hours on a somewhat clearer river, we emerge at Oxford Lake. My new trading post is located at the far end of this lake. A fresh wind is blowing, and we cut a couple of young trees to make masts and then rig a sail using the canoe's protective tarp. For half a day we can let the oars rest. Later the wind dies down, and we start the outboard motor and glide forward, ever forward. Points and islands fall behind us. Oxford Lake has an irregular shape. Tree-covered peninsulas stick out into the bay and make the landscape come to life. The terrain is hillier than what I have been used to so far. The rocks here have a relative abundance of minerals, and men hungry for gold do quite a bit of prospecting in this area.

Occasionally, the Indians stop the motor. A loon is crying nearby and this summons the Indians to hunt. This is not only because it is part of their nature to kill every wild creature, big and small, which comes into sight, but also because the loon takes fish and birds from the Indians. As a result, they feel particularly hostile towards this bird. There is also an extra excitement in hunting the loon. When the bird dives, the hunter must guess where it will reappear so he can be in the best position to shoot. The Indians are guided by the position of the loon's head. After diving, the bird swims underwater in the direction its head was pointing at the time it went under. But it is difficult to see the exact direction of the head.

The loon is not considered desirable for eating. The meat is tough and requires several hours of boiling. It is not very tasty either, but certainly edible. Despite this, an Indian always paddles with a certain pride to retrieve a loon he has shot. Even if he is in a hurry, he forgets about what he is doing when he hears the call of the loon.

Einar Odd Mortensen in northern Manitoba.

8 | *Days at Oxford Lake*

MY STATION AT OXFORD LAKE is larger than the one at Pine Bluff. Being larger means there is more fur trading that goes on here, because that is how trading posts are evaluated. The houses are also larger here, but the merchandise and appearance are somewhat similar to Pine Bluff. The primitive building style and extremely simple interiors are the same: one table, three chairs, a bunk, an oven, and some cooking utensils.

A half-breed Indian named Dooles McIver has been managing the post on a temporary basis. He is a big, good-natured, and presumably somewhat lazy fellow. He is a mix of an Indian mother and a Scot who was in H.B.'s service.

Dooles is a fine cook. He bakes fresh French bread in place of bannock and serves up a good variety of foods for dinner. Dooles speaks fluent English, and he is a handsome man who is very popular among the beauties of the region. I suspect that at times some of this admiration is also directed towards me, but I am bound by a hands-off rule.[1]

There is enough to do at the post in the coming days. Winter is just around the corner, and we have to make all kinds of preparations. One canoe load after another arrives from the south, and we are already preparing for the winter's trapping and sales. We send out small caches of goods, partly as supplies for trappers we consider trustworthy and partly to a few Indians who serve as assistant managers of sort. They receive a cache of goods and trade furs on our account, but this trading must be done by direct settlement. They are not allowed to grant credit, but sometimes they do so anyway. They actually do so most of the time.

Future sled dogs. Mortensen acquired six of these puppies, all males, to build his own dog team.

We try to move some of the merchandise that will be traded during this coming winter's sledding season as far as we can while the waters are still open. Transportation is easier by canoe than by toboggan. We have a temporary storage shed a couple of days' journey downstream where we primarily keep heavy goods such as flour, salt, sugar, and baking powder. The store is locked with a twenty-five-cent padlock, and that is good enough. There might be some shoplifting if the store were to be left open, but the Indians have a sense of honour, and they do not want to have a reputation as a thief or a crook. Only four Indian families live near the store, and if a burglary took place, we would hear about it. If this were to happen, the Mounted Police would come to take the trespasser into custody the next summer. It is inconceivable that any Indians living farther away would come to steal goods from the store.

We must also think about the winter supply of fish, mainly for our own dogs. The trading post has two dog teams and some puppies. Dooles is interested in raising puppies because he sells them. We also need a bit of fish to sell at a few other trading posts.

We estimate that we consume 10,000–12,000 fish over the winter, but we are also in one of the richest fishing areas in the North. Getting enough fish for the winter is a great problem in many other areas. There, hunters are only able to partially cover their requirements for the winter when they fish in the fall. This means they must later resort to the tiring and not so productive method of winter fishing with nets under the ice. However, we always have enough fish for the entire winter in advance.

One day at the beginning of October, I load three Indian families and their equipment onto a York boat. Pulling four canoes behind us, we travel south for a day to reach their regular fishing grounds. This trip is a colourful family affair. We have an oven in the middle of the boat, and use it to cook our food during the trip so we don't need to go ashore. A really pleasant family atmosphere develops between young and old alike.

We do not catch very much the first few days. The nets are almost empty since the whitefish haven't started spawning yet. We try various locations, but regardless of whether we set our nets in deep or shallow water, the catch is always poor. However, the fish may start spawning at any time and pass by. We use 30–40 nets, both deep-water nets and regular ones.

The fish arrive on the fourth day, and they are clearly visible. In the morning, as our canoes cut their way through the thin layer of ice that has formed overnight, the deep-water nets are adrift on the surface. The water glows white with shining fish bellies, and the bulging nets are completely full of whitefish weighing between half a kilogram and two kilos each.

The Indians pull in the nets with both hands, and then use their teeth to grab the fish. They jerk a fish free from the net with their teeth and flip it into the canoe. If they pull so hard that the head breaks off, they just open their mouths a little wider and bite further up on the fish. I have rarely seen such a well-developed work technique; it is the Taylor model in action.[2] They quickly turn their head and the fish is free and ready to be flipped into the canoe. As soon as the men fill up the canoe, we paddle one load after another ashore.

The other family members remain ashore and hang up the fish. We don't clean them but make a hole just above the tail. Ten fish are strung on metre-long sticks, and these sticks are raised onto two scaffolds that are about one and a half metres above the ground.

There is an abundance of this wonderful whitefish in the lake during the spawning season. We erect one full scaffold after another, and after fourteen days we have caught the twelve thousand fish we need.

I also work hanging fish from morning till night — it is of no use to be the *kitchi oogemoo*. Time is precious, winter is just around the corner, and we are happy for every day we wake up with no sign of an approaching storm. To be on the water with Indian families in stormy weather is not the most pleasant situation. They are far too clumsy to be useful sailors. With our canoes full of fine whitefish we turn towards home. Now winter can come as far as we are concerned.

Who hasn't had the experience of choking on a fishbone? As we sit coughing in front of a plate half filled with fish scraps, we can't but wonder. Why did Our Lord[3] create fish with so many bones and fins and such large heads? I have also wondered about this in the past, but now I know that I have been a bit unfair to Our Lord. He has, in addition to the pike and perch and the other fish that resemble them, also created the ideal fish. He has created a species of fish that has a minimal number of fins and bones: body parts that, though anatomically necessary, are merely inconvenient to diners. He has created the whitefish.[4]

The whitefish is the fish of the North. When we speak of fish we mean whitefish. No other fish exists for us. Whitefish. It is impossible for an outsider to comprehend all that this word entails. The name doesn't adequately describe this fish. The most misleading thing about the name is the colour. The fish should at least be called the silver-white fish, but that would not do them justice either. Maybe rainbow fish, but then some might confuse it with the rainbow trout. With their silvery white flanks, silvery grey backs, and pearly white bellies, a load of whitefish is like a material incarnation of parts of the rainbow, inviting and delicious.

The meat of the whitefish is all that its outer appearance promises. The whitefish is tasty and nourishing and one never tires of eating it. One can eat it year after year without craving other fish.

One might think it was the result of a multi-year breeding project to produce a truly excellent fish. A distinctive aspect of whitefish anatomy is the minimal size of its head, fins, entrails, and bones. The majority of the fish is edible.

The only thing that Our Lord appears not to have considered when He created the whitefish is the sport angler. Sport anglers comprise, as you know, a breed of their own, and their needs were not considered when the whitefish was created. These people look at the whitefish with unappreciative and critical eyes, because the whitefish can't be caught by fly-fishing. Yes, even regular fishermen, people who lower themselves and use a lure, will cast for it in vain. Their lure is of no interest to the whitefish. And worms on hooks don't interest whitefish either. It must be caught with a net, and that is a method of fishing that is sacrilegious from a sport angler's perspective. But even if the whitefish were to latch onto a fly, it would be a disappointment to the angler with a fishing rod. Due to its poor aerodynamics, it would not be able to put up much of a fight.

Here in the North, however, we need food, not sport fishing, and we rejoice when our nets are full of whitefish.

The Indians also appreciate the whitefish. If they catch "jockfish," "sucker," "cockerell" or "corries,"[5] they will keep them and eat them for the sake of variety. However, they can live on whitefish without complaining and whitefish make them strong. The Indian who gets a full scaffold[6] of fish in the autumn considers himself to be safe for the winter.

Some may have the impression that the rivers and lakes here in the North are like fish tanks, where one can simply go and take what they need. It is not quite that simple because sometimes there is a scarcity of fish. Even the Indians have to be satisfied with pike and perch during these winters. But when the whitefish are running in the fall, we catch large quantities of them. The Indians have their regular fishing spots where they scoop up large numbers of these fish.

When the winter storeroom is stocked full of fish, I begin to arrange for the winter firewood. I have the Indians bring three big loads of good dry pine and spruce to the house. With the passage of time, we must go farther and farther afield to find firewood, since all dry wood from around the trading post has already been cut and burned. Every year we have to go a greater distance for wood. But there is plenty for the taking if we just walk half an hour from the trading post.

I spread a clay mixture over the walls of the house and mix it with plenty of moose hair so the plaster sits more securely. The coating provides significant protection from the cold and saves firewood.

The dogs must also be dewormed before the season begins. A couple of them have gotten skinny and lazy, and they drink constantly. We treat all the dogs. First, we don't feed them for a day, and then we give them some tapeworm capsules we brought with us from Norway House. We have fun assisting with the tapeworm treatment. We wrap the tapeworm around a small stick and then spin it around. Often we make an entire small ball of yarn from a single tapeworm. It is incredible that dogs can have so many metres of tapeworm inside of them.

At the beginning of November, the Indians start to trap, and I will set out on my first trading trip to the camps later in the month. The most valuable fox furs are often caught early in the season. Then the skins are less rubbed or scuffed, and it is worth arriving before the other traders.

Oxford Lake still hasn't frozen over, but I am anxious to set out. To get a head start, we load the sled and dogs into canoes and paddle a few days towards the north. There we stop to wait for the snow. The ground has frozen solid, and the swamps and some rivers have iced over. Now we only need a little snow to have good travelling conditions.

We load merchandise from our storage locations and check in with some of our half-breed assistant managers as we wait to journey north. The assistants are running short of goods once again. Most of them have been traded on credit in spite of the rules, and the assistants have probably used some of the merchandise themselves. It is hard for them to say no to their own people, even though they are trading other people's wares. A few pathetic ermine skins are the entire result of their trading so far.

Due to their unreliability, Indians seldom achieve success as traders. One would think fur trading companies could recruit the staff they need from among the Indians, but that is not how it is. Even though some Indians learn to speak English very well, and should be able to serve as a fine link between white men and Natives, their unreliability in everything means they can rarely be used. Now I need to use my sharp tongue to scare them, and I set Christmas as a deadline for bringing in the furs. Otherwise they will not get more merchandise this season.

The hunters we visit have not trapped anything worth mentioning either. As a result, I return from my first trading trip with a modest load. But at least I have some good dogs, and I immediately notice how different it is to drive a team that has been well trained by a white man rather than a team of Indian dogs.

The Indian who is travelling with me as a runner is a lazy and sullen slouch, but on the way home he has to give it his all. The temperature has dropped and the hard, frozen, almost snowless river makes for fast running. The load is light and there is no need to hold back. The runner ends up behind the sled and this makes him a bit more humble. It is considered shameful for a runner to fall behind like that. Young Indians who eagerly take jobs as runners[7] want to be considered skillful, and it is a sought-after job to be the runner for a white man. The white men usually make short day trips. They have an abundance of good food along and the trips are, as a result, pleasant.

Back home at the trading post, Dooles tells us about the bountiful fur years and incredible hunting areas around Hudson Bay. Thousands upon thousands of white foxes migrate there every third year. At these times, a person can just about catch as many of them as he wants with any trapping method, down to the simplest one. The foxes can even be caught with a fishing line, he says. One only has to put a piece of pork on a fishing hook. A red rag will do if nothing else is available. If a person hides behind a small hill, rod in hand, it does not take long before there is a bite and a white fox is reeled in. This is how they tell the story, and I know that this has actually been done.

As the fire crackles in the oven in the evening, these stories awaken the desire in me for a long trip. I have become somewhat acquainted with this country, and I am curious to find out what lies northeast and southeast of the regions I have travelled through. The farther northeast we come, the greater our expectations, the fewer the traders, and the better the furs. Hunters always dream of having enough supplies to travel as far as possible in these directions.

Shortly after New Year's, I set out on my first long journey to the Hudson Bay region. I have an Indian runner with me who knows the area. He has not been at the exact place I am heading for, but he has been in that general direction and that is good enough around here. The map I have of the area is not detailed enough for our trip, so we mainly follow the rivers. This allows us to determine our general direction. We will primarily follow the Hayes River until we reach the Hudson Bay area with Port Nelson as our destination.[8] I bring two sleds with an inviting cargo: a good bit of clothing and a little food.

After having travelled four days down the Hayes River, we come across a camp. Here the Indians are living like counts if their lifestyle were to be measured by European standards. The standard silvery whitefish are not hanging on their cache but rather long, dark fish. These are sturgeon, the same species as the sturgeon in Russia. Even the dogs are fed sturgeon since there is such an abundance of them in the river. Every fall, the sturgeon run up the Hayes River from Hudson Bay. In the course of a few hectic days, the Indians net as many of this rare and highly desired fish as they need. It is of no use to leave the nets in the river overnight. If they did so, the nets would be shredded and there would be no fish. The Indians catch these sturgeon by the hundreds and hang them out to dry on their scaffolds.

They have prepared a wonderful sturgeon meal for me, one I will always remember. This cartilaginous fish, the sturgeon, seems to be a combination of the meat from various land animals. But I am not well acquainted with its natural history. Some parts of it taste like pork, some like veal, and some like moose. The sturgeon truly seems to combine the taste of all kinds of meat.

Here on the Hayes River it is also common for the Indians to fish using homemade fish traps. The traps are very simple and very useful in these fish-rich waters. First, the Indians build a lock in the rapids. The lock is wider at the top where the water flows into the rapids and narrower downstream. At the exit of the lock they set up a square frame—a network of thin branches with railings all around. When the fish enters the lock, it is carried by the current and ends up in the frame. The water passes through the branches, but the fish stays in the trap, ready to be picked up when needed.

The journey continues. I am in the true wilderness. We could travel for days without seeing people. What are the addresses of the people who live here? An example would be: Travel downstream on the river for two days, go over a hill, and then follow the river for half a day. The addressee is certain to be residing somewhere around there. Follow the tracks of the sled, and if the snow has wiped them away, the dogs will still find their way.

After travelling a few more days, we are in the Port Nelson area. One of the patriarchs of the wilderness, Noah the one-armed, lives here, together with his seven sons and sons-in-law. He is different from the Cree Indians and belongs to the Hudson Bay Indians.[9] He is barrel-chested[10] and this round, broad chest is supposedly the result of the mixing of Eskimos[11] and Norwegians—people from Stavanger,[12] to be exact.

They receive us with overwhelming hospitality, and a wonderful meal with several courses of fish and an abundance of meat is set out for us strangers. It is enough to satisfy at least ten thoroughly hungry men.

I never found out why Noah only had one arm. Nobody knew how he had lost it, only that it had happened during a hunting trip. No one had ever heard him tell the story. However, I have heard some things about him and his story goes something like this. Thomas Noah was originally from York Factory.[13] He had a wife, two children, and a brother-in-law. When his wife was eight months pregnant, Thomas had tired of his life around York Factory and wanted to settle in an area with better furs. First he took his family and some of his belongings with him, and then left the family in a place he had chosen on the Hayes River. There was an excellent fishing spot nearby, so his wife would be able to have fresh fish every day. Together with his brother-in-law, Thomas returned to York Factory to retrieve the remainder of his winter supplies.

One day after the men had left on their trip to the south, the wife discovered that a bear had taken over her fishing spot. It sat next to the trap and took the fish as they came by, and it stayed in that place the whole day. The next day another bear came along. The bears did not show any consideration for the lonely wife or the children, and they disturbed the family in the night by tramping around their teepee over and over again. In the end the wife became extremely distressed. To get away from the bears, she fled with her children in a small canoe farther up the river to another camp, taking some food and blankets. However, the bears followed them there, and they ended up having to flee from that place too. This time the wife was so unnerved that she hardly took any food or clothing along in her haste.

Meanwhile, Thomas was on his way back from York Factory, and because his wife was going to have a little one soon, he came as fast as he could. When he arrived at the first camp, he saw the bear tracks. From the other tracks, he realized that his family had fled upriver. He went off in hot pursuit and when he arrived at the second camp and went towards the teepee, he saw a bear coming out of it. He sent his brother-in-law down to the canoe to get the rifles, and they armed themselves before approaching the teepee again. All the same, the bear escaped and they didn't succeed in shooting it. As Thomas peeked into the teepee, he just managed to jump out of the other bear's way as it suddenly came charging out.

There was no sign of his family except their tracks, which indicated they had left the teepee in great haste. Now a feverish search began for the wife and children. The next day Thomas found them on the shore of a small lake. His little children were alone, almost frozen, and half starved. His wife had died a few hours earlier after giving birth to a stillborn child. She was not yet cold.

This was a hard blow to take out here in the wilderness. However, this man of the northern forests quietly bowed his head before his God's merciless will. Even so, he did not yield completely. The missionary's words had not instilled a very strong faith in him. Doubts began to gnaw at him. Was the white man's God really the right God for him and his people? The priest had surely not lied when he said, "My God is a merciful God." He was no doubt a merciful God for white people. But did his mercy and care also extend to others?

One night that winter, as the moon shone in the white wilderness, the silence was broken by the sound of monotonous drumming. It was Noah. In his unrelenting distress and despair, he was seeking to re-establish the connection with his old gods — the Indians' own gods from ancient times.

I stay at Noah's camp for a few more days, and we trade in the prescribed way. My trading merchandise seems equivalent in value to the furs he has stored away, so all his pelts are transferred to my sled and all my trading merchandise is stowed away in his cabin. The trappers here have valuable pelts, which gives me a toboggan load worth several thousand dollars.

My current load is the most valuable load of furs I have had so far, and it turned out later that this would be the most valuable single load of the season. Noah's solitary camp disappears behind me, vanishing in a thin cloud of swirling snow in the dawn of the winter morning.

The flat landscape before me is partially lit up by a weak and greyish flickering light. The bright snowflakes sparkle and flash, but the light has not quite overtaken the darkness. It will take eight days to travel back to my trading post by sled if we commit to long days. The temperature has dropped to below −50 degrees, and the icy, bitingly cruel arctic winter is all around us and in us. It takes great effort to stay warm, and we have to run behind the sled all day long. When I have breathed through the scarf covering my face for a short time, I have to turn it as my breath causes the scarf to freeze into an ice cake.

Under these conditions it is impossible to sleep for any length of time. In the evening we build a big bonfire and creep as close to it as we can. The Indian hardly sleeps at all. If I fall asleep around midnight, I have to get up after three hours because by then the cold has penetrated my sleeping bag, no matter how warm it is. The innermost layer of the bag is made of down and outside that there is a layer of woven rabbit skins with an external protective layer of canvas. But even this rabbit robe[14] is not enough to keep the frost away for more than a few hours.

Shivering from the cold, we haul more wood onto the bonfire, melt snow for tea, and also attempt to thaw the bannock. If the bread burns on the side towards the fire, it freezes on the other side,

Illustration by Birger Cranner. Used with permission from Birger Cranner's estate.

just as we do. I can't even smoke my pipe, since the smoke freezes in the pipe stem.

The journey is also exhausting for the dogs. First thing in the morning there is no sign of them. The snow usually drifts over them during the night, and only a small bump and a breathing hole for their snout indicate their location. They do not move when we get up. They just lie lifeless but always watchful. As soon as we begin to chop pieces of fish for them, the dogs' snouts emerge from the snow, and they make their presence known. They shake themselves and then attack the frozen fish.

On such frosty mornings, the dogs' spirits are usually below zero. They lack any incentive to work and a let's go attitude is nowhere to be seen. They lie reluctantly in their harnesses[15] while we break camp and prepare to leave. The dogs' hairless paws are their weak spot. When the dogs start to pull, we may suddenly hear little popping sounds. Their paws are cracking. We have to use the whip to get the dogs moving, but things improve once they have warmed up.

This is the hardest trip I have ever made. Even the dogs struggle. On the fourth day one of them dies in the harness. It has been driven too hard. In all probability, it had worms in its liver and now the illness has taken its toll.

On top of everything else, as an extra hardship, my stomach starts to act up. I need to crouch down every half hour, and that creates its own challenges in this temperature. Every time I do so, I have to light a piece of birch bark to thaw my fingers so I can pull my trousers down. I try to think of a simpler system, but I don't come up with anything.

The food rations are very low towards the end of the trip. I sold too much to Noah and we have not been able to travel as many miles each day as I had estimated. On the last two days, we scrape out tin cans and try to make soup from that. The situation is dismal. Then a heavy snowfall begins and the temperature rises a bit. The snow becomes sticky and heavy.

The last day of the trip is a long one. The Indian has given up running ahead of the sled. For these Indian runners it is a matter of honour to persevere, but the task is too much for him. He sits on the sled and mechanically whips the dogs onward. I am not able to get him to accompany me by any other method, and I must take over the runner's job. In the evening I get angry. The Indian wants to set up a camp, but I prefer to continue the journey. The lead dog frequently stops in his tracks. He has almost become accustomed to the whip and would like to give up too. But I force both the dogs and the Indian onward through the darkness, wanting to make it to the trading post before we take a rest. I have to trust that the dogs will stay on course.

It is already 1:30 in the morning when we arrive at the post and manage to wake up Dooles. We do not take time to eat but just fall into bed, letting Dooles take care of the dogs.

The next morning I see a black man[16] when I look in the mirror. The skin on my face has frozen and is completely black. Fortunately, as it turned out, my injuries were not so serious that they left any lasting scars.

Gerd Kjustad Mortensen at the Opaskwayak Cree Nation in northern Manitoba, June 2011. Photo by Ahti Tolvanen.

Epilogue
A Personal Perspective on the Author and the Book

GERD KJUSTAD MORTENSEN

EINAR ODD MORTENSEN WAS BORN IN 1902 in what was then called Kristiania. The Norwegian capital's name was changed to Oslo in 1925, which was the town's original name before 1624.

My father-in-law grew up in a family of five boys and four girls. Their mother took care of the big family, while their father was the manager of a furniture store in the centre of the town. The sons of the family were rather adventurous. The eldest one, Bjarne (b. 1893), went, among other places, to Zululand in Africa in 1910 and worked in a village shop there. In 1917, during the First World War, Bjarne went with Canadian troops to France. Bjarne also worked for a period of time in the fur trading business at Norway House, Manitoba. Here Bjarne's brother-in-law, Leif Sunde, was manager, having taken over after the death of Hans Christen Hyer (Høyer). Einar Odd's brother Bjarne might have encouraged my father-in-law to go to Canada. Another brother, Leif (b. 1901), participated in the Second World War. During the war, he sailed with the Kvarstadboats (*Kvarstadbåtene*) from Gothenburg in Sweden, but he was captured by the Germans and sent to different prisons with the prisoner's number 116668. Luckily, he returned to Norway in 1945. The five boys did not have much education, but the girls had professions in teaching and nursing. It is interesting to observe that, given the time period, it was the women in the family, not the men, who pursued professions requiring higher education.

Before Einar Odd decided to go westwards, he graduated from high school in 1922 and started studying medicine. He terminated his studies after one year, and from 1923 to 1925 he worked as a farmhand at a large farm with animals and a nursery garden.

During these years, he became acquainted with the local veterinarian's daughter, who was only sixteen years old at the time. She became his girlfriend, but when my father-in-law wanted to buy a farm close by, she told him she did not want to be a farmer's wife. So in 1925 he immigrated to Canada. He came by ship to Quebec via Bergen and London. This is verified by immigration records (1925–1935) at the National Archives of Canada. From Quebec he went on by train to Winnipeg, Manitoba.

The Norwegian Helge Ingstad went to Alberta in 1926—one year after Einar Odd came to Manitoba. Ingstad published a book about his stay in Alberta and the Northwest Territories in Norwegian, *Pelsjegerliv* (Life as a trapper), in 1931. Einar Odd gave up his book project after this. He thought there might be no interest anymore for his adventures in Manitoba during the years 1925–1928. Both my husband and his sister Lise told me this. Another reason for not going ahead with publishing might also have been that he was now busy in the store in Oslo, and also courting the girlfriend he had met sometime in 1923 and eventually married in 1930. I do not know if they had any contact with each other during his Canada-stay, however difficult that might have been! From his pencil-written notes, I understood that he started on his manuscript shortly after returning from Canada, and after a fishing trip in the mountains with a close friend of his.

My husband and I contacted the largest Norwegian publishing company, Gyldendal, in Oslo many years later after we had revised Einar Odd's draft manuscript. Gyldendal ended up publishing it as *Pelshandleren* [The fur trader] in 2007. Gyldendal thought that both Mortensen's and Ingstad's books gave a unique insight into different aspects concerning their lives in two different areas in Canada at the time. Gyldendal also maintained that the two books complemented each other in many ways. *Pelshandleren* was also translated into Finnish under the title *Turkiskauppiaana intiaanireservaatissa*, in 2009.

My husband, Einar Odd Jr., actually had the same name as his father, but I just called him Einar, like most of his friends did. He would have been the most appropriate person to write this epilogue about his father's story, but unfortunately became seriously ill during the process of editing the manuscript, so asked me to do so instead. He was, however, able to proofread all I wrote. Unfortunately, he died in 2009, but he provided valuable input along the way in the process of my writing. His father had not told much to his children about his stay in Manitoba. Luckily, my husband's sister, Lise Nordhagen, had taken care of an unfinished manuscript, notes, and pictures from that time. Shortly after Einar's retirement in 2002, she handed it all over to him to use as a basis for writing a book about their father's stay in Manitoba.

I have tried my best to capture my father-in-law's cognitive style of expressing himself. He had a specific way of using humour in his language usage. I attempted to put it into modern Norwegian according to a Norwegian governmental report issued in 1980–1981.[1] This report mainly focused on spelling. When it comes to usage, I think the translators and editors have done a good job in conveying his style in Canadian English. In 2007, Gyldendal also commented on Mortensen's straightforward language "in Mortensen's own distinctive and engaging voice." When I became acquainted with my father-in-law and his way of conversation, I noticed this particular linguistic trait in him, and how this was reflected in his personality. I am interested in language and learning, and I feel that both my father-in-law and my husband had that trait in common. Einar Odd understood and used some Cree words, which does not seem easy to me at all! I would also describe my husband Einar as a linguistic chameleon in the way he was able to change his language when communicating in different situations. Einar picked up variations of Norwegian dialects easily, both when it came to vocabulary and tones. I also noticed this ability in him when we were travelling and he tried to use other languages.

Relatives, friends, and acquaintances of Einar Odd have all contributed facts and impressions of the author that helped my late husband and me learn more about his Canadian experiences. From one of his cousins we heard that Einar Odd had been interviewed by journalist Johannes Borge for an article that appeared in a Norwegian magazine called *Hjemmet* in November 1940.[2] The article deals with Norwegians in Canada at Norway House, which was an old centre for fur trading in Manitoba. Einar Odd was promised a job there and he waited for an answer about it in Winnipeg. But since he got no reply from Norway House, he continued by train to The Pas. Here, a telegram finally reached him, saying "Not Wanted Here!" Instead he met with Isaac Benjamin Dembinsky in The Pas. Dembinsky was a businessman who had several trading posts in northern Manitoba. Einar Odd was hired by him to work at a post called Pine Bluff, or Piskominahikoska in the Cree language. My father-in-law noted that Dembinsky was a German Jew. I wondered why he made that remark. Perhaps he just did so because of his limited contact with Jewish people previously.

In Norway, Jewish people were not allowed into the country, according to the Norwegian Constitution of 1814, Article 2, also called the Religion Article. The article outlines that Jesuits, different monastic orders, and Jews were not allowed in the country. The section of this article referencing Jewish people was withdrawn in 1851, but only after much discussion and dissension in our parliament. The first Jewish settlers who came to Norway were mainly from northern Germany. The attitude in Norway at the time was that they were considered very competent, influential, and even tough businessmen. Maybe Einar Odd came with similar attitudes in his meeting with his new employer.

My father-in-law told the story about the first load of furs he delivered to Ben Dembinsky, his new boss. Furs were to be traded in for goods at the post. In the settlement, the new and inexperienced Norwegian fur trader felt he was somehow indebted to Dembinsky. In a humorous way, Einar Odd commented that he even got a two months' vacation, but without pay! He was quite aware he was no expert on furs yet, and he was also making fun of his own incompetence in the matter. He remembered that his mother had a boa, but he was not sure if it was made of furs or feathers. In spite of everything, Einar Odd was pleased to be hired by Dembinsky for another year.

After having been employed by Dembinsky in The Pas, my father-in-law continued his adventures in Canada around Norway House, where H.C. Hyer employed him. Here in these surroundings he experienced new and hard challenges. I really admired Einar Odd's stamina and endeavour in many of the ordeals he has described. Both my husband and I were very surprised he even got back to

Norway alive after the long and strenuous journey described in the last chapter of the book. This description of an eight-day trip with sledge and dogs seemed to us cruelly hard. He had a very heavy load with furs on this trip, maybe his heaviest so far, taking it through very challenging cold and changing weather. The description of that tour amazed us, especially with regard to his perseverance and effort. These were among his qualities partly unknown to us prior to the time of editing. At least I had not observed them in him. We certainly learned to know Einar Odd as a more versatile person when going through all the material left behind from his experiences in Manitoba.

Each chapter of this book can be looked upon individually. Each of them tells us different stories from Einar Odd's experiences and way of living in Manitoba—one of the Prairie provinces—almost a hundred years ago. The book about the adventures of Einar Odd Mortensen with the Cree and a number of other Nations ends in a rather abrupt way. He was asked by his father to come back to Norway to help him out in their store. As a loyal son he returned to Norway in 1928. Both my husband and I had for a long time thought of visiting Manitoba to look at the places where Einar Odd had worked as a fur trader. I got the opportunity to visit Manitoba in the late spring of 2011, after I had been at a conference in Fredericton, New Brunswick, presenting a paper about my father-in-law's experiences in Manitoba. I flew the last part of this trip on a small plane with Bearskin Airlines to The Pas, and I stayed at Kikiwak Inn at Opaskwayak Cree Nation.

In The Pas I visited the Sam Waller Museum. Here I got a lot of information about The Pas and its vicinity. For me it was thrilling to hear about my father-in-law's surroundings at the time he was a fur trader, and most of all to get a clearer picture of what he had been up against. Seeing the Saskatchewan River running past The Pas in June must have been quite different from how Einar Odd experienced it in November 1925, "with a biting, cold, northeast wind" ("North of the 53rd Parallel"). It was also fascinating to experience the vastness and wilderness around and north of The Pas. The countryside is still sparsely populated, and there are plenty of rivers and lakes. I could easily see the portages from the air, and the land seemed flat with wet ground all around. There were not many fir trees to be seen, but there was plenty of green vegetation. I could vividly imagine how transport to the trading posts was done during both summer and winter. In summer, canoes, and in winter, dog teams were used. Today, there are still not too many roads built, and snow trails are often used to go to places during the winter.

On my way back by plane to Winnipeg, we made a stop at Flin Flon. I had learned at the Sam Waller Museum that there was still a business there called Dembinsky's Ben, which is a clothing store. I understood that the Dembinsky family had been very influential in The Pas area over the years, and that family members had settled in Flin Flon. I have also read in H.S.M. Kemp's *Northern Trader* that Flin Flon was important in the days of fur hunting and trading.

I visited the Visitor Information Centre in The Pas as well. To a certain degree tourists can still go to the wilderness described by Einar Odd, but now planes are mostly used. I had rented a car and tried to find Pine Bluff, his first trading post, but unfortunately without any luck. I had contacted the government archives of Manitoba in Winnipeg before going to The Pas. I asked about the whereabouts of Pine Bluff and the trade post according to the descriptions mentioned by the author. The most likely place was at the mouth of the Piskominahikoska River,[3] according to the archives' staff, but today this area is unfortunately under water.

I was very pleased to be invited to a Cree ceremony in The Pas, and the celebration of an adoption in Opaskwayak Cree Nation across the Saskatchewan River from The Pas. Here I was introduced to certain aspects of the Cree culture, religion, and language. I felt a warm welcome, and I was most heartily received. I am glad they all spoke English to me, but the adoption ceremony was carried out in Cree. At this special celebration, they served, among other things, traditional food such as bannock and whitefish, which were essential to Einar Odd's diet throughout his stay in Manitoba. The celebration was held at the very spot where Einar Odd set out from, going to his first trading post in Pine Bluff in the early winter of 1925 with a dog team.

I also struck up an acquaintance with an Opaskwayak Elder, Rosalyn Ing, at this celebration. Rosalyn had travelled the farthest to attend from her home in Vancouver, BC. She and her husband George visited me in my home in Norway the following summer, and she kindly read an English translation of *The Fur Trader* at that time. She provided me with valuable advice as to how to proceed with my project, and for that I am extremely grateful.

My visit to The Pas really helped me to imagine the challenges and adventures my father-in-law experienced during his days as a fur trader in northern Manitoba. First of all, I must mention his descriptions about living close to the Cree people and learning to communicate with them. Later on, he had to learn how to cooperate with other Nations around Norway House. This must have been a vital challenge for him in order to succeed with his work.

Another adventurous experience he encountered was his fight with the mosquitoes during the summer. He describes their extremely annoying attacks on him with great humour. His seeking refuge in the water is masterfully put into words. In June, I experienced the mosquitoes' attacks as well. I had no trouble understanding how they could multiply in large numbers in this environment, and I certainly felt sympathy with my father-in-law in his fight against them during the summer!

In a way, I think Einar Odd was sad to leave this life behind, hard and tough as it must have been. But being the loyal son, he left Manitoba in 1928 and married his girlfriend in 1930, the one who had refused to be a farmer's wife in 1925. So my father-in-law started his trading experiences with fur trading in Manitoba and ended up in the furniture business at the A/S Einar Mortensen store in Oslo. He even had plans to start fur farming in Norway! But working in the store ended up taking all his time. Both my father-in-law and my husband were much alike in many ways. They had the same name, and from what I have understood, the two of them often shared the same view on how things ought to be done in the store. Their decision making, in business and other matters, was generally based on pragmatism and a rational way of thinking. I also think they communicated well. Einar worked in the store together with his

Gerd Kjustad Mortensen with Dr. Rosalyn Ing (centre) and Betsy Kematch (right). Opaskwayak Cree Nation, June 2011. Photo by Ahti Tolvanen.

father for some years. But in 1959 he decided to start studying veterinary medicine and graduated in 1964. Their personalities were somehow similar in the way both of them made some unexpected decisions in life.

My father-in-law died in 1969 at the age of sixty-seven without ever returning to Canada. My husband passed away in 2009, at seventy-five. They were both very dear to me, and I truly miss them.

Finally, I want to acknowledge the following for their encouragement, support, and contributions to this English translation of *The Fur Trader*: my close Finnish Canadian friends, Marja-Liisa and Ahti Tolvanen, who have both been active supporters from the very beginning of this project, as well as Dr. Ingrid Urberg and Dr. Daniel Sims who have edited this English edition. Their introduction, notes, and translation editing have given more insight and context to the events *The Fur Trader* describes, events that took place almost a hundred years ago. I am very thankful for all they have done and contributed to make possible the publication of this book in the country where it all was experienced.

Reading Guide and Discussion Questions

DEPENDING ON WHETHER YOU ARE READING Einar Odd Mortensen's *The Fur Trader* out of personal interest, as part of a book club, or in conjunction with a course, you will avail yourself of different lenses and approaches as you analyze this personal narrative. Below are some suggestions for examining and discussing the text.

Themes

Silences: A theme that is central to Indigenous studies and gender studies is silencing.

- Discuss the ways in which various voices and perspectives — particularly those of Indigenous men and women and settler women — are marginalized, even silenced, in the text. (Note Mortensen's lack of naming individuals.)
- Discuss the representations of Indigenous and non-Indigenous women in the text. Are they ever more than stereotypes? Does the pictorial material support these representations or challenge them?
- Can you identify any subtexts in the narrative? What are some possible explanations as to why Mortensen did not directly address these topics in *The Fur Trader*?

Disciplines

Literary Studies:
- John Tallmadge argues that in travel accounts the plot has to be uncovered rather than created.[1] Does Mortensen successfully

uncover the plot in his northern experiences? Support your position with specific textual examples.
- *The Fur Trader* starts in *media res* — in the middle of things — and ends abruptly in the same way. Do you find this strategy to be satisfying or unsatisfying? Why?
- What type of picture does Mortensen paint of himself? Do Mortensen's northern adventures appear to change him in any significant way? In other words, do you perceive a marked character development?
- How would you characterize the tone of the text? Discuss Mortensen's use of humour and satire in the narrative. What are his possible motivations for using these devices?
- Who does Mortensen's intended audience appear to be? Support your answer with specific textual examples.
- How do Mortensen's word choices reflect the time period in which he lived? How do you think he would edit the text if he wrote it today?
- Have you read other narratives written by fur traders or trappers? Compare and contrast *The Fur Trader* to these narratives.

History:
- How do Mortensen's experiences relate to the field of fur trade history? Where would you situate it in the literature?
- Do you think his memoirs would be different if he worked for a major fur trading company, like the Hudson's Bay Company?
- Why do you think Mortensen spends so little time talking about the day-to-day activities of the fur trade?
- Place Mortensen's adventures within the context of colonialism in Canada. What type of colonialism, if any, do you think he represents and why? What are the implications of Mortensen being aware or unaware of his role?
- How are Mortensen's choice of profession and activities in northern Canada, as well as his return to Norway, typical or atypical of the European immigrant experience in the early twentieth century in Canada?

Indigenous Studies:
- How do Mortensen's experiences fit into the field of Indigenous studies? How would you situate it in the literature?
- Is Mortensen's portrayal of Indigenous Peoples of historical importance? Does it matter that he never names a specific band/First Nation? What impact does his intended audience have on the information he provides?
- What does Mortensen's account indicate about the pervasiveness of colonial views in the early twentieth century? Is Mortensen truly sympathetic to his customers?
- How do Mortensen's memoirs intersect with theory? Do they confirm or challenge any particular theory or concept in Indigenous studies?

Environmental Studies:
- How do Mortensen's experiences fall into the field of environmental studies? How would you situate them in the literature?
- Discuss the role of the natural environment in the narrative.
- Mortensen attempts, at times, to make sense of his new surroundings by comparing them to the natural environment he is familiar with in Norway. Locate and discuss at least one example of this.
- How does Mortensen's memoir connect to the conservation and environmental movements? What are his views on hunting and trapping?

Additional Questions
- Which lens or combination of lenses did you find most beneficial while reading this text?
- Identify two reflective passages in the book that resonate with you and explain the reasons for this.
- Identify and discuss one or two passages that trouble you as a contemporary reader.
- If you could ask Einar Odd Mortensen a question about his time in the Canadian North, what would it be?

Notes

Introduction

1. According to family tradition, and the community-based research Gerd Kjustad Mortensen conducted in 2011, Pine Bluff was located in Manitoba, likely eighty kilometres southeast of The Pas on the Saskatchewan River. It is possible, however, that Mortensen served the Cumberland House Cree Nation at a trading post next to their Pine Bluff reserves (Pine Bluff 20A and Pine Bluff 20B) in Saskatchewan. The opening lines of Mortensen's narrative state that Pine Bluff was located a five to six day journey and two hundred miles north of The Pas. Strictly speaking, neither Pine Bluff fits this description, although the reserves in Saskatchewan are west northwest of The Pas. The fact that Pine Bluff is a frequently used place name, and the directional flow of the Saskatchewan River (The Pas is on a southern bend of the river as it flows west to east and therefore regardless of what direction you take you are heading "north" if you follow the river), makes it difficult to say with certainty which Pine Bluff Mortensen was referring to.
2. Einar Odd Mortensen, *Pelshandleren: Mitt liv blant indianere i Nord-Canada 1925–28* (Oslo: Gyldendal, 2007).
3. Helge Ingstad, *Pelsjegerliv blandt Nord-Kanadas indianere* (Oslo: Gyldendal, 1931); Helge Ingstad, *The Land of Feast and Famine*, trans. Eugene Gay-Tifft (New York: Alfred A. Knopf, 1933). McGill-Queen's University Press reissued this text in 1992. For details about this period of Ingstad's life, refer to Ingrid Urberg, "Helge Ingstad: Inspiration for a Life of Adventure in the Land of Feast and Famine," in *Pike's Portage: Stories of a Distinguished Place*, ed. Morten Asfeldt and Bob Henderson (Toronto: Natural Heritage Books, 2010), 192–204; Benedicte Ingstad, *A Grand Adventure: The Lives of Helge and Anne Stine Ingstad and Their Discovery of a Viking Settlement in North America* (Montreal: McGill-Queen's University Press, 2017), 41–81.
4. Eirik Ingstad Sandberg (Ingstad's grandson), Stein P. Aasheim, Vegard Ulvang, Sverre Hovind and most recently Jens Kvernmo, are other notable Norwegians who have retraced portions of Ingstad's travels in the Great Slave Lake region.
5. *Canada på tvers*, directed by Fridtjof Kjæreng, written by Lars Monsen, aired on NRK in 2005. Monsen also published a book based on his Canadian adventures. Lars Monsen, *Nådeløs villmark: Canada på tvers* [Merciless wilderness: across Canada] (Oslo: Lars Monsen Outdoors, 2002).

6. For a recent analysis of Ingstad's narrative refer to Fredrik Chr. Brøgger's article, "Re-enacting Modernity in the Wilderness of the Canadian North: An Ecocritical Examination of Helge Ingstad's *The Land of Feast and Famine*," in *Arctic Modernities: The Environmental, the Exotic and the Everyday*, ed. Heidi Hansson and Anka Ryall (Newcastle upon Tyne: Cambridge Scholars Publishing, 2017).
7. Michael Payne, "Fur Trade Historiography: Past Conditions, Present Circumstances and a Hint of Future Prospects," in *From Rupert's Land to Canada*, ed. Theodore Binnema, Gerhard Ens, and R.C. MacLeod (Edmonton: University of Alberta Press, 2001), 13.
8. H.S.M. Kemp, *Northern Traders: The Last Days of the Fur Trade* (Regina: University of Regina Press, 2014), xi.
9. Take, for example, Peter Baker, *Memoirs of an Arctic Arab: A Free Trader in the Canadian North: The Years 1907–1927* (Saskatoon: Yellowknife Publishing Co., 1976); Tom Boulanger, *An Indian Remembers: My Life as a Trapper in Northern Manitoba* (Winnipeg: Peguis Publishers, 1971); Carolyn Podruchny, *Making the Voyageur World: Travelers and Traders in the North American Fur Trade* (Lincoln: University of Nebraska Press, 2006), 293.
10. Podruchny, 14, 155–156, 293–294, passim.
11. In 1849, four Métis free traders were placed on trial in the Red River Colony for violating the Hudson's Bay Company's trade monopoly. Although the first person tried, Pierre-Guillaume Sayer, was found guilty by a jury of his peers, he was granted clemency. This decision, combined with the HBC's decision to drop charges against the other three, rendered its monopoly meaningless. John Foster, "Sayer Trial," *Canadian Encyclopedia*, Historica Canada, February 7, 2006, https://www.thecanadianencyclopedia.ca/en/article/sayer-trial.
12. Quite interestingly, Harold Innis does not mention the trial. Harold Innis, *The Fur Trade in Canada: With a New Introductory Essay by Arthur J. Ray* (Toronto: University of Toronto Press, 2001), 331, 363, 371; Michael Payne, *The Fur Trade in Canada: An Illustrated History* (Toronto: James Lorimer & Company Ltd., 2004), 75, 84–90.
13. Ron Maguire, *Pre-Confederation Upper Canada Treaties: Indian Annuities* (Ottawa: Treaties and Historical Research Centre, 1970), 2.
14. Arthur Ray, *The Canadian Fur Trade in the Industrial Age* (Toronto: University of Toronto Press, 1990), 39–40, 88–89.
15. H.C. Hyer changed his name upon immigrating to North America. His name in Norway was Høier, as noted by Einar Odd Mortensen in Chapter 6, "Hudson's Bay versus Free Trader." The spelling "Høyer" appears in an article in the magazine *Hjemmet*, referenced elsewhere in the introduction and epilogue (see Chapter 1, note 21 and Chapter 7, note 4).
16. Consider, for example, how 133 of the 159 citations found in Tough's chapter on competition from independent traders are from the Hudson's Bay Company. Frank Tough, *'As Their Natural Resources Fail': Native Peoples and the Economic History of Northern Manitoba, 1870–1930* (Vancouver: UBC Press, 2008), 251, 262, 357–360, 358nn55–56, 358nn58–61, passim.
17. Payne, "Fur Trade Historiography," 13.
18. Archives of Manitoba, "Hudson's Bay Company Archives," *Archives of Manitoba*, October 4, 2018, https://www.gov.mb.ca/chc/archives/hbca/.

19. Martin Hunter, *Canadian Wilds: Tells about the Hudson's Bay Company, Northern Indians and Their Modes of Hunting, Trapping, Etc.* (Columbus, OH: A.R. Harding, 1935), 18; Innis, *The Fur Trade in Canada*, 371; Tough, 'As Their Natural Resources Fail,' 250–257, 276.
20. Hunter, 18.
21. As George Colpitts points out, it does not help that free traders have not been extensively studied. George Colpitts, "Itinerant Jewish and Arabic Trading in the Dene's North, 1913–1930," *Journal of the Canadian Historical Association* 24, no. 1 (2013): 165.
22. Podruchny, *Making the Voyageur World*, 14, 155–156, 163.
23. Dembinsky's name is misspelled as Dernbentsky in Mortensen's notes and in the published Norwegian memoir. This edited translation contains the correct spelling throughout.
24. Manitoba Historical Society, "Isaac Benjamin 'Ben' Dembinsky (1885–1960)," *Memorable Manitobans*, February 16, 2021, http://www.mhs.mb.ca/docs/people/dembinsky_ib.shtml.
25. Mortensen is not the first individual to discuss fur trade protocols. In discussing their continuance into the twentieth century, he does, however, contribute to our understanding of them. A good place to start examining fur trade protocols is Bruce White, "A Skilled Game of Exchange: Ojibway Fur Trade Protocol," *Minnesota History* 50, no. 6 (1987), 229–240.
26. Alexander Mackenzie, *Voyages from Montreal on the River St. Laurence, Through the Continent of North America to the Frozen and Pacific Oceans; In the Years 1789 and 1793 with a Preliminary Account of the Rise, Progress and Present State of the Fur Trade of that Country* (London: R. Noble, 1801).
27. As Dennis McLeod, one of the Swampy Cree translators we consulted, pointed out, Swampy Cree is properly written in syllabics, so strictly speaking there is no correct spelling in the Roman alphabet. Thus, words written in the Roman alphabet are transliterations.
28. Leonard Bell, *Colonial Constructs: European Images of Maori, 1840–1914* (Auckland: Auckland University Press, 1992), 2.
29. Elizabeth Bird, "Introduction: Constructing the Indian, 1830s–1990s," in *Dressing in Feathers: The Construction of the Indian in American Popular Culture*, ed. Elizabeth Bird (Boulder: Westview Press, 1996), 3–4; Elizabeth Bird, "Not My Fantasy: The Persistence of Indian Imagery in *Dr. Quinn, Medicine Woman*," in *Dressing in Feathers: The Construction of the Indian in American Popular Culture*, ed. Elizabeth Bird (Boulder: Westview Press, 1996), 248; Patrick Brantlinger, *Dark Vanishings: Discourse on the Extinction of Primitive Races, 1800–1930* (Ithaca: Cornell University Press, 2003), 7–13, 101, passim; Sally Jones, "The First, but Not the Last of the 'Vanishing Indians': Edwin Forrest and Mythic Recreations of the Native Population," in *Dressing in Feathers: The Construction of the Indian in American Popular Culture*, ed. Elizabeth Bird (Boulder: Westview Press, 1996), 15, passim.
30. In using the term *frame*, I make reference to Joe Feagin's book, *White Racial Frame*. In it he argues that rather than being one component of a European world view, since the seventeenth century racism has underpinned all European perceptions of the world. Bird, "Introduction," 3–4; Bird, "Not My Fantasy," 248; John Bloom, "'There is Madness

in the Air': The 1926 Haskell Homecoming and Popular Representations of Sports in Federal Indian Boarding Schools," in *Dressing in Feathers: The Construction of the Indian in American Popular Culture*, ed. Elizabeth Bird (Boulder: Westview Press, 1996), 104–105; Steven Conn, *History's Shadow: Native Americans and Historical Consciousness in the Nineteenth Century* (Chicago: University of Chicago Press, 2004), 216, 226; Joe Feagin, *White Racial Frame: Centuries of Racial Framing and Counter-Framing*, 2nd ed. (New York: Routledge, 2013), 3, 10–19, passim; Daniel Francis, "The Imaginary Indian: The Image of the Indian in Canadian Culture," in *Race and Racialization: Essential Readings*, 2nd ed., ed. Tania Gupta et al. (Toronto: Canadian Scholars, 2018), 478–479; Alison Griffiths, "Science and Spectacle: Native American Representation in Early Cinema," in *Dressing in Feathers: The Construction of the Indian in American Popular Culture*, ed. Elizabeth Bird (Boulder: Westview Press, 1996), 80–83; Stuart Hall, "The West and the Rest: Discourse and Power," in *Race and Racialization: Essential Readings*, 2nd ed., ed. Tania Gupta et al. (Toronto: Canadian Scholars, 2018), 86–93; Jeffrey Steele, "Reduced to Images: American Indians in the Nineteenth-Century Advertising," in *Dressing in Feathers: The Construction of the Indian in American Popular Culture*, ed. Elizabeth Bird (Boulder: Westview Press, 1996), 61.

31. Conn, *History's Shadow*, 226; Francis, "The Imaginary Indian," 480; Peter Geller, "'Hudson's Bay Company Indians': Images of Native People and the Red River Pageant, 1920," in *Dressing in Feathers: The Construction of the Indian in American Popular Culture*, ed. Elizabeth Bird (Boulder: Westview Press, 1996), 68, 72; Griffiths, "Science and Spectacle," 79–83, 92.

32. Francis, "The Imaginary Indian," 480.

33. Bird, "Not My Fantasy"; Cynthia-Lou Coleman, "A War of Words: How New Frames Define Legitimacy in a Native Conflict," in *Dressing in Feathers: The Construction of the Indian in American Popular Culture*, ed. Elizabeth Bird (Boulder: Westview Press, 1996), 181; Feagin, *White Racial Frame*; Frank Goodyear, "The Narratives of Sitting Bull's Surrender: Bailey, Dix & Mead's Photographic Western," in *Dressing in Feathers: The Construction of the Indian in American Popular Culture*, ed. Elizabeth Bird (Boulder: Westview Press, 1996), 30; C. Richard King, "Segregated Stories: The Colonial Contours of the Little Bighorn Battlefield National Monument," in *Dressing in Feathers: The Construction of the Indian in American Popular Culture*, ed. Elizabeth Bird (Boulder: Westview Press, 1996), 175; Jay Mechling, "Florida Seminoles and the Marketing of the Last Frontier," in *Dressing in Feathers: The Construction of the Indian in American Popular Culture*, ed. Elizabeth Bird (Boulder: Westview Press, 1996), 149; Debra Merskin, "What Does One Look Like?" in *Dressing in Feathers: The Construction of the Indian in American Popular Culture*, ed. Elizabeth Bird (Boulder: Westview Press, 1996); Annette Taylor, "Cultural Heritage in *Northern Exposure*," in *Dressing in Feathers: The Construction of the Indian in American Popular Culture*, ed. Elizabeth Bird (Boulder: Westview Press, 1996); Peter van Lent, "'Her Beautiful Savage': The Current Sexual Images of the Native American Male," in *Dressing in Feathers: The Construction of the Indian in American Popular Culture*, ed. Elizabeth Bird (Boulder: Westview Press, 1996).

34. Goodyear, "The Narratives of Sitting Bull's Surrender," 30.

35. Theodore Jojola, "*Moo Mesa*: Some Thoughts on Stereotypes and Image Appropriation," in *Dressing in Feathers: The Construction of the Indian in American Popular Culture*, ed. Elizabeth Bird (Boulder: Westview Press, 1996), 277.

36. In recent years, institutions like Library and Archives Canada have started programs like Project Naming to try to rectify this situation. Library and Archives Canada, "Project Naming," *Library and Archives Canada*, May 30, 2019, bac-lac.gc.ca/eng/discover/aboriginal-heritage/project-naming/Pages/introduction.aspx; Carole Payne, "Lessons with Leah: Re-reading the Photographic Archive of Nation in the National Film Board of Canada's Still Photography Division," *Visual Studies* 21, no. 1 (2006): 11–12, 17–19; David Smith, "From Nunavut to Micronesia: Feedback and Description, Visual Repatriation and Online Photographs of Indigenous Peoples," *Partnership: The Canadian Journal of Library and Information Practice and Research* 3, no. 1 (2008): 2, 4.

37. Martha McCarthy, *Pine Bluff: A History* (Winnipeg: Manitoba Hydro and Pine Bluff Residents' Association, 1992), 1–3, 11–12, 29–30, passim.

38. Chris Andersen, *Métis: Race, Recognition, and the Struggle for Indigenous Peoplehood* (Vancouver: UBC Press, 2014), 6, 27–28, 38, 200.

39. Andersen, *Métis*.

40. Nicole St-Onge, Carolyn Podruchny, and Brenda MacDougall, eds., *Contours of a People: Family, Mobility, and Territoriality in Métis History* (Norman: University of Oklahoma Press, 2012).

41. Jennifer Adese and Chris Andersen, eds., *A People and a Nation: New Directions in Contemporary Métis Studies* (Vancouver: UBC Press, 2021).

42. For a lengthy examination of the legacy of *The Last of the Mohicans*, see Barker and Sabin's *The Lasting of the Mohicans*. Martin Barker and Roger Sabin, *The Lasting of the Mohicans: History of an American Myth* (Jackson: University Press of Mississippi, 1995), 21–22; Daniel Francis, *The Imaginary Indian: The Image of the Indian in Canadian Culture* (Vancouver: Arsenal Pulp Press, 1992), 38, 44, 73.

43. He does refer to them as Cree, but as the largest Indigenous ethnic group in Canada, with a traditional territory that stretches from Labrador to British Columbia, this noun without an adjective is somewhat vague.

44. It is also possible that he served the Cumberland House Cree Nation at a trading post next to their Pine Bluff reserves (Pine Bluff 20A and Pine Bluff 20B). This possibility, however, contradicts the community-based research conducted by Gerd Kjustad Mortensen and is based on taking Mortensen's reference to the community being a reserve literally. The equating of an Indigenous community to a reserve is all too common and reflects the fact that reserves represent official Indigenous space in Canada. For examination of the role reserves played in the colonial process, see Cole Harris, *Making Native Space: Colonialism, Resistance, and Reserves in British Columbia* (Vancouver: UBC Press, 2002).

45. Barker and Sabin, *The Lasting of the Mohicans*, 25–26; Francis, *The Imaginary Indian*, 44.

46. As John A. Macdonald famously stated on May 9, 1883, "When the school is on the reserve, the child lives with his parents who are savages; he is surrounded by savages, and though he may learn to read and write his habits, and [sic] training and mode of thought are Indian. He is simply a savage who can read and write." Canada, *House of Commons Debates*, May 5, 1883, 1107–1108 (John A. Macdonald, Prime Minister).

47. Truth and Reconciliation Commission of Canada, *Honouring the Truth, Reconciling for the Future: Summary of the Final Report of the Truth and Reconciliation Commission of Canada* (Winnipeg: Truth and Reconciliation Commission, 2015), 1, 3, 43, 55, passim.
48. In 1912, laws were passed that allowed for conscription if not enough volunteers enlisted. See Christian Koller, "Nationalism and Racism in Franco-German Controversies about Colonial Soldiers," in *Nations, Identities and the First World War: Shifting Loyalties to the Fatherland*, ed. Nico Wouters and Laurence van Ypersele (London: Bloomsbury Academic, 2018), 215, passim; Gregory Martin, "German and French Perceptions of the French North and West African Contingents, 1910–1918," *Militärgeschichtliche Mitteilungen* 56 (1997): 39, 57–58.
49. Bell, *Colonial Constructs*, 3.
50. Timothy Winegard, *For King and Kanata: Canadian Indians and the First World War* (Winnipeg: University of Manitoba Press, 2012), 6–9, 11, 168–169.
51. Robert Talbot, "'It Would Be Best to Leave Us Alone': First Nations Responses to the Canadian War Effort, 1914–18," *Journal of Canadian Studies* 45, no. 1 (2011): 100, 104, 108–116.
52. It important to point out that, under the Military Service Act of 1917, all male subjects between eighteen and sixty could be conscripted. At the time, Indigenous Peoples were considered subjects and it was not until after five months of protests following the passage of the act that Indigenous Peoples were deemed to be exempt from it. Nevertheless, they were still asked to register so they could officially receive their exemption. Brian MacDowall, "'A Flag That Knows No Colour Line': Aboriginal Veteranship in Canada, 1914–1939," (PhD diss., York University, 2017), 93–101, passim; Katharine McGowan, "'We Are Wards of the Crown and Cannot Be Regarded as Full Citizens of Canada': Native Peoples, the Indian Act and Canada's War Effort" (PhD diss., University of Waterloo, 2011), 22–23, 53–54, 131–159, 161, 164–165, 171–173, 180, 194–231, passim; Talbot, "It Would Be Best to Leave Us Alone," 106–107; Winegard, *For King and Kanata*, 168.
53. Winegard, *For King and Kanata*, 9.
54. Winegard, *For King and Kanata*, 10–11.
55. The entire general history is 132 pages long. We have included the starting points of the section itself, the details about Mackenzie, and his ethnographic/linguistic information. Mackenzie, *Voyages from Montreal on the River St. Laurence*, i, xix, cvii.
56. Mackenzie, 35.
57. W. Kaye Lamb discusses the editorial process in his introduction to the 1970 edition of Mackenzie's journal. Mackenzie, *Voyages from Montreal on the River St. Laurence*, iii–viii; Alexander Mackenzie, *The Journals and Letters of Sir Alexander Mackenzie*, ed. W. Kaye Lamb (Cambridge: University of Cambridge Press, 1970), 33–36; Samuel Black, *A Journal of a Voyage from Rocky Mountain Portage in Peace River to the Sources of Finlays Branch and North West Ward in Summer 1824*, ed. E.E. Rich (London: The Hudson's Bay Record Society, 1955), xix–xx.
58. Simon Fraser, *The Letters and Journals of Simon Fraser, 1806–1808*, ed. W. Kaye Lamb (Toronto: Dundurn Press, 2007), 17–18, 52–58.
59. Fraser, *The Letters and Journals of Simon Fraser*, 57; Mackenzie, *The Journals and Letters*, 35–36.

60. Mary Louise Pratt, *Imperial Eyes: Travel Writing and Transculturation*, 2nd ed. (London: Routledge, 2008), 3.
61. Bell, *Colonial Constructs*, 5–6.
62. Mackenzie, *Voyages from Montreal on the River St. Laurence*.
63. As historian W. Kaye Lamb points out, French translations were quickly made of them, ostensibly so that Napoleon could look for a military weakness in British North America. Mackenzie, *The Journals and Letters*, 35.
64. Daniel Sims, "Dam Bennett: The Impacts of the W.A.C. Bennett Dam and Williston Lake Reservoir on the Tsek'ehne of Northern British Columbia" (PhD diss., University of Alberta, 2017), 105–106.
65. Gulbrand Loken, "Norwegians," *The Canadian Encyclopedia*, Historica Canada, April 12, 2018, https://www.thecanadianencyclopedia.ca/en/article/norwegians.
66. The key difference between the two types of colonialism being that whereas extractive colonialism aims to extract raw resources, like furs, it is not concerned with replacing the Indigenous population with settlers—the defining characteristic of settler colonialism. Nancy Shoemaker, "A Typology of Colonialism," *Perspectives of History*, October 2015, https://www.historians.org/publications-and-directories/perspectives-on-history/october-2015/a-typology-of-colonialism.
67. Catherine Hall, *Civilising Subjects: Metropole and Colony in the English Imagination, 1830–1867* (Chicago: University of Chicago Press, 2002), 5–6, 14–15.
68. It harkens back to Edward Said's famous argument that the Orient helped define Europe and Europeans. Edward Said, *Orientalism* (London: Penguin Books, 2003); Hall, *Civilising Subjects*, 8–15; Anne McClintock, *Imperial Leather: Race, Gender and Sexuality in the Colonial Contest* (New York: Routledge, 1995), 4–5; Ann Laura Stoler and Frederick Cooper, "Between Metropole and Colony: Rethinking a Research Agenda," in *Tensions of Empire: Colonial Cultures in Bourgeois World*, ed. Frederick Cooper and Ann Laura Stoler (Berkeley: University of California Press, 1997), 1.
69. McClintock, *Imperial Leather*, 17, 207–231.
70. In particular, it was feared that such relationships would result in the loss of the man's European culture, which, although presented by Europeans as inherently superior, was also believed to be too weak to survive encounters with non-European cultures on such a level and/or intimate playing field. See Adele Perry, *On the Edge of Empire: Gender, Race and the Making of British Columbia, 1849–1871* (Toronto: University of Toronto Press, 2001), 49, 78, passim; Ann Laura Stoler, "Sexual Affronts and Racial Frontiers: European Identities and the Cultural Politics of Exclusion in Colonial Southeast Asia," in *Tensions of Empire: Colonial Cultures in a Bourgeois World*, ed. Frederick Cooper and Ann Laura Stoler (Berkeley: University of California Press, 1997), 199.
71. The National Archives of Norway do have a record of Einar Odd Mortensen emigrating on November 4, 1925, from Oslo to Canada, travelling via Bergen and England. "Person: Einar Odd Mortensen—Emigrants from Oslo 1867–1930," *The Digital Archives*, November 22, 2018, http://www.digitalarkivet.no/en/view/8/pe00000000562579.
72. In a 2007 interview with journalist Lena Storvand from the Norwegian tabloid *Verdens Gang*, Einar Odd Mortensen Jr. stated that he would not be surprised to learn that he had some half-siblings in Canada. He made this comment while looking at a picture of his father with a young Cree woman, but he also stated that his father never broached

this topic. Lena Storvand, "Farens fortid var tabu" [Father's past was taboo], *Verdens Gang*, March 18, 2007.

73. The Sámi are the Indigenous Peoples of Sápmi, an area that encompasses the northern regions of Norway, Sweden, Finland, and Russia's Kola Peninsula. At the time that Mortensen was in Canada, the terms *Lapp* and *Lappland* were primarily used by non-Sámi to denote the Sámi People and their traditional cultural territory Sápmi. The former terms are considered to be derogatory today. For more information on the Sámi, please refer to John Trygve Solbakk, *The Sámi People—A Handbook* (Karasjok, Norway: Davvi Girji, 2006).

74. This is part of the Mortensen family oral history, and the Cranner illustrations bookend this English edition of *The Fur Trader*. There is also evidence that while Mortensen mentioned his years as a fur trader in Canada to other friends, and was even interviewed for a magazine article in *Hjemmet* about Norway House, he did not necessarily share his personal experiences in any depth. For example, in an obituary written by "a friend," the friend mistakenly writes that Mortensen worked for the HBC while in Canada. "Obituary," *Aftenposten*, January 4, 1969. Johannes Borge, "Nordmenn i Kanada: Norway House" [Norwegians in Canada: Norway House], *Hjemmet* 23, no. 47 (1940): 3–5.

75. Henning Howlid Wærp, "Fridtjof Nansen, *First Crossing of Greenland* (1890): Bestseller and Scientific Report," in *Arctic Discourses*, ed. Anka Ryall, Johan Schimanski, and Henning Howlid Wærp (Newcastle upon Tyne: Cambridge Scholars Publishing, 2010), 43–44. This article is a valuable source of information about the 1888–1889 Nansen-led Greenland expedition.

76. Wærp, "Fridtjof Nansen," 43.

77. Ellen Rees, *Cabins in Modern Norwegian Literature: Negotiating Place and Identity* (Madison: Fairleigh Dickinson University Press, 2014), 83. Rees makes the point that Nansen contributed more than anyone else to this ideal's development.

78. Rees, *Cabins in Modern Norwegian Literature*, 85.

79. Rees, *Cabins in Modern Norwegian Literature*, 85.

80. The choice of this location and company was likely informed by Mortensen's familial connections: his eldest brother Bjarne worked for a time in Norway House and was married to manager Leif Sunde's sister. Though Mortensen does not mention Leif Sunde—an immigrant from Norway—in his text, Sunde appears in at least one of Mortensen's photos. The lives and work of the Sunde family are documented in home movies, a video, photographs, and travel accounts housed in the Archives of Manitoba.

81. Silje Solheim Karlsen, "Fangstmannsbiografien og heltelitteratur. Med et skråblikk på sjangeren: Wanny Wolstad, Henry Ette, Thorleif Bjertnes og Henry Rudi" [The hunter/trapper biography and hero literature. A new way of looking at the genre: Wanny Wolstad, Henry Ette, Thorleif Bjertnes and Henry Rudi], *Nordlit* 32 (2014): 1, https://doi.org/10.7557/13.3077. A number of the better known trapper and hunter biographies—including Wanny Wolstad's *Første kvinne som fangstmann på Svalbard* [The first woman trapper on Svalbard] (Oslo: Tanum, 1956), and Henry Rudi's *Isbjørnkongen* [Polar bear king] (Oslo: Gyldendal, 1958)—were published in the latter part of Einar Odd Mortensen's life.

82. Peter Elia, "Svalbard: In Search of Europe's Last Great Wilderness," *The Local*, November 2, 2019, https://www.thelocal.no/20191102/svalbard-europes-last-great-wilderness-norway/; "See the Sights of Svalbard, Europe's Last Wilderness," *Independent*, December 5, 2017, https://www.independent.co.uk/travel/visit-norway/see-sights-svalbard-europe-s-last-true-wilderness-a8019396.html.
83. In his seminal study, *The Idea of Wilderness*, ecological philosopher Max Oelschlaeger provides a survey of the wilderness concept over the millennia and emphasizes the need for carefully considering the "different, sometimes inconsistent, and even contradictory ideas of wilderness." Max Oelschlaeger, *The Idea of Wilderness: From Prehistory to the Age of Ecology* (New Haven: Yale University Press, 1991), 3.
84. For example, see William Cronon, "The Trouble with Wilderness: Or, Getting Back to the Wrong Nature," *Environmental History* 1, no. 1 (1996): 7–28.
85. Barbara Kelcey, *Alone in Silence: European Women in the Canadian North before World War II* (Montreal: McGill-Queen's University Press, 2001).
86. One of Mortensen's photos contains a picture of children on a sled in Norway House.
87. Cronon, "The Trouble with Wilderness," 14.
88. Liza Piper, "Knowing Nature through History," *History Compass* 11, no. 12 (2013): 1140.
89. Piper, 1141, 1145, passim.
90. Gregory Smithers, "Beyond the 'Ecological Indian': Environmental Politics and Traditional Ecological Knowledge in Modern North America," *Environmental History* 20, no. 1 (2015): 85–92.
91. Mortensen was married three times and had four children. His first wife was Astrid Heggenhaugen (m. 1930), his second wife was Anny Elle (m. 1944), and his third wife was Margaret Ulstrup Dahle (m. 1960). He had three children with Astrid and one child with Anny. The information here has been gleaned from published interviews with his oldest son, Einar Odd Mortensen Jr. (1933–2009), daughter Lise Nordhagen, and his daughter-in-law Gerd Kjustad Mortensen. The newspaper interviews are all cited later in this introduction.
92. Ivar Bae, "Landbrukslærlingen som ble pelshandler i Canada" [The farming apprentice who became a fur trader in Canada], *Ringsaker Blad*, April 21, 2007.
93. These terms are taken from Smith and Watson's discussion of "The Autobiographical 'I,'" in "A Tool Kit: Twenty Strategies for Reading Life Narratives." This chapter provides a wide variety of helpful strategies and questions to ask while reading life narratives. Sidonie Smith and Julia Watson, *Reading Autobiography: A Guide for Interpreting Life Narratives*, 2nd ed. (Minneapolis: University of Minnesota Press, 2010), 238–239.
94. Adventurer, writer, and ethnologist Thor Heyerdahl (1914–2002) is best known for his 1947 crossing of the Pacific Ocean from Peru to Polynesia on *Kon-Tiki*, a balsawood raft. Heyerdahl's book about this six-person expedition became an international bestseller, and a documentary film from the voyage received the 1951 Academy Award for Best Documentary Feature.
95. Mortensen, *Pelshandleren*, 12.
96. "10 største nettaviser" [10 largest online newspapers], *MedieNorge-Fakta om Norske Medier*, NORDICOM, November 26, 2018, http://www.medienorge.uib.no/statistikk/medium/avis/395; "Ti største papiraviser" [Ten largest print newspapers],

MedieNorge-Fakta om Norske Medier, NORDICOM, November 26, 2018, http://www.medienorge.uib.no/statistikk/medium/avis/353.

97. Jan Harbu, "Pelshander i Canada" [Fur trader in Canada], *Vi Menn*, 2007; Henrik Munthe, "Pelshandler i Canadas ødemark" [Fur trader in Canada's Wilderness], *Snø & Ski*, May 2007.
98. Lasse Stang, "Kom Ingstad i forkjøpet" [Preempted Ingstad], *Oppland Arbeiderblad*, April 3, 2007.
99. Per Haddal, "Pels, mygg og kulde" [Furs, mosquitoes and cold], *Aftenposten*, April 15, 2007.
100. Kåre Bulie, "Norsk pelshandlerprosa" [Norwegian fur trader prose], *Dagbladet*, April 9, 2007.
101. Bae, "Landbrukslærlingen som ble pelshandler i Canada."
102. Jon Michelet, "Mortensen i villmarka" [Mortensen in the wilderness], *Klassekampen*, April 13, 2007, 18–19. Michelet (1944–2018) was the senior editor of *Klassekampen* from 1997 to 2002.
103. Torstein Paulsen, "Verdt å vite spesial: *Pelshandleren*" [Worth knowing (special): *The Fur Trader*], Oslo: NRK, April 6, 2007.
104. Einar Odd Mortsensen, *Turkiskauppiaana intiaanireservaatissa* (Helsinki: Minerva, 2009).
105. Einar Haugen, "Language and Immigration," *Norwegian-American Studies and Records* 10 (1938), https://www.naha.stolaf.edu/pubs/nas/volume10/vol10_1.htm. Haugen's pre-1960 research and published works, including *Bilingualism in the Americas: A Bibliography and Research Guide*, are considered to have been instrumental in providing some of the groundwork for future research on code switching. See Einar Haugen, *Bilingualism in the Americas: A Bibliography and Research Guide* (Gainesville, FL: American Dialect Society, 1956); Jose Mercado, "Code Switching," in *Encyclopedia of Cross-Cultural School Psychology*, ed. C.S. Clauss-Ehlers, 2010 ed. (Boston: Springer, 2015), https://doi.org/10.1007/978-0-387-71799-9_74.
106. Though she was unable to visit the site due to hydroelectric development, Kjustad Mortensen was able to view the general area from the air.
107. To learn more about Rosalyn Ing's life and career, please refer to "In Memoriam—Dr. Rosalyn Ing" on the University of British Columbia's website: https://edst.educ.ubc.ca/in-memoriam-dr-rosalyn-ing/.
108. For a comprehensive study of Norwegian American literature, see Orm Øverland, *The Western Home: A Literary History of Norwegian America* (Northfield, MN: The Norwegian American Historical Association, 1996).
109. Janice Dickin, introduction to *Looking for Country: A Norwegian Immigrant's Alberta Memoir*, by Ellenor Ranghild Merriken (Calgary: University of Calgary Press, 1999), 6.
110. Odd Lovoll, *The Promise of America: A History of the Norwegian-American People* (Minneapolis: University of Minnesota Press, 1984), 8.
111. Knut Djupedal, "Report on the Returned Emigrant Project," in *Essays on Norwegian-American Literature and History Volume II*, eds. Øyvind Gulliksen, Ingeborg R. Kongslien, and Dina Tolfsby (Oslo: NAHA-Norge, 1990), 191.
112. It is impossible to determine the exact number of Norwegian immigrants in Canada during this period due to the nature of record keeping by the Department of

Citizenship and Immigration. For a look a migration trends during this time frame, refer to Gulbrand Loken, *From Fjord to Frontier: A History of the Norwegians in Canada* (Toronto: McClelland and Stewart, 1988), 223–226; Loken, "Norwegians."

1 | *North of the 53rd Parallel*

1. Here Mortensen uses the Norwegian term *skinn*. *Skinn* can be translated as hide, fur, or pelt. Both *skinn* and *pels*, another Norwegian word for fur or hide, are frequently used throughout the narrative.
2. Historically used in Canada to refer to First Nations individuals but considered offensive today. "Indian" still exists as a legal category under the Indian Act.
3. Located on the Saskatchewan River, The Pas is the home of the Opaskwayak Cree Nation. Around 1741 the La Verendyre established Fort Paskoyac in the area. Historical geographer Frank Tough argues the construction of a railway to the Pas in 1908 made it possible for independent traders to easily compete with the HBC. This view can be found as early as 1935 in the memoirs of fur trader Martin Hunter. Hunter, *Canadian Wilds*, 18; Opaskwayak Cree Nation, "History," *Opaskwayak Cree Nation*, October 23, 2018, http://opaskwayakcreenation.ca/history.html; The Pas Chamber of Commerce, *The Pas…A History: Adventure & Romance* (The Pas: The Pas Chamber of Commerce, 1970), 26, 63–80; Tough, 'As Their Natural Resources Fail,' 253.
4. Mortensen used both imperial and metric measurements in his original text, and we have chosen to be faithful to his original notations here. Norway adopted the metric system in 1875, so Mortensen grew up with it. His mixing of imperial and metric references appears to reflect his navigation of multiple cultures.
5. Here Mortensen uses the English word *greenhorn*, followed by its Norwegian equivalent *grønnskolling*. In the rest of the narrative he only uses *greenhorn*.
6. Established in 1670, the Hudson's Bay Company was making the transition to a regular retail company during this period in time. For more information on how this rebranding evolved, please see James Opp, "Branding 'the Bay/la Baie': Corporate Identity, the Hudson's Bay Company, and the Burden of History in the 1960s," *Canadian Historical Review* 96, no. 2 (2015): 223–256.
7. The Revillon family had been involved in the fur trade since 1723 as retailers in France. In the nineteenth century they moved to make fur not only fashionable but also affordable. To this end they opened a warehouse in Edmonton in 1899 and quickly expanded their business across Canada. In 1903, they established the Revillon Canada Far Northern Company, which became Revillon Brothers in 1904. In 1912, it was formally incorporated as Revillon Frères Trading Company Limited and was a rival of the Hudson's Bay Company until the Hudson's Bay Company began buying it out in 1926. According to Tough, the store in The Pas closed in 1923. Archives of Manitoba, "Hudson's Bay Company: Revillon Frère Trading Company," *Archives of Manitoba*, February 1, 2018, http://pam.minisisinc.com/scripts/mwimain.dll/144/PAM_AUTHORITY/AUTH_DESC_DET_REP/SISN%202044?sessionsearch; Ray, *The Canadian Fur Trade in the Industrial Age*, 92–93, 160–161; Tough, 'As Their Natural Resources Fail,' 251.
8. One of the last gold rushes to occur in western North America, the Klondike gold rush peaked in 1899 and led to the establishment of Yukon Territory in 1898. Perhaps more

importantly, it caught the public's imagination due to the fact it serves as the setting of numerous literary works by authors such as Jack London and Robert Service. Robert Jarvenpa examines how both authors laid the ground for modern tourism in the Klondike. Robert Jarvenpa, "Commoditization versus Cultural Integration: Tourism and Image Building in the Klondike," *Arctic Anthropology* 31, no. 1 (1994): 29.

9. In 1911, the Province of Manitoba closed the sturgeon fishery due to overfishing. Manitoba Hydro, *Lake Sturgeon in Manitoba: A Summary of Current Knowledge* (Winnipeg: Manitoba Hydro, 2016), 21.

10. Considered offensive today, it is unclear if Mortensen is referring to Métis individuals or Indigenous People with European ancestry when he uses this noun phrase. As mentioned in the introduction, although Mortensen's term and the term *Métis* are often equated to each other, the two terms are not synonymous and the presumption that they are reflects stereotypes surrounding the Métis. For a larger examination of what it means to be Métis, please see Andersen, *Métis*.

11. Originally totalling 8,128 acres, the original Pas reserve was located on both sides of the Saskatchewan River. Of the 1559.19 acres on the south side of the river, 500 acres were surrendered on August 21, 1906, followed by an additional 540 acres being sold in March 1913. Dominion of Canada, *Annual Report of the Department of Indian Affairs for the Year Ended June 30 1906* (Ottawa: S.E. Dawson, 1906), 88–89; Dominion of Canada, *Annual Report of the Department of Indian Affairs for the Year Ended 31 March 1907* (Ottawa: S.E. Dawson, 1907), 34; Dominion of Canada, *Annual Report of the Department of Indian Affairs for the Year Ended 31 March 1914* (Ottawa: J. de L. Taché, 1914), 46–47; Indian Claims Commission, "Opaskwayak Cree Nation: Streets and Lanes Inquiry," February 2007, Part II.

12. As the name suggests, reserves are quite literally parcels of land reserved for First Nations in Canada. Strictly speaking, they do not exist for the Inuit or Métis, although both groups do at times have their own land base. It should be noted that not every First Nation has a reserve, some First Nations have more than one reserve, and there is no standard reserve size in Canada. Furthermore, as historian George Stanley's 1950 article "The First Indian 'Reserves' in Canada" demonstrates, reserves were very much foundational to Indigenous policy in what became Canada. The end result has been that reserves play a complicated role for many First Nations as their land base on one hand, and as a tool of colonialism on the other. George Stanley, "The First Indian 'Reserves' in Canada," *Revue d'Histoire de l'Amerique Française* 4, no. 2 (1950): 178–210.

13. Mortensen provides the Norwegian word *pelsjeger*, immediately followed by the English equivalent *trapper*. This is the only time he uses the word *trapper* in the text.

14. Signs like the one Mortensen describes historically existed on the border of many reserves in Canada. Most have been taken down, but it depends on the community and their current bylaws, which might differ from adjacent jurisdictions.

15. In this paragraph Mortensen is directly challenging some of the stereotypes about Indigenous Peoples identified at the time as Indians. His comments about Indigenous poverty are problematic, but do reflect the outcomes of Canadian Indigenous policy at the time that either wanted to eliminate Indigenous Peoples through assimilation or death. See James Daschuk, *Clearing the Plains: Disease, Politics of Starvation, and the Loss of Indigenous Life* (Regina: University of Regina Press, 2013); Hugh Shewell, *'Enough*

to Keep Them Alive': Indian Social Welfare in Canada, 1873–1965 (Toronto: University of Toronto Press, 2004).

16. *Allez* means "Let's go!" or "Off you go!" in French. It is commonly used by dog mushers to get their teams moving.
17. Mortensen does not mention what language he and the Icelander used to communicate. Modern Icelandic and Norwegian are related but are not mutually intelligible. The Icelander may well have learned Danish if he had attended school in Iceland, since Danish was taught at most primary and other schools such as secondary schools once they were established in the second part of the nineteenth century. Danish and Norwegian are mutually intelligible. It is also possible Mortensen and the Icelander spoke English. Auður Hauksdóttir, "The Role of the Danish Language in Iceland," *Linguistik Online* 79, no. 5 (2016): http://dx.doi.org/10.13092/lo.79.3335.
18. Mortensen uses the English word *willow* in the original text, and explains that this is a type of *pil*, the Norwegian word for willow.
19. Mortensen uses the English *log-house* in his Norwegian account.
20. Cross-country skiing is closely linked to modern Norwegian national identity, and "*Nordmenn er født med ski på beina*" (Norwegians are born with skis on their feet) is a well-known Norwegian saying. For detailed information on the history of skiing in what is now Norway, a tradition dating back thousands of years, see Olav Bø, *På ski gjennom historia* [On skis through history] (Oslo: Det Norske Samlaget, 1993).
21. Commonly known simply as Hyers, this trading company flourished between 1875 and the Great Depression. Its founder, Hans Christian Hyer, died in 1922 and was remembered as John Hire by local residents. Tough, 'As Their Natural Resources Fail,' 251, 262; Manitoba, "Detailed Death Information: Registration Number 1922-022380," *Manitoba Vital Statistics Agency*, February 12, 2018, https://vitalstats.gov.mb.ca/DetailView.php.
22. Founded in 1918 with the merger of Riley-Ramsay Company and A. Macdonald Company, this food supply company was purchased in 1955 by George Weston Limited and became part of the Loblaw brand. Manitoba Historical Society, "Western Grocers Limited/Westfair Food Limited," *Manitoba Business*, February 12, 2018, http://www.mhs.mb.ca/docs/business/westerngrocers.shtml.
23. Easily confused with the Pine Bluff reserves in Saskatchewan that belong to Cumberland House Cree Nation—see the map in the Norwegian edition for example—this Pine Bluff was located about eighty kilometres southeast of The Pas on the Saskatchewan River. Martha McCarthy describes it as a Métis community in her 1992 report for Manitoba Hydro and the Pine Bluff Residents' Association, but also notes that most residents arrived between 1910 and 1940, and that many recalled finding evidence of prior settlement when they arrived. As she notes, the location was ideal as a settlement site and involvement in the fur trade. In what might seem paradoxical to some, she makes the argument that the residents were distinct from local First Nations and English-speaking Métis, while later on discussing their close connection to both groups in an imagined community. As mentioned in the introduction, although distinct, the Métis and First Nations were connected. Pine Bluff, Manitoba, was destroyed by flooding and environmental devastation caused by the Grand Rapids dam in the 1960s. Although much of the community remains

above water, its residents were forced to relocate without government compensation. Library and Archives Canada, "Finding Aid 10-12: Guide to Indian Bands and Agencies in Western Canada, 1871–1959" (Ottawa: Library and Archives Canada, n.d.), 56; McCarthy, *Pine Bluff*, 1–3, 11–12, 29–30, passim.

24. According to Arthur Ray, this simple fact was one of the reasons why Hudson's Bay Company district and post managers resisted attempts to restrict Indigenous credit. Ray, *The Canadian Fur Trade in the Industrial Age*, 87–88.
25. The winter coat of the stoat or short-tailed weasel.
26. Based on the location, this most likely refers to the "n" dialect of Cree, commonly known as Swampy Cree.

2 | *Alone at the Trading Post*

1. No doubt a reference to the consumption of chewing tobacco, dipping tobacco, or snus.
2. Traditional sled dogs were bred to be aggressive and hardy. Although they played an important role in Indigenous culture, and were cared for deeply, they were not pets in the modern sense of the word.
3. No Indian reserve existed at Pine Bluff. It would appear that Mortensen employed the faulty logic that any place where people identified as Indians live must be a reserve. Mortensen is not unique in employing this logic, and even today, when Google Maps accurately marks the location of reserves, some people challenge their accuracy. As noted earlier in this chapter, the 1992 report by Martha McCarthy states that Pine Bluff was a Métis community. Although it is almost certain that some of Mortensen's customers were Métis, it is also very likely that some of his customers were First Nations. We can make this assumption given the proximity of Pine Bluff to the Opaskwayak Cree Nation, combined with the fact that traplines were often off reserve. Greater precision is near impossible given what is in the text. It does not help that Mortensen does not provide any names. McCarthy, *Pine Bluff*, iv, 1.
4. *Gooshoo* appears to be Mortensen's transliteration of *kōsiw*, which is a contraction of *wēmistikōsiw*, the Swampy Cree word for someone identified as white.
5. Although it is a shining example of extractive colonialism, the fur trade in Canada developed certain conventions, such as negotiations and gifts, which gave Indigenous People limited agency. By this point in time, Mortensen's customers would have been familiar with these conventions and prepared to negotiate. Please see Arthur Ray, *Indians in the Fur Trade: Their Role as Trappers, Hunters, and Middlemen in the Lands Southwest of Hudson Bay, 1660–1870* (Toronto: University of Toronto Press, 1998); and White, "A Skilled Game of Exchange."
6. Although overcrowding is an issue on many reserves today, the communal nature of many First Nations complicates the matter. As a result, it is important not to draw too many conclusions from Mortensen's statement here, especially since the number twelve seems to be figurative.
7. A *stabbur* is a traditional Norwegian wooden storehouse that sits on pillars of stone or wood. These pillars—as well as a sizeable gap between the top of the last step and entrance—were designed to prevent mice, rats, and other animals from entering the building and damaging food and clothing. The use of *stabbur* was widespread in

8. Mortensen spells cache "cash."
9. Based on the fact this form of fishing was practised across Canada, and before the arrival of Icelanders, this comment appears to be incorrect. Mortensen seems aware of this reality, but nonetheless, like David Mandelbaum and Alanson Skinner, feels the need to report the claim that net fishing might have originated with Europeans. In doing so, he gives a nod to diffusion theory, without making any firm commitment. David Mandelbaum, *The Plains Cree: An Ethnographic, Historical, and Comparative Study* (Regina: University of Regina, 2012), 276; Alanson Skinner, *Notes on the Eastern Cree and Northern Saulteaux*, vol. ix, part 1, *Anthropological Papers of the American Museum of Natural History* (New York: Order of the Trustees, 1911), 137.
10. Skunks are not native to Norway, so it is not surprising Mortensen lacked basic knowledge about their behaviour.

3 | *From Camp to Church*

1. As evidenced by the following sentences, these trips were fairly extended seasonal affairs with the food and supplies mentioned referring to items not available at these hunting grounds. It should be noted that, although it is not entirely clear if the pass system was enforced on the "Pine Bluff reserve," it would appear that, given their northern location, it was not.
2. Mortensen uses the word *geitost* in his narrative. *Geitost* or *brunost*, as it is commonly called today, is still a staple of the Norwegian diet, often eaten on bread for breakfast, lunch, and/or an evening snack.
3. In making these statements, Mortensen is, perhaps unknowingly, falling into a common narrative of the fur trade that presented Indigenous consumption of goods as problematic and wasteful. See Mary Black-Rogers, "Varieties of 'Starving': Semantics and Survival in the Subarctic Fur Trade, 1750–1850," *Ethnohistory* 33, no. 4 (1986): 353–383; Elizabeth Vibert, *Trader's Tales: Narratives of Cultural Encounters in the Columbia Plateau, 1807–1846* (Norman: University of Oklahoma, 2000).
4. During this period in time, tuberculosis cases were increasing across Canada and would eventually peak in 1946 with 103.6 cases per one hundred thousand Canadians. Public Health Agency of Canada, *Tuberculosis in Canada, 2012* (Ottawa: Public Health Agency of Canada, 2015), https://www.canada.ca/en/public-health/services/infectious-diseases/tuberculosis-canada-2012.html.
5. Commonly known as the Wendigo or Windigo, this spirit was said to possess individuals, usually as a result of cannibalism.
6. An often-cited exchange rate, which although undoubtedly based on real events, was not universal.
7. Mortensen uses the English word *teepee* in his text.
8. Mortensen uses three Norwegian words for muskrat: the abbreviated term *rotte* or rat, *moskusrotte*, and *bisamrotte*. The translations in this English edition do not necessarily mirror Mortensen's usage. Here, for example, Mortensen uses the abbreviated *rotte* in the original.

9. More correctly spelled as *ēhē*, the Swampy Cree word for yes.
10. Though the Norwegian word *visdom* could arguably be translated as education in this context, this translation would not capture Mortensen's sarcastic tone. The quotation marks have been inserted by the editor. A smoother translation of the last line of this paragraph would be "if they receive an education," but this would not accurately capture Mortensen's tone either.
11. Although residential schools of Indigenous children existed prior to Confederation, it was not until 1883 that the federal government in conjunction with various Christian denominations began to operate its own residential schools. Official means to enforce mandatory attendance began to emerge in 1894 and culminated with an amendment to the Indian Act in 1920. Technically, they would remain until 2014, even though the last residential school closed in 1996. For a thorough history of the residential school system, please see the final report of the Truth and Reconciliation Commission. Bill c-428, *Indian Act Amendment and Replacement Act*, 2014; Truth and Reconciliation Commission of Canada, *Final Report of the Truth and Reconciliation Commission of Canada* (Winnipeg: Truth and Reconciliation Commission of Canada, 2015).
12. The muskrat was introduced to the Austro-Hungarian Empire in 1905 and is currently considered an invasive species in Europe. It did not reach Norway, however, until the 1980s. Gintare Skyriene and Algimantas Paulauskas, "Distribution of Invasive Muskrats (*Ondatra zibethicus*) and Impact on Ecosystem," *Ekologija* 58, no 3 (2012): 358.
13. Burial customs varied from nation to nation.
14. *Sámi* is the term that has replaced *Lapp*, now considered to be a derogatory term.
15. This paragraph highlights Mortensen's misunderstanding of Indigenous views on gratitude and sled dog care.
16. The Norwegian word is *tyttebær*. Picking wild berries was, at Mortensen's time, a popular outdoor activity in Norway, and it continues to be so today.
17. It is unclear how literal Mortensen is being in this paragraph. As with the previous section on sled dogs, it appears he misunderstands and is critiquing Indigenous views on sled dogs and their care.
18. This appears to be Mortensen's transliteration of *okimáw*, which means boss or chief. It can also be used to refer to white people, as a sign of respect and/or to refer to one's in-laws. Depending on the tone, this can be used sarcastically in much the same way as *boss* and/or *chief* can in English today.
19. Throughout his narrative, Mortensen uses the English term *old-timer*.

4 | *From Greenhorn to Old-Timer*

1. Here Mortensen is echoing the sentiment found in a well-known Norwegian proverb, "*Det finnes ikke dårlig vær, bare dårlige klær*" [There is no bad weather, only bad (inappropriate) clothing].
2. Boiled fish and potatoes were and are typical Norwegian foods, so it is understandable that Mortensen comments on the quality of these foods in his new environment.
3. The English term *spring pool* is used in the original.
4. Mortensen uses the English word *cash* in the original.
5. It is unclear why Mortensen came to this conclusion. It is similar to arguing non-Indigenous people do not trade among themselves because they purchase their

goods from a store rather than directly from the manufacturer. The entire matter is complicated by the credit system employed by many fur traders. Referred to as "debt peonage" by Frank Tough, fur trade companies used credit to maintain loyalty and compete with rival traders. According to Tough and others, the system also promoted dependency among Indigenous Peoples, which many scholars argue caused or contributed to underdevelopment and dependency in the contemporary period. Tough, 'As Their Natural Resources Fail,' 8–9, 273–276, 300–302, 309, passim; Arthur Ray, "Periodic Shortages, Native Welfare and the Hudson's Bay Company, 1670-1930," in *The Subarctic Fur Trade: Native Social and Economic Adaptations*, ed. Shepard Krech III (Vancouver: UBC Press, 1984); Shewell, 'Enough to Keep Them Alive,' 30, 32–36, 61, 67, 97–99, 124, passim.

6. Given the fluctuating cost of furs, another way of looking at this decision is that Mortensen's customers are hoping to maximize their profit. Indeed, some scholars have used Indigenous manipulation of the fur trade to argue dependency was limited or did not exist. See Eleanor Blain, "Dependency: Charles Bishop and the Northern Ojibwa," in *Aboriginal Resource Use in Canada: Historical and Legal Aspects*, ed. Kerry Abel and Jean Friesen (Winnipeg: University of Manitoba Press, 1991).

7. Traditionally a sign of interdependency among Indigenous Peoples, gift-giving was not only adopted by fur traders but, as seen in this passage, continued long after the traders had forgotten its significance. See Susan Brophy, "Reciprocity as Dispossession: A Dialectical Materialist Analysis of the Fur Trade," *Settler Colonial Studies* (2018): 6–9.

8. Mortensen uses the English phrase *catch and catch*.

9. This phrase appears to be Mortensen's transliteration of *mino-kīsikāw*.

10. *Misteet makeso* appears to be Mortensen's transliteration of *miscēt mahkēsiw(ak)*.

11. This appears to be Mortensen's transliteration of *nēma kiskēnimāw mōniyāw okimāw*, which strictly means that one is known as the white man. It is very similar to *nīna (ni) kiskēnimāw mōniyāw okimāw*, though, which means "I will know the white man," or "I am dying to do something to the white man."

12. This appears to be Mortensen's transliteration of *na-mimikonāw wīpac nēhēntamān, nimāh-mimikonāw wīpac nēhēntamān, nika-minwēnihtamawāw wīpac*, or something similar. All of these phrases refer to satisfying Mortensen.

13. Mortensen's apparent transliteration of *kēhcināt*.

14. This entire section might sound risqué to non-Indigenous readers, but at the risk of overgeneralizing Indigenous Peoples in what became Canada, it is important to note that most Indigenous Peoples have a wicked sense of humour, to the point where newcomers to an Indigenous community are told to expect to be bugged if people like them. As the Indigenous radio comedy *The Dead Dog Café Comedy Hour* indicates in its name, everything is open to joking, including sex. This willingness to joke about sex, however, does not necessarily indicate an actual desire for sex and/or consent.

15. Mortensen uses the Norwegian word *foreteelse*, which is most frequently translated as *phenomenon*. Mortensen's use of this word indicates that George Dane's visit was a colourful affair.

16. The Norwegian *buhund* is a medium-sized dog in the spitz family. It was originally bred in Norway, and is best known as a farm and herding dog.

17. It is not entirely clear whether these individuals told Mortensen all of this information, if he did some of his own research upon return to Norway, or if he assumed it. Often due to the pre-existing alliances and treaties, many Indigenous groups pledged their support to the imperial Crown when war was declared. Still more volunteered due to material incentives, both real and promised, as well as propaganda from their social network or the state. As a result, over a third of Indigenous males of military age fought for Canada, despite the fact that until December 1915 their enlistment was actively discouraged. See Talbot, "'It Would Be Best to Leave Us Alone,'" 100, 104, 108–116; Winegard, *For King and Kanata*, 6–11, passim.

5 | *Sons of the Wilderness*

1. A racist term for Indigenous Peoples in what is now known as North and South America, based on the rhetoric that each "race" had a different skin colour, either literally or figuratively. The common explanation is that it stemmed from Indigenous Peoples in the Americas wearing red paint and/or pigment, although there are competing theories of origin. Much of the contemporary scholarship deals with the Washington Football Team and their use of the term in their name prior to July 2020. See James Fenelon, *Redskins? Sports Mascots, Indian Nations and White Racism* (New York: Routledge, 2017); C. Richard King, *Redskins: Insult and Brand* (Lincoln: University of Nebraska Press, 2016); Nancy Shoemaker, "How Indians Got To Be Red," *The American Historical Review* 102, no. 3 (1997): 625–644.

2. James Fenimore Cooper's *The Leatherstocking Tales*, a series of five novels, were published between 1823 and 1841. Mortensen refers to two of these—*The Last of the Mohicans* (1826) and *The Deerslayer* (1841)—in this passage, as well as to one of the major characters in four of the novels, namely Chingachgook. Note Mortensen's misspelling. These books were first translated into Norwegian in 1909, so Mortensen would have read Norwegian translations of them. Fenimore Cooper repeatedly refers to the happy, glorious, and/or blessed hunting grounds while discussing Indigenous views on the afterlife. At best it is a simplification of actual Indigenous beliefs and by no means universal. "Hva kunne barn og unge lese i 1905?" [What could children and young people read in 1905?] *Bergen Offentlige Bibliotek*, December 15, 2018, https://bergenbibliotek.no/barn/tips-og-nytt/barn-tema-1905.

3. A noted Hunkpapa Lakota leader who was famously involved in the Battle of the Greasy Grass/the Battle of the Little Bighorn in 1876. He was later involved in Buffalo Bill's Wild West show.

4. Old Waverly was a fictional character found in German children's books during the early twentieth century. Kaspar Maase, *Die Kinder Der Massenkultur: Kontroversen um Schmutz und Schund Seit Dem Kaiserreich* [The children of mass culture: controversies about filth and rubbish since the German empire] (Frankfurt: Campus Verlag, 2012), 267–268. Mortensen's comment reveals these texts were translated into Norwegian as well.

5. The above section evokes a number of stereotypes about Indigenous People. It is fitting that Mortensen mentions the fictional *Last of the Mohicans* and *The Deerslayer*, books that not only appropriated Mohegan history and culture but also employed the noble savage, savage, ecological Indian, and vanishing Indian tropes. Numerous scholars

have studied these books, but an important thing to bear in mind, as Daniel Francis put so eloquently, is for "travelers whose imaginations had been nurtured on the paintings of Catlin and Kane and the novels of Fenimore Cooper...actual Native people could not hope to measure up to the standards set by art." J. Fenimore Cooper, *The Last of the Mohicans: A Narrative of 1757*, new ed., vol. 1–2 (New York: Stringer and Townsend, 1852); Francis, *The Imaginary Indian*, 44; Thomas King, *The Inconvenient Indian: A Curious Account of People in North America* (New York: Doubleday, 2012); Paige Raibmon, *Authentic Indians: Episodes of Encounter from the Late-Nineteenth-Century Northwest Coast* (Durham: Duke University Press, 2005).

6. It is unclear if Mortensen was aware that Plains (or Prairie) Indians were the source of many of these stereotypes.

7. A fairly common practice with some flagship events, including Banff Indian Days and the Calgary Stampede. See Susan Joundrey, "Hidden Authority, Public Display: Representations of First Nations People at the Calgary Stampede, 1912–1970" (PhD diss., Carleton University, 2013); Courtney Mason, "The Construction of Banff as a 'Natural' Environment: Sporting Festivals, Tourism, and Representations of Aboriginal Peoples," *Journal of Sport History* 35, no. 2 (2008): 221–239.

8. The exonym *Cree* denotes the largest Indigenous Nation in Canada, with multiple dialects, cultural practices, and ways of life, depending on where they live. Based on the location of the two trading posts Mortensen worked at, Pine Bluff and Oxford House, it is likely he primarily worked with the Swampy Cree, although as mentioned it is possible many of his customers were actually Métis. It is important to bear in mind that Mortensen is recounting his own impressions of the Cree groups he encountered while in Canada, which may have included Plains Cree, Woods Cree, Rocky Cree, and/or Swampy Cree.

9. "The Oslo Breakfast" was first introduced in 1926 at Sandaker outdoors school for physically weak children. By 1932, this breakfast was offered at all Oslo schools, and the program gradually spread to schools around Norway and in many other countries where it was popular in the 1930s and 1940s. "Skolemåltidets historie" [History of the school meal], *Skolefrukt*, December 15, 2018, https://www.skolefrukt.no/om-skolefruktordningen/skolemaltidets-historie.html.

10. This statement is logical since these clothes are often worn for festive events.

11. It is unclear how serious Mortensen is in making this statement, or how he would "know" this detail. It does, however, fit into larger perceptions of Indigenous Peoples as unclean due to the simple fact that they are Indigenous, especially when one considers the next paragraph and other sections of the text. James D. Waldram, Ann Herring, and T. Kue Young, *Aboriginal Health in Canada: Historical, Cultural, and Epidemiological Perspectives*, 2nd ed. (Toronto: University of Toronto Press, 2007), 183, 196. For additional reading, see Alison Bashford, *Imperial Hygiene: A Critical History of Colonialism, Nationalism and Public Health* (New York: Palgrave MacMillan, 2004); Mary-Ellen Kelm, *Colonizing Bodies: Aboriginal Health and Healing in British Columbia, 1900–50* (Vancouver: University of British Columbia Press, 1998); Maureen Lux, *Medicine That Walks: Disease, Medicine and Canadian Plains Native People, 1880–1940* (Toronto: University of Toronto Press, 2001); Roy MacLeod and Milton James, eds., *Disease,*

Medicine, and Empire: Perspectives on Western Medicine and the Experience of European Expansion (London: Routledge, 1988).

12. This is one of only a few instances in which Mortensen names an Indigenous individual in his text. Please see the discussion about "the unnamed Indian" in the introduction.
13. The perception that Indigenous men are not physically strong and/or are lazy is still a common stereotype in popular perceptions of Indigenous Peoples. Both are contradicted not only on this page but also in other sections of this text. Goodyear, "The Narratives of Sitting Bull's Surrender," 36–37.
14. Not to be confused with modern-day Nipigon. Nipigon House was located northwest of present-day Nipigon on the western shore of Lake Nipigon.
15. This English phrase and the quotation marks appear in the Norwegian text.
16. Species of these mammals—mink, otter, beaver, fox, lynx, and marten—are all indigenous to Norway. This could well be why Mortensen focuses on them here. While the American mink is now widespread in Norway, the European mink is critically endangered and is no longer found there.
17. Mortensen uses the Norwegian term *potetbrenneriet*.
18. In 1868, the federal government prohibited "the sale or barter of liquor" to status Indians. Six years later it was made a specific criminal offence for a status Indian to be publicly intoxicated. Both restrictions would be included in the first Indian Act and would continue in subsequent versions until the 1951 Indian Act, which contained provisions for provincial liquor laws to prevail off reserve. Wendy Moss and Elaine Gardner-O'Toole, "Aboriginal People: History of Discriminatory Laws," May 4, 2018, http://publications.gc.ca/Collection-R/LoPBdP/BP/bp175-e.htm.
19. As many scholars and Indigenous activists have noted, the Chief and council system was often imposed by Indian Affairs, who used it to their own advantage. See Vic Satzewich and Linda Mahood, "Indian Affairs and Band Governance: Deposing Indian Chiefs in Western Canada, 1896–1911," *Canadian Ethnic Studies* 26, no. 1 (1994): 40–58.
20. Mortensen uses the English words *the Indian agent* in his account. He accurately describes their role, especially in comparison to the Chief. For additional information on Indian agents, see Robin Brownlie, *A Fatherly Eye: Indian Agents, Government Power, and Aboriginal Resistance in Ontario, 1918–1939* (Oxford: Oxford University Press, 2003); John Steckley, *Indian Agents: Rulers of the Reserve* (New York: Peter Lang, 2016); Brian Titley, *The Indian Commissioners: Agents of the State and Indian Policy in Canada's Prairie West, 1873–1932*, 1st ed. (Edmonton: University of Alberta Press, 2009).
21. The number of counsellors varies from band to band.
22. It is not entirely clear what "past" or "customs" Mortensen is referring to.
23. Once again Mortensen uses the English term.
24. It would appear this "tax" is not official. It is important to note, however, that neither the 1924 nor the 1927 Indian Act provided a tax exemption, except on reserve. As historian Shirley Tillotson points out in her book, *Give and Take*, during this period there was disagreement regarding the exact nature of this exemption and what exactly it covered. Shirley Tillotson, *Give and Take: The Citizen-Taxpayer and the Rise of Canadian Democracy* (Vancouver: UBC Press, 2017), chapter 5, passim.

25. Mortensen uses the term *allfader*, an apparent reference to the Old Norse god Odin, known as *Alfödr* (Old Norse) or *All-father*.
26. It is not clear how extensive Mortensen's knowledge of Indigenous spiritual beliefs was. The Swampy Cree of the region believed in a Great Spirit and were far from passive when it came to spiritual matters. For more information see Louis Bird, *The Spirits in the Mind: Omushkego Stories, Lives, and Dreams*, ed. Susan Gray (Montreal: McGill-Queen's University Press, 2007).
27. It is important to bear in mind that many Cree speakers challenge the claim that Evans invented syllabics. See Lesley Crossingham, "Cultural Director Says Missionaries Didn't Invent Syllabics, Indians Did," *Windspeaker* 5, no. 21 (1987).
28. It is unclear where Mortensen got this information from, but anyone fluent in a Cree dialect knows that swear words exist.
29. It is not entirely clear where Mortensen got this information. It appears to refer to the myth that the Cree only moved west after contact. As anthropologist James Smith points out, however, there is no evidence for this myth. See James Smith, "The Western Wood Cree: Anthropological Myth and Historical Reality," *American Ethnologist* 14, no. 3 (1987): 434–448.
30. Mortensen calls this "the mokasin wire."
31. Mortensen uses the English term *treaty*, followed by the Norwegian term *ting*, which could be translated as assembly. The *ting* was a term that originated in the Scandinavian Middle Ages and was used for a regional assembly of free men that had both legislative and judicial functions. The modern Norwegian parliament (legislative function only) is called *Stortinget* (the Big Assembly). "Treaty"-et (the Treaty) has been translated as "the treaty assembly" later in this text.
32. It appears Mortensen is referring to the annual payment of annuities, an event that still exists today for those Indigenous groups who signed a treaty that contains provisions for them.
33. This section is a good example of the colonial view that the only authentic Indigenous culture was one unaffected by outside influence. It ignores the fact that cultures are ever evolving and change over time and in doing so presents authentic "Indians" as being stuck in the past and unchanging. Paige Raibmon examines this view and its continuance into the present day in her book; see Raibmon, *Authentic Indians*.
34. This section is a good example of the contradictory colonial view that, although "superior" to nonwhite cultures, white culture was considered to be weaker. According to this view, unless steps were taken to prevent it, white culture was in danger of being assimilated by nonwhite cultures. In reference to Mortensen's earlier comments regarding the "prohibition" between romantic relationships with Indigenous women, it was often feared that such relationships would result in this loss of white culture, not only for the man but also for the children. For a further examination of how gender and race interacted with each other in a colonial situation, see Perry, *On the Edge of Empire*.

35. Though this is a commonly held romanticized view of Indigenous Peoples, such a state of affairs never existed.

6 | *Hudson's Bay versus Free Trader*

1. Mortensen uses this English phrase in his account.
2. As can be seen from the title of this chapter and this sentence, Mortensen and/or the original Norwegian editors do not see the Hudson's Bay Company in the best light. This sentiment should be noted when reading through the rest of this chapter.
3. Charles II is listed as Karl II in the original text.
4. Though Mortensen used these quotation marks in his original manuscript, he did not record where he retrieved this information.
5. Adam Gaudry wonderfully deconstructs claims of Hudson's Bay Company sovereignty in Adam Gaudry, "Fantasies of Sovereignty: Deconstructing British and Canadian Claims to Ownership of the Historic North-West," *Native American and Indigenous Studies* 3, no. 1 (2016): 46–74.
6. The colonial governments of Upper and Lower Canada had little to no say regarding the matter.
7. The official transfer occurred on June 23, 1870, due to the Red River Resistance.
8. This statement is dependent on how you define "rise up." For example, in 1823 local Indigenous people wiped out Fort St. John. This event could be considered a rising. If you define rising up as a general insurrection, then that never happened.
9. By American, Mortensen is referring to what is now the United States of America. Norwegians still tend to use the term *America(n)* to refer to the United States.
10. Arguably, the most common form of relief was via credit, but other forms existed as well. Following Confederation, the Hudson's Bay Company began to move away from independently providing relief, although it still helped the federal government in providing aid. Ray, "Periodic Shortages, Native Welfare, and the Hudson's Bay Company, 1670-1930," 10–17. For a history of how this transition is believed to have led to contemporary dependency in some Indigenous communities, see Shewell, *'Enough to Keep Them Alive.'*
11. A common slur used to denounce European men who formed anything close to an actual relationship with Indigenous women. This expression, as well as "the bush takes him," appear in English in the original.
12. Mortensen uses the Norwegian term *gjenstand*, which actually means thing or object. This is a very strange passage. Painting the man blue may refer to giving him a severe beating.

7 | *Towards New Hunting Grounds*

1. Oxford House, Manitoba, is a village of the Bunibonibee (Oxford House) Cree Nation. Located on the Hayes River, which until the advent of the railway was a major transportation route in this part of the world, the Hudson's Bay Company initially established a supply depot here in 1798. Soon, however, it became a trading post and the company's successor company, the North West Company, currently operates a Northern Store in the community. Mortensen never uses the name Oxford House in his narrative, referring only to Oxford Lake. Christopher Hanks maintains the

Bunibonibee Cree Nation moved to the location after the supply depot was opened. It should be noted, however, that this claim does not mean they did not live in the area and has more to do with Hanks's understanding of a semi-nomadic lifestyle. Christopher Hanks, "The Swampy Cree and the Hudson's Bay Company at Oxford House," *Ethnohistory* 29, no. 2 (1982): 103, passim.

2. Outposts were generally smaller, often semi-permanent, trading posts associated with larger permanent ones. Given that Mortensen was working for an independent trading company it is unclear where this outpost was located exactly.

3. This length of time can be misleading to modern readers. Unlike highways, the Hayes River meanders and therefore more time is spent on the water than one would expect.

4. Norway House was named after the Norwegian axemen charged with cutting a road from Lake Winnipeg to York Factory in the early 1800s. The original Norway House was located on Lake Winnipeg itself. It was relocated to its current location in 1826 following a fire, and would become an important trading post of the HBC. In 1875, Treaty 5 was signed at this location with the Saulteaux and Swampy Cree. A 1940 article in the magazine *Hjemmet* examined the continued Norwegian presence at Norway House and indeed the entire fur trade. Among the individuals featured in it was H.C. Hyer. When he passed away in 1922, his partner Leif Sunde took over management of the H.C. Hyer Company, a position he would continue to hold until it was sold to the Hudson's Bay Company in 1938. See Archives of Manitoba, "Leif and John Sunde fonds," Archives of Manitoba, March 24, 2021, http://pam.minisisinc.com/scripts/mwimain.dll/144/PAM_DESCRIPTION/WEB_DESC_DET_REP/REFD%20%2218755%22?SESSIONSEARCH; Archives of Manitoba, "Sunde, Leif," Archives of Manitoba, March 24, 2021, http://pam.minisisinc.com/scripts/mwimain.dll/144/PAM_AUTHORITY/AUTH_DESC_DET_REP/SISN%202425?sessionsearch; Borge, "Nordmenn i Kanada"; Parks Canada, "Norway House Historic Site of Canada," *Canada's Historic Places*, March 24, 2021, https://www.historicplaces.ca/en/rep-reg/place-lieu.aspx?id=12401; Parks Canada, "Norway House National Historic Site of Canada," *Directory of Federal Heritage Designations*, March 24, 2021, https://www.pc.gc.ca/apps/dfhd/page_nhs_eng.aspx?id=125; George Penner, "Historic Sites of Manitoba: Norway House Plaques (Norway House, Northern Manitoba)," *Manitoba Historical Society*, December 20, 2018, http://www.mhs.mb.ca/docs/sites/norwayhouse.shtml.

5. Though Norwegian American Ole Evinrude is often given credit for inventing the outboard motor, historian Kenneth Bjørk more accurately describes him as the "inventor of the first practical outboard motor," which was first produced in 1909. Evinrude was born in Norway and immigrated to Wisconsin with his family when he was five years old. Kenneth Bjørk, "Ole Evinrude and the Outboard Motor," *Norwegian-American Studies and Records* 12 (1941): 168, 172.

6. This appears to be Mortensen's transliteration of *kihci-okimāw*.

7. Mortensen does not explain why he thinks the cabin and/or the dogs are abandoned.

8. Although water bombers existed as early as the 1920s, the first practical design did not exist until the 1950s. Stephan Wilkinson, "Firebombers!" *Aviation History* 28, no. 4 (2018): 32–35.

9. Mortensen uses the English term *muskeg* throughout the text. To cite the *Oxford English Dictionary*, muskeg is "a swamp or bog consisting of a mixture of water and partly dead vegetation, often covered by a layer of sphagnum or other mosses." The OED notes it is a term most commonly used in Canada. See "muskeg, n.," *Oxford English Dictionary Online*, December 2021, https://www-oed-com.prxy.lib.unbc.ca/view/Entry/124156?redirectedFrom=muskeg.
10. Named after York Factory, the York boat was "based on an old Orkney design, that in turn derived from the Viking longship. [T]he boats were built by Orkneymen recruited by the Company specifically for their boat building skills." Capable of carrying "more than three tons," they dominated trade in western Canada until the railway arrived. Hudson's Bay Company, "York Boat," *Hudson's Bay Company History Foundation*, December 20, 2018, http://www.hbcheritage.ca/things/technology/the-york-boat.
11. Based on Mortensen's description of this portage being at the height of land, he is referring to Painted Stone Portage. Similar car systems were used as major portages. Indeed, Anthony Dalton describes a similar rail system at the "Longest Portage," a.k.a. Robinson Portage, in his book, *River Rough, River Smooth*. Anthony Dalton, *River Rough, River Smooth: Adventures on Manitoba's Historic Hayes River* (Toronto: Natural Heritage Books, 2010), 109–114, passim; Manitoba Geographic Names Program, "Geographic Names of Manitoba," July 30, 2018, http://www.gov.mb.ca/sd/lands_branch/geo_names/document/cdgnm.pdf.
12. The Devil's Fall appears to be Hell Gate, which was also historically known as Devil's Gate and/or Wetikoweskwattam, which means Devil's Doorway. Mortensen uses the English name. Manitoba Geographic Names Program, "Geographic Names of Manitoba."
13. It is unclear which lake Mortensen is referring to. It does not help that the names of many lakes were changed in the interwar period. See Manitoba Geographic Names Program, "Geographic Names of Manitoba." As is his practice, Mortensen uses the English name for this natural formation, though in the following paragraphs he uses a Norwegian translation—*Rottesjøen*.
14. As Mortensen indicates, the northern (Finnmark) and interior (Røros is one example) regions of Norway have the highest mosquito populations in his home country. As the following sections demonstrate, however, Mortensen is convinced there is no comparison with the situation in northern Canada.
15. While there are some traditional mosquito repellents that Indigenous People used, body odour was not one of them. This sentence highlights the racist views Mortensen held. Sarah Moore and Mustapha Debboun, "History of Insect Repellents," in *Insect Repellents: Principles, Methods, and Uses*, ed. Mustapha Debboun, Stephen Frances, and Daniel Strickman (New York: CRC Press, 2007), 4–5.

8 | *Days at Oxford Lake*

1. This English phrase appears in the original text.
2. This appears to be a reference to the scientific management theory developed by Frederick Winslow Taylor (1856–1915), an American mechanical engineer often called the "Father of Scientific Management." Taylor's principles were developed to maximize efficiency in the performance of specific tasks. For more detail, see Hakan

Turan, "Taylor's 'Scientific Management Principles': Contemporary Issues in Personnel Selection Period," *Journal of Economics, Business and Management* 3, no. 11 (2015): 1102–1105.

3. *Vår Herre*—translated into English as "Our Lord"—is a phrase that occurs in a number of Scandinavian "Origin and Hope for Salvation" narratives from the oral tradition, classified at times as legends and other times as religious folktales. Reimund Kvideland and Henning K. Sehmsdorf, eds., *Scandinavian Folk Belief and Legend* (Minneapolis: University of Minnesota Press, 1988), 205–206. Einar's contemporaries would have been familiar with this phrase and context.

4. Einar uses both the English word *whitefish* and the Norwegian equivalent *hvitfisken* in his account.

5. The spellings and quotation marks are from the Norwegian text.

6. The English term *scaffold* appears throughout the Norwegian text.

7. Einar uses three terms for runner: the English word *runner*, and the Norwegian words *løpegutt* (running boy) and *forløper* (forerunner).

8. This harbour was connected to two failed Hudson's Bay Company forts in the area. Port Nelson is located on the mouth of the Nelson River and was chosen to be the terminus of the Hudson Bay Railway in 1912. Work continued until 1918, when expenses combined with low wheat prices and a lack of support led to the project being put on hold. It would remain on hold until 1927, when Churchill was selected as the terminus and Port Nelson was completely abandoned. Hudson's Bay Company, "York Factory," *Hudson's Bay Company History Foundation*, July 30, 2018, http://www.hbcheritage.ca/places/forts-posts/york-factory; David Malaher, "Port Nelson and the Hudson Bay Railway," *Manitoba History*, no. 8 (1984); Manitoba Geographic Names Program, "Geographic Names of Manitoba."

9. It is unclear what Mortensen means by the Hudson Bay Indians. It is likely he is referring to the Denésoliné, but he could be unknowingly talking about another Cree group.

10. Mortensen uses the English phrase *barrel-chested*.

11. A historic exonym for the Indigenous Peoples of the Arctic, commonly known as the Inuit or Yupik. Today it is considered offensive. A big reason is the potential etymology of the word stemming from the Anishinaabe word for "eaters of raw meat." It should be noted, however, that etymologists are still debating whether or not this is true. See E. Benveniste, "The 'Eskimo' Name," *International Journal of American Linguistics* 19, no. 3 (1953): 242–245; Zach Parrott, "Eskimo," *The Canadian Encyclopedia*, Historica Canada, April 11, 2021, https://www.thecanadianencyclopedia.ca/en/article/eskimo.

12. Stavanger is on the southwestern coast of Norway. The first group of emigrants from Norway to North America in modern times sailed from Stavanger on July 4, 1825, on the sloop *Restauration*.

13. Located at the mouth of the Hayes River, York Factory was established by the Hudson's Bay Company in 1784 and served as the de facto headquarters of the HBC in North America. Manitoba Geographic Names Program, "Geographic Names of Manitoba."

14. The English words *rabbit robe* appear in the original text.

15. Mortensen uses *harnessen* in the original, blending Norwegian (*en*—a definite article) and English (harness).

16. Mortensen used *neger* (negro) in his notes, and it also appears in the Norwegian publication. This word was in widespread use in Norway during Mortensen's time to describe a Black person and was not considered to be offensive. Today it has racist connotations.

Epilogue

1. Kirke- og Undervisningdepartementet, *Endringer i Rettskrivningen og Læreboknormalen for Bokmål: Stortingsmelding nr. 100, 1980–81* [Changes in (the) spelling and textbook standards for (the written language) bokmål: parliamentary white paper nr. 100, 1980–81] (Oslo: Kirke- og Undervisningdepartementet, 1981).
2. Borge, "Nordmenn i Kanada."
3. There are two different rivers called Piskominahikoska. The river mentioned here is not the better-known Piskominahikoska River, which is located further north in Manitoba.

Reading Guide and Discussion Questions

1. Henning Howlid Wærp, *Arktisk litteratur—fra Fridtjof Nansen til Anne B. Ragde* [Arctic literature—from Fridtjof Nansen to Anne B. Ragde] (Stamsund, Norway: Orkana, 2017), 124.

Bibliography

Primary Sources

Baker, Peter. *Memoirs of an Arctic Arab: A Free Trader in the Canadian North: The Years 1907–1927.* Saskatoon: Yellowknife Publishing Co., 1976.

Bill C-428. *Indian Act Amendment and Replacement Act.* 2014.

Black, Samuel. *A Journal of a Voyage from Rocky Mountain Portage in Peace River to the Sources of Finlays Branch and North West Ward in Summer 1824.* Edited by E.E. Rich. London: The Hudson's Bay Record Society, 1955.

Boulanger, Tom. *An Indian Remembers: My Life as a Trapper in Northern Manitoba.* Winnipeg: Peguis Publishers, 1971.

Canada. *House of Commons Debates*, May 5, 1883, 1107–1108 (John A. Macdonald, Prime Minister).

Cooper, James Fenimore. *The Last of the Mohicans: A Narrative of 1757.* New edition. Volumes 1–2. New York: Stringer and Townsend, 1852.

Cooper, James Fenimore, and H. Daniel Peck. *The Deerslayer.* Oxford: Oxford University Press, 1993.

Dickin, Janice. Introduction to *Looking for Country: A Norwegian Immigrant's Alberta Memoir*, by Ellenor Ranghild Merriken, 5–33. Calgary: University of Calgary Press, 1999.

Dominion of Canada. *Annual Report of the Department of Indian Affairs for the Year Ended June 30 1906.* Ottawa: S.E. Dawson, 1906.

———. *Annual Report of the Department of Indian Affairs for the Year Ended 31 March 1907.* Ottawa: S.E. Dawson, 1907.

———. *Annual Report of the Department of Indian Affairs for the Year Ended 31 March 1914.* Ottawa: J. de L. Taché, 1914.

Fraser, Simon. *The Letters and Journals of Simon Fraser, 1806–1808.* Edited by W. Kaye Lamb. Toronto: Dundurn Press, 2007.

Hunter, Martin. *Canadian Wilds: Tells about the Hudson's Bay Company, Northern Indians and Their Modes of Hunting, Trapping, Etc.* Columbus, OH: A.R. Harding, 1935.

Ingstad, Helge. *The Land of Feast and Famine.* Translated by Eugene Gay-Tifft. New York: Alfred A. Knopf, 1933.

———. *Pelsjegerliv blandt Nord-Kanadas indianere* [Life as a trapper among the Indians of northern Canada]. Oslo: Gyldendal, 1931.

Kemp, H.S.M. *Northern Traders: The Last Days of the Fur Trade.* Regina: University of Regina Press, 2014.

Kirke- og Undervisningdepartementet. *Endringer i Rettskrivningen og Læreboknormalen for Bokmål: Stortingsmelding nr. 100, 1980–81* [Changes in (the) spelling and textbook standards for (the written language) bokmål: parliamentary white paper nr. 100, 1980–81]. Oslo: Kirke- og Undervisningdepartementet, 1981.

Mackenzie, Alexander. *The Journals and Letters of Sir Alexander Mackenzie.* Edited by W. Kaye Lamb. Cambridge: University of Cambridge Press, 1970.

———. *Voyages from Montreal on the River St. Laurence, Through the Continent of North America to the Frozen and Pacific Oceans; In the Years 1789 and 1793 with a Preliminary Account of the Rise, Progress and Present State of the Fur Trade of that Country.* London: R. Noble, 1801.

Manitoba. "Detailed Death Information: Registration Number 1922-022380." Manitoba Vital Statistics Agency. February 12, 2018. https://vitalstats.gov.mb.ca/DetailView.php.

Monsen, Lars. *Nådeløs villmark: Canada på tvers* [Merciless wilderness: across Canada]. Oslo: Lars Monsen Outdoors, 2002.

Mortensen, Einar Odd. *Pelshandleren: Mitt liv blant indianere i Nord-Canada 1925–28* [The fur trader: my life among Indians in northern Canada, 1925–28]. Oslo: Gyldendal, 2007.

———. *Turkiskauppiaana intiaanireservaatissa* [A fur trader on an Indian reservation]. Helsinki: Minerva, 2009.

"Person: Einar Odd Mortensen—Emigrants from Oslo 1867–1930." *The Digital Archives.* November 22, 2018. http://www.digitalarkivet.no/en/view/8/pe00000000562579.

Rudi, Henry. *Isbjørnkongen* [Polar bear king]. Oslo: Gyldendal, 1958.

Wolstad, Wanny. *Første kvinne som fangstmann på Svalbard* [The first woman trapper on Svalbard]. Oslo: Tanum, 1956.

Secondary Sources

"10 største nettaviser" [10 largest online newspapers]. *MedieNorge-Fakta om Norske Medier*, NORDICOM. November 26, 2018. http://www.medienorge.uib.no/statistikk/medium/avis/395.

Adese, Jennifer, and Chris Andersen, eds. *A People and a Nation: New Directions in Contemporary Métis Studies.* Vancouver: UBC Press, 2021.

Andersen, Chris. *Métis: Race, Recognition, and the Struggle for Indigenous Peoplehood.* Vancouver: UBC Press, 2014.

Archives of Manitoba. "Hudson's Bay Company Archives." *Archives of Manitoba.* October 4, 2018. https://www.gov.mb.ca/chc/archives/hbca/.

———. "Hudson's Bay Company: Revillon Frère Trading Company." *Archives of Manitoba.* February 1, 2018. http://pam.minisisinc.com/scripts/mwimain.dll/144/PAM_AUTHORITY/AUTH_DESC_DET_REP/SISN%202044?sessionsearch.

———. "Leif and John Sunde Fonds." Archives of Manitoba. March 24, 2021. http://pam.minisisinc.com/scripts/mwimain.dll/144/PAM_DESCRIPTION/WEB_DESC_DET_REP/REFD%20%2218755%22?SESSIONSEARCH.

———. "Sunde, Leif." Archives of Manitoba. March 24, 2021. http://pam.minisisinc.com/scripts/mwimain.dll/144/PAM_AUTHORITY/AUTH_DESC_DET_REP/SISN%202425?sessionsearch.

Bae, Ivar. "Landbrukslærlingen som ble pelshandler i Canada" [The farming apprentice who became a fur trader in Canada]. *Ringsaker Blad.* April 21, 2007.

Barker, Martin, and Roger Sabin. *The Lasting of the Mohicans: History of an American Myth.* Jackson: University Press of Mississippi, 1995.

Bashford, Alison. *Imperial Hygiene: A Critical History of Colonialism, Nationalism and Public Health.* New York: Palgrave MacMillan, 2004.

Bell, Leonard. *Colonial Constructs: European Images of Maori, 1840-1914.* Auckland: Auckland University Press, 1992.

Benveniste, E. "The 'Eskimo' Name." *International Journal of American Linguistics* 19, no. 3 (1953): 242-245.

Bird, Elizabeth. "Introduction: Constructing the Indian, 1830s-1990s." In *Dressing in Feathers: The Construction of the Indian in American Popular Culture*, edited by Elizabeth Bird, 1-12. Boulder: Westview Press, 1996.

———. "Not My Fantasy: The Persistence of Indian Imagery in *Dr. Quinn, Medicine Woman.*" In *Dressing in Feathers: The Construction of the Indian in American Popular Culture*, edited by Elizabeth Bird, 245-262. Boulder: Westview Press, 1996.

Bird, Louis. *The Spirits in the Mind: Omushkego Stories, Lives, and Dreams.* Edited by Susan Gray. Montreal: McGill-Queen's University Press, 2007.

Bjørk, Kenneth. "Ole Evinrude and the Outboard Motor." *Norwegian-American Studies and Records* 12 (1941): 167-177.

Black-Rogers, Mary. "Varieties of 'Starving': Semantics and Survival in the Subarctic Fur Trade, 1750-1850." *Ethnohistory* 33, no. 4 (1986): 353-383.

Blain, Eleanor. "Dependency: Charles Bishop and the Northern Ojibwa." In *Aboriginal Resource Use in Canada: Historical and Legal Aspects*, edited by Kerry Abel and Jean Friesen, 93-106. Winnipeg: University of Manitoba Press, 1991.

Bloom, John. "'There is Madness in the Air': The 1926 Haskell Homecoming and Popular Representations of Sports in Federal Indian Boarding Schools." In *Dressing in Feathers: The Construction of the Indian in American Popular Culture*, edited by Elizabeth Bird, 97-110. Boulder: Westview Press, 1996.

Bø, Olav. *På ski gjennom historia* [On skis through history]. Oslo: Det Norske Samlaget, 1993.

Borge, Johannes. "Nordmenn i Kanada: Norway House" [Norwegians in Canada: Norway House]. *Hjemmet* 23, no. 47 (1940): 3-5.

Brantlinger, Patrick. *Dark Vanishings: Discourse on the Extinction of Primitive Races, 1800-1930.* Ithaca: Cornell University Press, 2003.

Brøgger, Fredrik Chr. "Re-enacting Modernity in the Wilderness of the Canadian North: An Ecocritical Examination of Helge Ingstad's *The Land of Feast and Famine.*" In *Arctic Modernities: The Environmental, the Exotic and the Everyday*, edited by Heidi Hansson and Anka Ryall, 64-86. Newcastle upon Tyne: Cambridge Scholars Publishing, 2017.

Brophy, Susan. "Reciprocity as Dispossession: A Dialectical Materialist Analysis of the Fur Trade." *Settler Colonial Studies* 9, no. 3 (2018): 1-19.

Brownlie, Robin. *A Fatherly Eye: Indian Agents, Government Power, and Aboriginal Resistance in Ontario, 1918-1939.* Oxford: Oxford University Press, 2003.

Bulie, Kåre. "Norsk pelshandlerprosa" [Norwegian fur trader prose]. *Dagbladet.* April 9, 2007.

Coleman, Cynthia-Lou. "A War of Words: How New Frames Define Legitimacy in a Native Conflict." In *Dressing in Feathers: The Construction of the Indian in American Popular Culture*, edited by Elizabeth Bird, 181-194. Boulder: Westview Press, 1996.

Colpitts, George. "Itinerant Jewish and Arabic Trading in the Dene's North, 1913–1930." *Journal of the Canadian Historical Association* 24, no. 1 (2013): 163–213.

Conn, Steven. *History's Shadow: Native Americans and Historical Consciousness in the Nineteenth Century*. Chicago: University of Chicago Press, 2004.

Cronon, William. "The Trouble with Wilderness: Or, Getting Back to the Wrong Nature." *Environmental History* 1, no. 1 (1996): 7–28.

Crossingham, Lesley. "Cultural Director Says Missionaries Didn't Invent Syllabics, Indians Did." *Windspeaker* 5, no. 21 (1987): 2.

Dalton, Anthony. *River Rough, River Smooth: Adventures on Manitoba's Historic Hayes River*. Toronto: Natural Heritage Books, 2010.

Daschuk, James. *Clearing the Plains: Disease, Politics of Starvation, and the Loss of Indigenous Life*. Regina: University of Regina Press, 2013.

Department of Educational Studies. "In Memoriam—Dr. Rosalyn Ing." Faculty of Education: Department of Educational Studies. January 7, 2021. https://edst.educ.ubc.ca/in-memoriam-dr-rosalyn-ing/.

Djupedal, Knut. "Report on the Returned Emigrant Project." In *Essays on Norwegian-American Literature and History Volume II*, edited by Øyvind Gulliksen, Ingeborg R. Kongslien, and Dina Tolfsby, 189–199. Oslo: NAHA-Norge, 1990.

Elia, Peter. "Svalbard: In Search of Europe's Last Great Wilderness." *The Local*. November 2, 2019. https://www.thelocal.no/20191102/svalbard-europes-last-great-wilderness-norway/.

Feagin, Joe. *White Racial Frame: Centuries of Racial Framing and Counter-Framing*, 2nd edition. New York: Routledge, 2013.

Fenelon, James. *Redskins? Sports Mascots, Indian Nations and White Racism*. New York: Routledge, 2017.

Foster, John. "Sayer Trial." *The Canadian Encyclopedia*. Historica Canada. February 7, 2006. https://www.thecanadianencyclopedia.ca/en/article/sayer-trial.

Francis, Daniel. *The Imaginary Indian: The Image of the Indian in Canadian Culture*. Vancouver: Arsenal Pulp Press, 1992.

———. "The Imaginary Indian: The Image of the Indian in Canadian Culture." In *Race and Racialization: Essential Readings*, 2nd edition, edited by Tania Gupta et al., 234–249. Toronto: Canadian Scholars, 2018.

Frøysaa, Tellef. "10 Favoritter" [10 favourites]. *Hamar Arbeiderblad*. June 20, 2007.

Gabrielsen, Bjørn. "Et blodtørstig liv" [A bloodthirsty life]. *Dagens Næringsliv*. March 22, 2007.

Gaudry, Adam. "Fantasies of Sovereignty: Deconstructing British and Canadian Claims to Ownership of the Historic North-West." *Native American and Indigenous Studies* 3, no. 1 (2016): 46–74.

Geller, Peter. "'Hudson's Bay Company Indians': Images of Native People and the Red River Pageant, 1920." In *Dressing in Feathers: The Construction of the Indian in American Popular Culture*, edited by Elizabeth Bird, 65–78. Boulder: Westview Press, 1996.

Goodyear, Frank. "The Narratives of Sitting Bull's Surrender: Bailey, Dix & Mead's Photographic Western." In *Dressing in Feathers: The Construction of the Indian in American Popular Culture*, edited by Elizabeth Bird, 29–44. Boulder: Westview Press, 1996.

Griffiths, Alison. "Science and Spectacle: Native American Representation in Early Cinema." In *Dressing in Feathers: The Construction of the Indian in American Popular Culture*, edited by Elizabeth Bird, 79-96. Boulder: Westview Press, 1996.

Haddal, Per. "Pels, mygg og kulde" [Furs, mosquitoes and cold]. *Aftenposten*. April 15, 2007.

Hall, Catherine. *Civilising Subjects: Metropole and Colony in the English Imagination, 1830-1867*. Chicago: University of Chicago Press, 2002.

Hall, Stuart. "The West and the Rest: Discourse and Power." In *Race and Racialization: Essential Readings*, 2nd edition, edited by Tania Gupta et al. Toronto: Canadian Scholars, 2018.

Hanks, Christopher. "The Swampy Cree and the Hudson's Bay Company at Oxford House." *Ethnohistory* 29, no. 2 (1982): 103-115.

Harbu, Jan. "Pelshander i Canada" [Fur trader in Canada]. *Vi Menn*. 2007.

Harris, Cole. *Making Native Space: Colonialism, Resistance, and Reserves in British Columbia*. Vancouver: UBC Press, 2002.

Haugen, Einar. *Bilingualism in the Americas: A Bibliography and Research Guide*. Gainesville, FL: American Dialect Society, 1956.

———. "Language and Immigration." *Norwegian-American Studies and Records* 10 (1938). https://www.naha.stolaf.edu/pubs/nas/volume10/vol10_1.htm.

Hauksdóttir, Auður. "The Role of the Danish Language in Iceland." *Linguistik Online* 79, no. 5 (2016). http://dx.doi.org/10.13092/lo.79.3335.

Hudson's Bay Company. "York Boat." *Hudson's Bay Company History Foundation*. December 20, 2018. http://www.hbcheritage.ca/things/technology/the-york-boat.

———. "York Factory." *Hudson's Bay Company History Foundation*. July 30, 2018. http://www.hbcheritage.ca/places/forts-posts/york-factory.

"Hva kunne barn og unge lese i 1905?" [What could children and young people read in 1905?]. *Bergen Offentlige Bibliotek*. December 15, 2018. https://bergenbibliotek.no/barn/tips-og-nytt/barn-tema-1905.

Indian Claims Commission. "Opaskwayak Cree Nation: Streets and Lanes Inquiry." February 2007. Part II.

Ingstad, Benedicte. *A Grand Adventure: The Lives of Helge and Anne Stine Ingstad and Their Discovery of a Viking Settlement in North America*. Montreal: McGill-Queen's University Press, 2017.

Innis, Harold. *The Fur Trade in Canada: With a New Introductory Essay by Arthur J. Ray*. Toronto: University of Toronto Press, 2001.

Jarvenpa, Robert. "Commoditization versus Cultural Integration: Tourism and Image Building in the Klondike." *Arctic Anthropology* 31, no. 1 (1994): 26-46.

Johanson, Helge. "Levende om pelshandler" [(A) vivid (account) about a fur trader]. *Stavanger Aftenblad*. April 26, 2007.

Jojola, Theodore. "*Moo Mesa*: Some Thoughts on Stereotypes and Image Appropriation." In *Dressing in Feathers: The Construction of the Indian in American Popular Culture*, edited by Elizabeth Bird, 263-280. Boulder: Westview Press, 1996.

Jones, Sally. "The First, but Not the Last of the 'Vanishing Indians': Edwin Forrest and Mythic Recreations of the Native Population." In *Dressing in Feathers: The Construction of the Indian in American Popular Culture*, edited by Elizabeth Bird. Boulder: Westview Press, 1996.

Joundrey, Susan. "Hidden Authority, Public Display: Representations of First Nations People at the Calgary Stampede, 1912–1970." PHD diss., Carleton University, 2013.

Karlsen, Silje Solheim. "Fangstmannsbiografien og heltelitteratur. Med et skråblikk på sjangeren: Wanny Wolstad, Henry Ette, Thorleif Bjertnes og Henry Rudi" [The hunter/trapper biography and hero literature. A new way of looking at the genre: Wanny Wolstad, Henry Ette, Thorleif Bjertnes and Henry Rudi]. *Nordlit* 32 (2014): 1–16. https://doi.org/10.7557/13.3077.

Kelcey, Barbara. *Alone in Silence: European Women in the Canadian North before World War II*. Montreal: McGill-Queen's University Press, 2001.

Kelm, Mary-Ellen. *Colonizing Bodies: Aboriginal Health and Healing in British Columbia, 1900–50*. Vancouver: University of British Columbia Press, 1998.

King, C. Richard. *Redskins: Insult and Brand*. Lincoln: University of Nebraska Press, 2016.

———. "Segregated Stories: The Colonial Contours of the Little Bighorn Battlefield National Monument." In *Dressing in Feathers: The Construction of the Indian in American Popular Culture*, edited by Elizabeth Bird, 167–180. Boulder: Westview Press, 1996.

King, Thomas. *The Inconvenient Indian: A Curious Account of People in North America*. New York: Doubleday, 2012.

Kjæreng, Fridtjof, dir. *Canada på tvers* [Across Canada]. Oslo: NRK, 2005.

Koller, Christian. "Nationalism and Racism in Franco-German Controversies about Colonial Soldiers." In *Nations, Identities and the First World War: Shifting Loyalties to the Fatherland*, edited by Nico Wouters and Laurence van Ypersele, 213–232. London: Bloomsbury Academic, 2018.

Kvideland, Reimund, and Henning K. Sehmsdorf, eds. *Scandinavian Folk Belief and Legend*. Minneapolis: University of Minnesota Press, 1988.

Library and Archives Canada. "Finding Aid 10-12: Guide to Indian Bands and Agencies in Western Canada, 1871–1959." Ottawa: Library and Archives Canada, n.d.

———. "Project Naming." *Library and Archives Canada*. May 30, 2019. bac-lac.gc.ca/eng/discover/aboriginal-heritage/project-naming/Pages/introduction.aspx.

Loken, Gulbrand. *From Fjord to Frontier: A History of the Norwegians in Canada*. Toronto: McClelland and Stewart, 1988.

———. "Norwegians." *The Canadian Encyclopedia*. Historica Canada. April 12, 2018. https://www.thecanadianencyclopedia.ca/en/article/norwegians.

Lovoll, Odd. *The Promise of America: A History of the Norwegian-American People*. Minneapolis: University of Minnesota Press, 1984.

Lux, Maureen. *Medicine That Walks: Disease, Medicine and Canadian Plains Native People, 1880–1940*. Toronto: University of Toronto Press, 2001.

Maase, Kaspar. *Die Kinder Der Massenkultur: Kontroversen um Schmutz und Schund Seit Dem Kaiserreich* [The children of mass culture: controversies about filth and rubbish since the German empire]. Frankfurt: Campus Verlag, 2012.

MacDowall, Brian. "'A Flag That Knows No Colour Line': Aboriginal Veteranship in Canada, 1914–1939." PHD diss., York University, 2017.

MacLeod, Roy, and Milton James, eds. *Disease, Medicine, and Empire: Perspectives on Western Medicine and the Experience of European Expansion*. London: Routledge, 1988.

Maguire, Ron. *Pre-Confederation Upper Canada Treaties: Indian Annuities*. Ottawa: Treaties and Historical Research Centre, 1970.

Malaher, David. "Port Nelson and the Hudson Bay Railway," *Manitoba History*, no. 8 (1984).

Mandelbaum, David. *The Plains Cree: An Ethnographic, Historical, and Comparative Study*. Regina: University of Regina, 2012.

Manitoba Geographic Names Program. "Geographic Names of Manitoba." July 30, 2018. http://www.gov.mb.ca/sd/lands_branch/geo_names/document/cdgnm.pdf.

Manitoba Historical Society. "Isaac Benjamin 'Ben' Dembinsky (1885–1960)." *Memorable Manitobans*. February 16, 2021. http://www.mhs.mb.ca/docs/people/dembinsky_ib.shtml.

———. "Western Grocers Limited/Westfair Food Limited." *Manitoba Business*. February 12, 2018. http://www.mhs.mb.ca/docs/business/westerngrocers.shtml.

Manitoba Hydro. *Lake Sturgeon in Manitoba: A Summary of Current Knowledge*. Winnipeg: Manitoba Hydro, 2016.

Martin, Gregory. "German and French Perceptions of the French North and West African Contingents, 1910–1918." *Militärgeschichtliche Mitteilungen* 56 (1997): 31–68.

Mason, Courtney. "The Construction of Banff as a 'Natural' Environment: Sporting Festivals, Tourism, and Representations of Aboriginal Peoples." *Journal of Sport History* 35, no. 2 (2008): 221–239.

McCarthy, Martha. *Pine Bluff: A History*. Winnipeg: Manitoba Hydro and Pine Bluff Residents' Association, 1992.

McClintock, Anne. *Imperial Leather: Race, Gender and Sexuality in the Colonial Contest*. New York: Routledge, 1995.

McGowan, Katharine. "'We Are Wards of the Crown and Cannot Be Regarded as Full Citizens of Canada': Native Peoples, the Indian Act and Canada's War Effort." PhD diss., University of Waterloo, 2011.

Mechling, Jay. "Florida Seminoles and the Marketing of the Last Frontier." In *Dressing in Feathers: The Construction of the Indian in American Popular Culture*, edited by Elizabeth Bird, 149–166. Boulder: Westview Press, 1996.

Mercado, Jose. "Code Switching." In *Encyclopedia of Cross-Cultural School Psychology*, edited by C.S. Clauss-Ehlers. 2010 ed. Boston: Springer, 2015. https://doi.org/10.1007/978-0-387-71799-9_74.

Merskin, Debra. "What Does One Look Like?" In *Dressing in Feathers: The Construction of the Indian in American Popular Culture*, edited by Elizabeth Bird. Boulder: Westview Press, 1996.

Michelet, Jon. "Mortensen i villmarka" [Mortensen in the wilderness]. *Klassekampen*. April 13, 2007.

Moore, Sarah, and Mustapha Debboun. "History of Insect Repellents." In *Insect Repellents: Principles, Methods, and Uses*, edited by Mustapha Debboun, Stephen Frances, and Daniel Strickman, 3–30. New York: CRC Press, 2007.

Moss, Wendy and Elaine Gardner-O'Toole. "Aboriginal People: History of Discriminatory Laws." May 4, 2018. http://publications.gc.ca/Collection-R/LoPBdP/BP/bp175-e.htm.

Munthe, Henrik. "Pelshandler i Canadas ødemark" [Fur trader in Canada's wilderness]. *Snø & Ski*. May 2007.

Oelschlaeger, Max. *The Idea of Wilderness: From Prehistory to the Age of Ecology*. New Haven: Yale University Press, 1991.

Opaskwayak Cree Nation. "History." *Opaskwayak Cree Nation*. October 23, 2018. http://opaskwayakcreenation.ca/history.html.

Opp, James. "Branding 'the Bay/la Baie:' Corporate Identity, the Hudson's Bay Company, and the Burden of History in the 1960s." *Canadian Historical Review* 96, no. 2 (2015): 223–256.

Øverland, Orm. *The Western Home: A Literary History of Norwegian America*. Northfield, MN: The Norwegian American Historical Association, 1996.

Oxford English Dictionary Online. December 2021. https://www-oed-com.prxy.lib.unbc.ca/view/Entry/124156?redirectedFrom=muskeg.

Parks Canada. "Norway House Historic Site of Canada." *Canada's Historic Places*. March 24, 2021. https://www.historicplaces.ca/en/rep-reg/place-lieu.aspx?id=12041.

———. "Norway House National Historic Site of Canada." *Directory of Federal Heritage Designations*. March 24, 2021. https://www.pc.gc.ca/apps/dfhd/page_nhs_eng.aspx?id=125.

Parrott, Zach. "Eskimo." *The Canadian Encyclopedia*. Historica Canada. April 11, 2021. https://www.thecanadianencyclopedia.ca/en/article/eskimo.

The Pas Chamber of Commerce. *The Pas...A History: Adventure & Romance*. The Pas: The Pas Chamber of Commerce, 1970.

Paulsen, Torstein. "Verdt å vite spesial: *Pelshandleren*" [Worth knowing (special): *The Fur Trader*]. Oslo: NRK, April 6, 2007.

Payne, Carole. "Lessons with Leah: Re-reading the Photographic Archive of Nation in the National Film Board of Canada's Still Photography Division." *Visual Studies* 21, no. 1 (2006): 4–22.

Payne, Michael. "Fur Trade Historiography: Past Conditions, Present Circumstances and a Hint of Future Prospects." In *From Rupert's Land to Canada*, edited by Theodore Binnema, Gerhard Ens, and R.C. MacLeod, 2–22. Edmonton: University of Alberta Press, 2001.

———. *The Fur Trade in Canada: An Illustrated History*. Toronto: James Lorimer & Company Ltd., 2004.

Penner, George. "Historic Sites of Manitoba: Norway House Plaques (Norway House, Northern Manitoba)." *Manitoba Historical Society*. December 20, 2018. http://www.mhs.mb.ca/docs/sites/norwayhouse.shtml.

Perry, Adele. *On the Edge of Empire: Gender, Race and the Making of British Columbia, 1849–1871*. Toronto: University of Toronto Press, 2001.

Piper, Liza. "Knowing Nature through History." *History Compass* 11, no. 12 (2013): 1139–1149.

Podruchny, Carolyn. *Making the Voyageur World: Travelers and Traders in the North American Fur Trade*. Lincoln: University of Nebraska Press, 2006.

Pratt, Mary Louise. *Imperial Eyes: Travel Writing and Transculturation*, 2nd edition. London: Routledge, 2008.

Public Health Agency of Canada. *Tuberculosis in Canada, 2012*. Ottawa: Public Health Agency of Canada, 2015. https://www.canada.ca/en/public-health/services/infectious-diseases/tuberculosis-canada-2012.html.

Raibmon, Paige. *Authentic Indians: Episodes of Encounter from the Late-Nineteenth-Century Northwest Coast*. Durham: Duke University Press, 2005.

Ray, Arthur. *The Canadian Fur Trade in the Industrial Age*. Toronto: University of Toronto Press, 1990.

———. *Indians in the Fur Trade: Their Role as Trappers, Hunters, and Middlemen in the Lands Southwest of Hudson Bay, 1660–1870*. Toronto: University of Toronto Press, 1998.

———. "Periodic Shortages, Native Welfare and the Hudson's Bay Company, 1670–1930." In *The Subarctic Fur Trade: Native Social and Economic Adaptations*, edited by Shepard Krech III, 1–20. Vancouver: UBC Press, 1984.

Rees, Ellen. *Cabins in Modern Norwegian Literature: Negotiating Place and Identity*. Madison: Fairleigh Dickinson University Press, 2014.

Said, Edward. *Orientalism*. London: Penguin Books, 2003.

Satzewich, Vic, and Linda Mahood. "Indian Affairs and Band Governance: Deposing Indian Chiefs in Western Canada, 1896–1911." *Canadian Ethnic Studies* 26, no. 1 (1994): 40–58.

"See the Sights of Svalbard, Europe's Last Wilderness." *Independent*. December 5, 2017. https://www.independent.co.uk/travel/visit-norway/see-sights-svalbard-europe-s-last-true-wilderness-a8019396.html.

Shewell, Hugh. *'Enough to Keep Them Alive': Indian Welfare in Canada, 1873–1965*. Toronto: University of Toronto Press, 2004.

Shoemaker, Nancy. "How Indians Got To Be Red." *The American Historial Review* 102, no. 3 (1997): 625–644.

———. "A Typology of Colonialism." *Perspectives of History*. October 2015. https://www.historians.org/publications-and-directories/perspectives-on-history/october-2015/a-typology-of-colonialism.

Sims, Daniel. "Dam Bennett: The Impacts of the W.A.C. Bennett Dam and Williston Lake Reservoir on the Tsek'ehne of Northern British Columbia." PHD diss., University of Alberta, 2017.

Skinner, Alanson. *Notes on the Eastern Cree and Northern Saulteaux*. Volume IX, part 1. Anthropological Papers of the American Museum of Natural History. New York: Order of the Trustees, 1911.

"Skolemåltidets historie" [History of the school meal]. *Skolefrukt*. December 15, 2018. https://www.skolefrukt.no/om-skolefruktordningen/skolemaltidets-historie.html.

Skyriene, Gintare, and Algimantas Paulauskas. "Distribution of Invasive Muskrats (*Ondatra zibethicus*) and Impact on Ecosystem." *Ekologija* 58, no 3 (2012): 357–367.

Smith, David. "From Nunavut to Micronesia: Feedback and Description, Visual Repatriation and Online Photographs of Indigenous Peoples." *Partnership: The Canadian Journal of Library and Information Practice and Research* 3, no. 1 (2008): 1–19.

Smith, James. "The Western Wood Cree: Anthropological Myth and Historical Reality." *American Ethnologist* 14, no. 3 (1987): 434–448.

Smith, Sidonie, and Julia Watson. *Reading Autobiography: A Guide for Interpreting Life Narratives*, 2nd edition. Minneapolis: University of Minnesota Press, 2010.

Smithers, Gregory. "Beyond the 'Ecological Indian': Environmental Politics and Traditional Ecological Knowledge in Modern North America." *Environmental History* 20, no. 1 (2015): 83–111.

Solbakk, John Trygve. *The Sámi People — A Handbook*. Karasjok, Norway: Davvi Girji, 2006.

St-Onge, Nicole, Carolyn Podruchny, and Brenda MacDougall, eds. *Contours of a People: Family, Mobility, and Territoriality in Métis History*. Norman: University of Oklahoma Press, 2012.

Stang, Lasse. "Kom Ingstad i forkjøpet" [Preempted Ingstad]. *Oppland Arbeiderblad*. April 3, 2007.

Stanley, George. "The First Indian 'Reserves' in Canada." *Revue d'Histoire de l'Amerique Française* 4, no. 2 (1950): 178–210.

Steckley, John. *Indian Agents: Rulers of the Reserve*. New York: Peter Lang, 2016.

Steele, Jeffrey. "Reduced to Images: American Indians in the Nineteenth-Century Advertising." In *Dressing in Feathers: The Construction of the Indian in American Popular Culture*, edited by Elizabeth Bird, 45–64. Boulder: Westview Press, 1996.

Stoler, Ann Laura. "Sexual Affronts and Racial Frontiers: European Identities and the Cultural Politics of Exclusion in Colonial Southeast Asia." In *Tensions of Empire: Colonial Cultures in a Bourgeois World*, edited by Frederick Cooper and Ann Laura Stoler, 198–237. Berkeley: University of California Press, 1997.

Stoler, Ann Laura, and Frederick Cooper. "Between Metropole and Colony: Rethinking a Research Agenda." In *Tensions of Empire: Colonial Cultures in Bourgeois World*, edited by Frederick Cooper and Ann Laura Stoler, 1–58. Berkeley: University of California Press, 1997.

Storvand, Lena. "Farens fortid var tabu" [Father's past was taboo]. *Verdens Gang*. March 18, 2007.

Talbot, Robert. "'It Would Be Best to Leave Us Alone': First Nations Responses to the Canadian War Effort, 1914–18." *Journal of Canadian Studies* 45, no. 1 (2011): 90–120.

Taylor, Annette. "Cultural Heritage in *Northern Exposure*." In *Dressing in Feathers: The Construction of the Indian in American Popular Culture*, edited by Elizabeth Bird, 229–244. Boulder: Westview Press, 1996.

"Ti største papiraviser" [Ten largest print newspapers]. *MedieNorge-Fakta om Norske Medier*, NORDICOM. November 26, 2018. http://www.medienorge.uib.no/statistikk/medium/avis/353.

Tillotson, Shirley. *Give and Take: The Citizen-Taxpayer and the Rise of Canadian Democracy*. Vancouver: UBC Press, 2017.

Titley, Brian. *The Indian Commissioners: Agents of the State and Indian Policy in Canada's Prairie West, 1873–1932*, 1st edition. Edmonton: University of Alberta Press, 2009.

Tough, Frank. *'As Their Natural Resources Fail': Native Peoples and the Economic History of Northern Manitoba, 1870–1930*. Vancouver: UBC Press, 2008.

Truth and Reconciliation Commission of Canada. *Honouring the Truth, Reconciling for the Future: Summary of the Final Report of the Truth and Reconciliation Commission of Canada*. Winnipeg: Truth and Reconciliation Commission, 2015.

———. *Final Report of the Truth and Reconciliation Commission of Canada*. Winnipeg: Truth and Reconciliation Commission of Canada, 2015.

Turan, Hakan. "Taylor's 'Scientific Management Principles': Contemporary Issues in Personnel Selection Period." *Journal of Economics, Business and Management* 3, no. 11 (2015): 1102–1105.

Urberg, Ingrid. "Helge Ingstad: Inspiration for a Life of Adventure in the Land of Feast and Famine." In *Pike's Portage: Stories of a Distinguished Place*, edited by Morten Asfeldt and Bob Henderson, 192–204. Toronto: Natural Heritage Books, 2010.

van Lent, Peter. "'Her Beautiful Savage': The Current Sexual Images of the Native American Male." In *Dressing in Feathers: The Construction of the Indian in American Popular Culture*, edited by Elizabeth Bird, 211–228. Boulder: Westview Press, 1996.

Vibert, Elizabeth. *Trader's Tales: Narratives of Cultural Encounters in the Columbia Plateau, 1807-1846*. Norman: University of Oklahoma, 2000.

Wærp, Henning Howlid. *Arktisk litteratur—fra Fridtjof Nansen til Anne B. Ragde* [Arctic literature—from Fridtjof Nansen to Anne B. Ragde]. Stamsund, Norway: Orkana, 2017.

———. "Fridtjof Nansen, *First Crossing of Greenland* (1890): Bestseller and Scientific Report." In *Arctic Discourses*, edited by Anka Ryall, Johan Schimanski, and Henning Howlid Wærp, 43-58. Newcastle upon Tyne: Cambridge Scholars Publishing, 2010.

Waldram, James D., Ann Herring, and T. Kue Young. *Aboriginal Health in Canada: Historical, Cultural, and Epidemiological Perspectives*, 2nd edition. Toronto: University of Toronto Press, 2007.

White, Bruce. "A Skilled Game of Exchange: Ojibway Fur Trade Protocol." *Minnesota History* 50, no. 6 (1987): 229-240.

Wilkinson, Stephan. "Firebombers!" *Aviation History* 28, no. 4 (2018): 32-41.

Winegard, Timothy. *For King and Kanata: Canadian Indians and the First World War*. Winnipeg: University of Manitoba Press, 2012.

Other Titles from University of Alberta Press

Masters and Servants
The Hudson's Bay Company and Its North American Workforce, 1668–1786
SCOTT P. STEPHEN
An essential examination of the role of labourers in early modern Atlantic political-economic history.

A Son of the Fur Trade
The Memoirs of Johnny Grant
JOHN FRANCIS GRANT
Edited by GERHARD J. ENS
Johnny Grant (1833–1907), Metis, fur trader, rancher, and Riel-Resistance participant, documented his historical experiences in the northwestern US and Canada.

Fur Trade Letters of Willie Traill 1864–1893
WILLIAM EDWARD TRAILL
Edited by K. DOUGLAS MUNRO
Gritty, deeply touching, fascinating, informative; these letters show the joys and heartbreaking challenges of family life in the fur trade.

More information at uap.ualberta.ca

www.ingramcontent.com/pod-product-compliance
Ingram Content Group UK Ltd.
Pitfield, Milton Keynes, MK11 3LW, UK
UKHW041630100725
460640UK00004B/120